PEARL HARBOR REVISITED

The Franklin and Eleanor Roosevelt Institute Series on Diplomatic and Economic History

General Editors: Arthur M. Schlesinger, Jr., William vanden Heuvel, and Douglas Brinkley

1. FDR AND HIS CONTEMPORARIES
Foreign Perceptions of an American President
Edited by Cornelis A. van Minnen and John F. Sears

2. NATO: THE FOUNDING OF THE ATLANTIC ALLIANCE AND THE INTEGRATION OF EUROPE
Edited by Francis H. Heller and John R. Gillingham

3. AMERICA UNBOUND
World War II and the Making of a Superpower
Edited by Warren F. Kimball

4. THE ORIGINS OF U.S. NUCLEAR STRATEGY, 1945–1953
Samuel R. Williamson, Jr. and Steven L. Rearden

5. AMERICAN DIPLOMATS IN THE NETHERLANDS, 1815–50
Cornelis A. van Minnen

6. EISENHOWER, KENNEDY, AND THE UNITED STATES OF EUROPE
Pascaline Winand

7. ALLIES AT WAR
The Soviet, American, and British Experience, 1939–1945
Edited by David Reynolds, Warren F. Kimball, and A. O. Chubarian

8. THE ATLANTIC CHARTER
Edited by Douglas Brinkley and David R. Facey-Crowther

9. PEARL HARBOR REVISITED
Edited by Robert W. Love, Jr.

10. THE UNITED STATES AND THE INTEGRATION OF EUROPE
Legacies of the Postwar Era
Edited by Francis H. Heller and John R. Gillingham

PEARL HARBOR REVISITED

Edited by Robert W. Love, Jr.

St. Martin's Press
New York

PEARL HARBOR REVISITED

ISBN 0-312-09593-7

Library of Congress Cataloging in Publication Data:

Pearl Harbor revisited / edited by Robert W. Love, Jr. — 1st ed.
p. cm. — (The Franklin and Eleanor Roosevelt Institute series on diplomatic and economic history)
Includes index.
ISBN 0-312-09593-7
1. Pearl Harbor (Hawaii), Attack on, 1941—Congresses. I. Love, Robert William, 1940- . II. Series.
D767.92.P3985 1995
940.54'26—dc20 94-42890
CIP

Book design by Acme Art, Inc.

First Edition: August 1995
10 9 8 7 6 5 4 3 2 1

CONTENTS

Introduction vii
Robert W. Love, Jr.

1. The Relationship between the Far Eastern and European Wars, 1922–1941 1
Donald Cameron Watt

2. The Royal Navy and the Japanese Threat 13
G. A. H. Gordon

3. Prelude to Pearl Harbor: The Diplomatic Dress Rehearsal 37
Frederick W. Marks III

4. Japanese Wartime Rhetoric in the Traditional Philosophical Context 61
Marleen Kassel

5. Moscow on the Pacific: Soviet Historians and the War in the Pacific, 1941–1945 75
J. Thomas Sanders

6. "Just Dumb Luck": American Entry into World War II 93
Stephen E. Ambrose

7. Pearl Harbor in a Global Context 103
Waldo Heinrichs

8. The Debacle in the Philippines 111
Michael Schaller

9. The United States, Japan, and the Panama Canal 131
John Major

10. Saturday, December 6, 1941 143
Jon Bridgeman

11. FDR as Commander in Chief 173
Robert W. Love, Jr.

About the Authors 193

Index 195

INTRODUCTION

Few events in American history excite as much interest or sustain such enduring controversy as the Japanese attack on the U.S. Navy's Pacific Fleet at Pearl Harbor on December 7, 1941. "Remember Pearl Harbor" quickly became a rallying cry for Americans during World War II and a postwar catchphrase of those who, as a matter of policy, urged vigilance against a sneak attack by an overseas enemy. Yet one of the ironies of Pearl Harbor was that it was relatively unremarkable as a military event. A large Japanese carrier task force conducted a tactically sloppy strike against a poorly defended enemy fleet and base, sinking or crippling old, slow World War I-era battleships that posed no serious threat whatsoever to Tokyo's broader, long term strategic plan. As an operation of war, the concept was neither novel, particularly well executed, or in any way decisive. At a tactical level, moreover, the Japanese clearly accepted a mere victory of attrition by failing to continue the attack and win a victory of annihilation. Another of the ironies of the attack on Pearl Harbor was, of course, its immense political significance. Having failed to conquer China after a costly four-year offensive, the Japanese decided to make war on the United States and, not incidentally, the British Empire. The attack fused separate conflicts theretofore confined to Europe and Asia, creating the nearly global struggle known subsequently as the Second World War.

To commemorate the fiftieth anniversary of the Pearl Harbor attack, the Franklin and Eleanor Roosevelt Institute sponsored a one-day symposium of scholars at Hofstra University, Hempstead, New York. This gathering occurred on December 7, 1991, the last day of a larger three-day conference that considered the broader topic of the United States and Japan in World War II. The charge to the scholars who attended was to consider the Pearl Harbor attack as a unique international event and to approach the issues it raised for historians from unconventional, oblique, or eccentric angles. Aware that each generation rewrites and reinterprets history, the authors hope that these contributions enrich the understanding of this most transfiguring landmark of our times.

Professor Douglas Brinkley, formerly of Hofstra University and now director of the Eisenhower Center at the University of New Orleans, managed the conference; he deserves our thanks. So does Simon Winder, senior editor at St. Martin's Press, who stuck with the project to the end. Lastly, editing these papers would not have been possible without the encouragement and patient support of my wife, Rose Seals Love.

Robert W. Love, Jr.
United States Naval Academy, Annapolis

1.

The Relationship between the Far Eastern and European Wars, 1922–41

Donald Cameron Watt

The establishment of a link between war in the Far East involving Britain and war in Europe was made likely by the outcome of the Washington Conference of 1921-22. The conference did two things. It ended the Anglo-Japanese Alliance of 1902, which at least British policy makers had come to see as a way of controlling Japanese expansionism in the Far East. Without British support, so it was believed in London, no Japanese regime would challenge the United States. And the text of the 1911 revision of the 1902 treaty made it clear that Britain would not allow the alliance to operate against the United States. Unfortunately for British policy in this respect, this point was never accepted in the United States, especially by the American "big navy" advocates and naval planners; the latter continued to plan for a Pacific war against Britain and Japan until well into the late 1920s. More sophisticated minds than these preferred to have Britain dependent on America, rather than the other way around.

This dependency was achieved by the second of the two "accomplishments" of the Washington Conference: the establishment of the principle of parity in naval tonnage at the capital and aircraft-carrier level between the British and American navies, and the fixing of Japanese and French naval strengths respectively at three-fifths and seven-twentieths of the permitted construction levels of British and American tonnage in these categories. Theoretically, this left Britain with a superiority of 150,000 tons over a combined French-Japanese lineup, preserving the two-power standard that British naval planners sought against potentially hostile powers. In practice it forced a major change in British naval strategy. From 1922 onward, British naval planning envisaged the dispatch of the British battle fleet or a major part of it to the Far East if war broke out there and no obvious warning was given. The fleet would be centered on a new naval base at Singapore and fortified to hold out against Japanese seaborne attack for a minimum of 70 days.

The subsequent course of international negotiations on naval arms limitation was troubled and stormy. The first attempt to apply the limitations accepted at Washington to the other categories of warship (cruisers, destroyers, etc.) broke down at Geneva in 1927 in bitter, bellicose mutual recriminations between Britain and the United States. Wiser counsels on both sides of the Atlantic brought agreement in London in 1930. But some naval men on both sides of the Atlantic spoke against the ratification of the treaty, while in Japan the imposition on Japanese naval strength was regarded as a national humiliation, and those who had advised the Emperor to accept it were seen as traitors. By 1934 nearly all those figures in Japanese politics or the navy who had so advised the Emperor had been assassinated or driven into private life.

In 1931 a group of Japanese army colonels provoked the Japanese takeover of Manchuria and brought down the Japanese government. Not to be outdone, the Japanese navy, taking action against a Chinese blockade of Japanese goods, landed a naval division in Chinese Shanghai, instigating bitter fighting that threatened both the international settlement and the British and American naval squadrons protecting it. London received intelligence reports of Japanese plans for a preemptive coup against Singapore, where the financial exigencies that had weighed on British defense budgets in the 1920s had held up completion of fortifications. The gold crisis of 1931, which had forced the pound sterling off gold, had led the national government to introduce cuts in British naval pay. This, in turn, led to mutiny in the British Grand Fleet lying at Scapa Flow at the north of Scotland, the first mutiny in the Royal Navy since 1795. These reports appear to have been untrue, but they were alarming in the extreme.

The events of the year 1933 were even more alarming. Condemned by the Lytton report, Japan left the League of Nations. In Germany Hitler was appointed chancellor. Reports of his taking immediate steps to break the 1919 Treaty of Versailles prohibition on Germany's possession of a military air force multiplied during the summer of 1933, and evidence of his campaign to destabilize the Austrian government and substitute one led by Nazis or fellow traveling nationalists was daily visible and audible. In November he took Germany in turn out of the League of Nations.

In the autumn of 1933 the British cabinet set up a secret committee, the Defence Requirements Sub Committee (DRC), to examine the deficiencies in Britain's defenses and to advise on their remedy. The committee consisted of the chiefs of staff of the three armed services and the three most powerful career public servants, the head of the Treasury, Sir Warren Fisher; the head of the Foreign Office, Sir Robert Vansittart; and the head of the Cabinet Office and the Committee of Imperial Defence, responsible for organizing and planning Britain's war effort in a future war, Sir Maurice Hankey. The politico-strategic side of their report was prophetic. Japan seemed the more immediate danger, Germany by far the greater, although it would take a little time before she was ready for war. The year of maximum danger, they said, would be 1939.

The problem with their report lay in its financial and military sections. Britain's financial strength, it was argued, was an essential part of its war-making capacity, as it had been in 1914-18. To maintain this strength Britain's leaders would need to choose between the military recommendations. The first priority became to remedy Britain's vulnerability to air attack, the actual and psychological effects of which were greatly overestimated. This ruled out any return to a genuine two-ocean navy; it ruled out too any new large-scale military intervention in a continental war. The Air Ministry believed that Germany would be deterred if Britain could match her in the air.

The implications for this in the Far East were dire. The senior public servants on the DRC and the chancellor of the exchequer, Neville Chamberlain, pressed hard for a new agreement with Japan. They were encouraged by the failure of the British foreign secretary, Sir John Simon, to get any support from the U.S. secretary of state, Cordell Hull, for a joint reply to the statement by Mr. Amau, the spokesman for the Japanese Foreign Ministry, claiming a "Japanese Monroe Doctrine" over China. Chamberlain fought a losing battle with his colleagues in the Cabinet on this issue. The majority of the Cabinet, strongly supported by the presence in London of South African statesman General Jan Smuts, took the view that in a future war with Germany, American support would be essential. Nothing should be done to alienate American opinion or President Roosevelt.

They had one piece of evidence to set against the skepticism and hostility toward the United States felt by the three knights, Vansittart, Fisher, and Hankey. By 1935 both the Washington and London naval treaties would expire. Unless there was to be a free-for-all in naval construction and a new naval race, there would have to be a new naval conference and a new naval arms limitation agreement. The matter was rendered the more urgent because all but three of the 15 British battleships and battle cruisers had been built before World War I in the great naval arms race with Imperial Germany. In 1936 or 1937 Britain would have to begin replacing them, or at the very least rebuilding them from the bottom up. For ten years Britain had been trying to get the upper size, displacement, and gun caliber limited by treaty, so as to get more ships for the pound. They had very little success with their American counterparts, many of whom were still bitter over the cruiser issue.

Preliminary talks with the Americans, the Japanese, the French, and the Italians in the summer of 1934 had suggested that there might be some basis for a new settlement. In the second round of talks, held in the winter of 1934-35, the U. S. Navy's new chief of naval operations, Admiral Standley, had begun by assuring his British opposite number, Admiral Chatfield, that the U. S. Navy would make no more difficulties over the British cruiser program. It would be overstating the case to say that the Anglophile faction in the U. S. Navy had won, but it was certainly in the ascendant.

This was just as well. Britain's prime anxiety in the Far East centered on two quite separate issues. The first was the protection of British investments in China, which were enormous. The second was the maintenance of the Commonwealth, to the defense of whose members Britain was still committed, but which had been divided since 1921 on the issue of relations with the United States. Canada and South Africa had put the abandonment of the British alliance with Japan and the maintenance of good relations with United States foremost on their list. Australia's and New Zealand's priorities were their defense against Japanese seaborne invasion. Without an alliance with Japan, only Anglo-American naval cooperation against Japan could appease these two sets of anxieties.

Seen from Tokyo, the existence of the Anglo-American lineup seemed much more convincing than the reality warranted. Alarmist naval planners anticipated a preemptive naval strike to keep Japanese fleet size inferior to that of Britain and America. An enormous armaments budget was proposed for 1934. This the Japanese Ministry of Finance succeeded in putting off until the outcome of the new naval conference was clear. Japan agreed to attend the conference, but its position, disguised under the slogan of a "common upper limit," a round figure for total naval tonnage, hid both a demand for parity with the Anglo-Saxon powers and freedom to dispose of that tonnage however they wished. The Japanese navy leadership dictated this demand as the price for attending the conference. And when the demand was rejected, Japan walked.

It was at this point that some of the various factions in Japan began to interest themselves in distracting Japan's opponents by encouraging her potential allies. One faction had tried to interest the foreign trade office of the Nazi Party in investment in Manchuria. The Japanese military attaché in Berlin, General Oshima, a devoted admirer of Nazism, took up private negotiations with the rising star in the Nazi foreign policy firmament, Joachim von Ribbentrop. Both fell afoul at first of the opposition of the German Foreign Ministry and of the German Army, deeply involved as the latter was in the rehabilitation of the Chinese Army, the maintenance in China of a high-level military mission, and the conclusion of a barter agreement, exchanging German arms for Chinese raw materials of considerable importance to German rearmament. Ribbentrop secured a portentous anti-Comintern agreement in October 1936. But the German Foreign Ministry trumped his move by concluding the Axis agreement with Mussolini's Italy and making sure the various commissions set up by the anti-Comintern agreement never met. In the meantime Ribbentrop languished as German ambassador to London.

The outbreak of the Sino-Japanese conflict in 1937 and the relentless onrush of the Japanese armies into China's coastal provinces threatened British investments, aroused American indignation, and alarmed the Soviet Union. All three powers began to send aid to China. Bowed down by their failure to bring China to surrender and increasingly crippled by the costs of military occupation, the Japanese army and the Ministry of Finance began to join forces. Chinese morale was kept going, so they believed, by foreign aid; therefore it was necessary to distract Britain, America, and the Soviet Union. An alliance with Germany became steadily more attractive. The Japanese Foreign Ministry and the Japanese navy did not share this view. Taking advantage of their opponents' preoccupations in other parts of the world was one thing, exposing Japan to the risk of involvement in a European war over which Japan would have no control was another. The stage was set for the prolonged German-Japanese negotiations of 1938-39, in which Hitler sought an alliance so as to distract Britain and America, while the Japanese cabinet repeatedly tried and failed to arrive at a formula that would satisfy Hitler without alarming London and Washington. In the meantime Stalin's agents kept him informed of the vital fact that these negotiations were not aimed at the Soviet Union. He felt free both to destroy the Japanese army in Manchuria at the Nomonhan battles and to reject British and French offers of an alliance in favor of concluding a nonaggression pact dividing Eastern Europe with Hitler in August 1939.

Anglo-American cooperation in the Far East seemed increasingly desirable to the British as the threat from Hitler grew and was made much more so by the formation of the Axis. With the Italian army and air force loose against Malta, Egypt, and Alexandria, and the Italian navy dominating the central Mediterranean, Britain now faced a possible war in Europe, the Mediterranean, and the Far East. The chiefs of staff judged such a war as beyond Britain's capacities. At the very least it made any move of the battle fleet to the Far East impossible without the abandonment of the Mediterranean. This, in turn, was impossible without the agreement of France, Britain's one firm ally against Germany. Placating, or, as the jargon had it, appeasing Japan appeared impossible: It would mean that the Pacific dominions would leave the Commonwealth. The Japanese were unappeasable. There remained only two options: to manage any European conflict between the European powers, at least until British rearmament began to exercise a deterrent affect on Germany; or to work for American support against Japan, so that British strength would register earlier in Europe.

Seen from London, Washington and the president gave out conflicting signals. From the White House and the president's minions there were to come the October 1937 quarantine speech; the proposal in December for a distant blockade of Japan put by the president and Admiral Leahy to the British ambassador in Washington; the mission to London in January 1938 of the director of the U. S. Navy's War Plans Division, Captain Royal S. Ingersoll; and the progressively closer and warmer relations obtaining between the officers commanding the British and American naval squadrons in Chinese waters. To these were added the very broad hints from the president's special emissary to the Brussels Conference in November 1937, Norman Davis, of joint Anglo-American action in the Far East. From Cordell Hull, Sumner Welles, and the State Department, by contrast, there came nothing but put-offs and put-downs. Cordell Hull put off a British proposal for concerted action against Japan the very morning of the quarantine speech. Sumner Welles quashed a British follow-up of the quarantine speech. Hull called Norman Davis to order and ended Roosevelt's employment of him as his personal intermediary with Britain. The State Department view was that it was for Britain to defend her interests in the Far East herself. Any attempt to rope in America was to be resisted. It was immoral in itself and potentially disastrous in Congress. Besides, the British were, as always, dragging their feet on the trade negotiations, the apple of Hull's eye. To a man who could write in his memoirs that had the Anglo-American trade agreement of November 1938 been concluded in 1935 there would have been no Second World War, anything that happened to Britain was richly deserved.

Fortunately for Britain, Roosevelt took a different view. Historians agree that to fathom what was going on at any time in Roosevelt's mind is not easy. But the evidence now available suggests three things: firstly, that from the summer of 1936 he was increasingly aware of the threat to the New Deal and to America constituted by Nazi Germany and war in Europe; secondly, that he saw Britain and France as the first lines of American defense against this threat; thirdly, that he thought that "world opinion" and the economic pressures the democracies could generate on the dictatorships could well restrain Germany and Japan without the need to resort to war arising or at least without the involvement of American armed forces. Only this last can explain how in the winter of 1938-39 he was prepared to release America's first advanced war planes to the French or, for that matter, his unsuccessful attempt the previous year to override the ingrained Sovietophobia of the U.S. Navy's procurement officers in order to get two battleships built for the Soviet Union in American shipyards for use with the Soviet Far Eastern fleet. The discussion he held in the summer of 1939 with the British with a view to leasing naval and air bases in the British West Indies—discussions that foreshadowed not only the Destroyer Deal of 1940 but also the neutralization against German submarine activity of the Western Atlantic—are part of this same strategy.

So too was the move of the American battle fleet to Hawaii in May 1940 and the denunciation in August of the American-Japanese trade agreement. Both decisions were taken in the context of the German-Japanese negotiations of which Roosevelt was made generally aware both by the British and by his ambassador in Tokyo, Joseph Grew. These acts were warning guns, fired across the Japanese bows to warn them against adding to the pressure on Britain by concluding an open-ended alliance with Germany, and they were taken as such in Tokyo. That the Japanese government of the day fell at the end of August, to be replaced by one more balanced and more cautious, and that Germany found herself at war with Britain and France with Italy and Japan neutral, at least insofar as Japan was concerned, were situations for which Roosevelt shared responsibility.

Unfortunately, even had he inclined toward compromise, the rising American public revulsion against Japan's presence in China made it impossible to capitalize on that success. American policy steadily increased the economic pressure on Japan, irrespective of the political complexity of individual Japanese governments. The attractiveness to Japan of taking advantage of the disasters that overtook France, Belgium, and the Netherlands in Europe in 1940 was the greater in that these nations' colonial possessions fell into the area coveted both by the Japanese army and navy. From northern Indochina a new military road seemed open toward Chiang Kai-shek's new capital. The oil and rubber of the

East Indies were essential to the Japanese navy and army alike. Both lay in the south seas area of expansion the Japanese navy had been dreaming of since 1936. Under Japanese pressure, Britain felt obliged in the summer of 1940 to yield over the closure of the Burma Road, by which Chiang Kai Shek received British and American military aid at a time when the U.S. president, let alone his military advisors, were far from convinced that Britain would hold out against Hitler for more than a few weeks longer. As for the French, they were left to beg in vain for the aircraft they had already bought and paid for but which had got no further than the French West Indies. All they met in Washington was Hull at his most sanctimonious. Ten thousand French casualties, many of them Indochinese troops, were the price France paid for the Japanese occupation of northern Indochina.

The autumn of 1940 saw Roosevelt determined to back Britain. By Plan Dog it was decided that in the event of a war with Germany and Japan, Germany would be the first target for the American military effort. The destroyers-for-bases deal and Lend-Lease kept Britain in the war against Germany. The ABCD staff talks in the Pacific stiffened British and Dutch resolve in the Pacific and maintained Australia and New Zealand's willingness to deploy the bulk of their armies and air forces in the defense of the Middle East against Italy and Germany. And as the leading British scholar of the Pacific war, Professor Christopher Thorne, has maintained, Roosevelt, still sure that economic pressure would restrain Japan, anxious about the disastrous effect on Britain's war effort of the loss of Malaya's tin and rubber, and still more anxious of the possible effect on Britain's ability to stand off Germany of a Japanese attack on Britain's Southeast Asian possessions, came to assume the dominant role in dealing with Japan. Churchill, anxious only to draw America deeper into the war in any way he could, acquiesced.

The British ambassador in Tokyo, Sir Robert Craigie, distrustful of American diplomatic finesse, protested and was told to mind his own business and to leave matters to the Americans. American strategy in the Atlantic extended to the occupation of Iceland and the escort of convoys into the mid-Atlantic. The main fear in London over the Far East was that America might settle for a compromise with Japan. Craigie was isolated, and when he returned to Britain from Japanese internment, his ideas were disowned and his final report, with its criticisms of the policies that had led to Pearl Harbor, suppressed for thirty years.

Much of American policy, from the summer of 1940 onward, was, as Paul Schroeder argued in the 1960s, based on the erroneous assumption that German and Japanese policy was coordinated under the terms of the 1940 Tripartite Alliance. In fact there was little or no coordination of policy. The Japanese were not notified of the German attack on the Soviet Union in advance. German pressure on Japan to follow suit and attack the Soviet Union's Pacific provinces was ignored. Instead the Japanese resumed their pressure on Indochina, bringing about the American counteraction, the oil embargo, and the freezing of all Japanese assets, which gave the Japanese government and military the choice of war or total withdrawal. This move was acquiesced in by a British government that had voluntarily abandoned all initiative in dealing with Japan to Roosevelt and Hull.

The attention of the British Cabinet and chiefs of staff was fixed on North Africa, on the eventually disastrous British attempt to open a new front in the Balkans, and on the complex of moves necessary to block Syria, Iraq, and Iran from German penetration. Beyond that there was the question of whether the Soviet state could survive the German attack and the losses of men, material, and land suffered between June and November 1941, and what would have to be done if Soviet resistance collapsed and the Wehrmacht threatened the boundaries of Iraq, Iran, and India. Two new armies, the Ninth and the Tenth, had to be formed to occupy Syria and Iraq and to share with the Soviets in the occupation of Iran. Troops had to be found for the new armies, as well as money to consolidate the economies of the individual Middle Eastern states and to run them in a world where all trade had to funnel through the U-boat–ridden oceans. The cultivation of American support took Churchill to Argentia. The apportionment of American Lend-Lease between Britain and the Soviet Union (which meant inevitably the diversion of American production promised to Britain to the new opponent of Hitler) had to be settled and the goods delivered past the German blockade of the Soviet's Arctic ports.

It is hardly surprising, therefore, that British attention was diverted from the Far East. In any case almost all the British experts on the Far East were ideologically anti-Japanese. Thinking in categories such as "aggression" and "appeasement," they were emotional Sinophiles, though skeptical where the Kuomintang leadership was concerned; furthermore, for a British diplomatic service whose senior figures had been taking part in politico-strategic discussions on European and Mediterranean issues with the British defense establishment, they were remarkably ignorant of military or strategic considerations.

Indeed it has to be said that the British machinery for coordinating military and policy considerations was never properly applied to the Far East or Southeast Asia. In part this was because the prewar machinery, the so-called Committee of Imperial Defence, had tended to compartmentalize issues of defense in the area east of Suez into Indian issues on the one hand and the defense of colonial bases against seaborne raids on the other. The problems of a major war in the Far East had been the exclusive concern of the Admiralty.

The Air Ministry had never even begun to consider them. The army had thought of them solely in terms of the defense of Singapore and Hong Kong.

The matter was complicated by the existence of separate and independent governments in Australia and New Zealand and the entire formally independent structure of the government and armed forces of India, with its separate ministry represented at cabinet level in London. The result was that the chiefs of staff in London had no single command structure to deal with east of Suez. The intelligence structure was fragmented and dispersed. Churchill's reorganization of the whole defense machinery in 1940-41 did not really take in the India/Southeast Asia/Pacific region until after the Japanese onrush had swamped Southeast Asia and arrived at the land and maritime frontiers of India and Australia. His first attempt at a Southeast Asian command structure was broken in that onrush. Australia and her approaches, New Guinea, and the Solomons passed into an American command area under General MacArthur, the only military figure besides the later Field Marshall Lord Alexander of Tunis whose career and reputation survived initial defeat.

This British inattention to the perils with which their position in Southeast Asia was fraught was compounded by a serious intelligence failure in the appreciation of Japanese military strength and capability. British Admiralty estimates of the capacity of the Japanese battle fleet contained a built-in assumption of an "Oriental inefficiency" factor that equated seven British capital ships with Japan's eight and still gave the British superiority. Where Japanese naval airpower was concerned, the long battle for control of British naval air forces between the Admiralty and the Air Ministry, which returned seaborne aircraft to the control of the Royal Navy only in 1936, meant that Britain's fleet commanders still saw them as ancillary to, rather than a more powerful substitute for, the broadside of the capital ships, an extension of the area of reconnaissance rather than of the fleet's firepower. Royal Navy aircraft carriers still carried aircraft only in penny packets rather than in the massed squadrons that were to fight Midway with distances of hundreds of miles separating the fleets. While British land-based aircraft still remained under Air Force command, the aircraft of the Fleet Air Arm were only just emerging from the era of "stick-and-string" biplanes, whose torpedoes were notoriously erratic and whose bomb load was more suited to the Western Front of 1918. The destruction of the HMS *Prince of Wales* and HMS *Repulse,* caught off Malaya without fighter escort by Japanese naval aircraft, illustrated only too well the failures of British naval intelligence. The success of the Japanese army in Malaya and Burma attested to similar failures on the part of the army leadership, underlined by the surrender at Singapore of the bewildered and broken British and Commonwealth defense forces to a numerically inferior Japanese enemy.

The revolution in British army training and discipline apparent in the Eighth Army in Egypt and Cyrenaica in 1941, which was to produce by 1944 British jungle-trained troops who could outfight, outmaneuver, and outmarch the Japanese, had not yet touched British military thinking or preparations in Malaya. British thinking, British training, British weapon design, and British supply patterns followed British strategy and British diplomacy in concentrating on the European and Atlantic war and on containing it within the confines of the Mediterranean littoral.

Thus, of the future belligerents in the Far East, Britain had virtually abandoned the Pacific and the containment of Japan to their future ally America. The Soviet Union, informed by its own espionage ring in Tokyo that there was no Japanese threat to Soviet Pacific provinces, stripped the Red Amy in the Far East of forces so as to defend Moscow and roll the German invaders back once winter had set in. Japanese efforts to exploit the war in Europe to its own benefit had led to a direct confrontation with America, for which in 1941 the fate of Indochina had assumed an importance that it had lacked the previous year. For Japan the only solution to the China incident was to connect it with the European war. The event they waited for was a successful German invasion of Britain. When Germany attacked the Soviet Union, the Japanese hedged their bets at first. But the decision to occupy southern Indochina, seen in the vital Imperial Conference of July 2, 1941, as a move that would make possible a war with Britain and America, was only part of a complex series of moves reflecting an internal debate between the military and the naval high commands on how best to exploit the new German victory they anticipated, a debate in which for a time some army factions considered a new attack on the Soviets.

This move was nevertheless fateful since it provoked the American embargo. There is a good deal of evidence to suggest that Roosevelt and the British did not intend the embargo to be applied as ruthlessly as Dean Acheson, who was in charge, made sure it was. Their motivation was to control, not to cripple, the Japanese war-making capacity. It was heavily influenced by British anxieties expressed most peacefully at Argentia both to the president and Sumner Welles. Information on the July 2 Imperial Conference obtained from Allied decipherment of Japanese codes had given Britain advanced warning of a Japanese attack on British and Dutch possessions and of a Japanese attack on British and Dutch possessions, and of a Japanese declaration of war on Britain in fact. This was something that would make the British military position, stretched to the limit as it was, impossible. As Churchill told Sumner Welles at Argentia, "Japan would immediately be in a position to seize or destroy all of the British merchant shipping in the Indian Ocean and in the Pacific and cut the lifelines between the British Dominions and the British Isles." Without an American move, "the blow to the British Government might be decisive."

That move was made. An American confrontation with Japan became inevitable. The problems between the two countries were resolvable only by diplomatic or military defeat on one side or the other. Domestic politics made a compromise impossible. But without the events in Europe, that confrontation might never have taken place.

2.

The Royal Navy and the Japanese Threat

G. A. H. Gordon

The disasters that overtook the British Empire in the Far East in 1941-42 have been described as "one of the most outstanding examples of strategic overstretch in history."[1] What is remarkable is that it took Britain's rivals until then to exploit that overstretch, since it had been an institutionalized state of affairs for two decades and its earliest symptoms had been apparent for four.

Alfred von Tirpitz's Navy Law of 1900 had promised the creation of a German "Risk-Fleet" (as it was called), strong enough to inflict losses on the Royal Navy in the event of war, which would leave the British Empire a hostage to other predators. In January 1902 Great Britain signed an alliance with Japan—the first one between them in two generations.

These two events were not, at first, connected. In 1902 the kaiser's navy was not yet taken seriously by the British, and it was against a combination of France and Russia that the alliance had been framed.[2] For Britain, the need for the alliance was the first innocuous sign of imperial overstretch, and it derived from the mere fact that countries that had started later in naval industrialization were now catching up. To the Japanese, their exclusive partnership with the world's greatest (and normally aloof) imperial power was a source of pride, for it gave them a place at the top table of international affairs and ensured that other nations would not combine to push them around. In technical matters the Imperial Japanese and Royal Navies grew close over the next few years, with the latter gaining an almost exclusive consultant/supplier relationship with its ally.

The alliance had a "two-enemies" clause that did not oblige Britain to join with Japan against Russia in 1904 (although it nearly happened anyway, when a paranoid Russian fleet shot up Humber fishing boats in the North Sea, mistaking them for Japanese destroyers); and with Admiral Togo's crushing defeat of Rozhestvensky at Tsushima in 1905, its original raison d'être passed. However, to allow the alliance to lapse was unthinkable to the Japanese; and for the British, owing to the momentum of Tirpitz's construction programs, the German factor was now paramount in strategical calculations.

Fisher was about to startle the world by unveiling HMS *Dreadnought.* His next ploy in the North Sea arms race would be the scrapping of scores of old ships on imperial policing duties, so that their personnel could be redistributed to modern ships in home waters—a process that would be made easier if the Japanese underwrote Britain's liabilities while she outfaced Germany. The Admiralty therefore welcomed the alliance's reaffirmation in 1905 because, as Lord Selborne, the First Lord of the Admiralty from 1900 to 1905, said, "it made a satisfactory disposition of our fleets easier."[3] But a subtle change had already taken place in the roles of patron and patronized.

Japan's partnership with Britain brought her into the war against Germany and her allies in August 1914. Imperial Japanese Navy warships searched for von Spee's cruiser squadron and escorted Australian troops across the Indian Ocean. Japan captured the German port of Tsingtao, on the Shantung peninsula, and seized Germany's Pacific islands—the Marianas, Carolines, and Marshalls. But she was reluctant to get involved in the real war outside the Western Pacific area,[4] and the impression that she regarded the Far East, in the absence of supervision, as an adventure playground gained credence from the "Twenty-one Demands" with which she confronted China, and which brought Washington and London together in protest. The war

> effectively removed the European presence and left Japan with considerably strengthened industrial and financial infrastructures, mainly as a result of Japan taking over Asian markets that the Europeans could no longer supply. In addition, the war allowed Japan to make certain territorial gains that left her in a very strong position to dominate the Far East.[5]

Not least suspicious about Japan's agenda was the United States, and notwithstanding the two countries' status as allies in the closing months of the Great War, "Japanese-American relations at the end of the First World War were strained."[6] Both embarked upon huge construction programs and appeared committed to the path of naval arms competition. American popular opinion, agitated by the usual inventory of anti-British pressure groups, set itself the goal of breaking up the Anglo-Japanese Alliance, which was due for review in 1921.

It became clear that war-exhausted Britain would have to stop the new naval race or win it, for otherwise she would find herself shoved from first to third among nations and her empire a hostage to the unlikely indulgence of others. Her predicament was heightened by the fact that much of the Royal Navy's stock of capital ships comprised first-generation "dreadnoughts"—coal-burners with 12-inch guns—which were no match for the hardware taking shape on postwar drawing boards. When the Americans invited the Pacific powers to discuss their differences, the British readily agreed. But the seeds of future British appeasement were sown in the Five- and Four-Power Treaties signed at the Washington Conference.

The Americans had little real desire to pay for the massive program bandied about by their naval lobby, and they confronted the British with the concept of parity in capital ship tonnages at a level economically convenient to them rather than commensurate with Britain's global defense liabilities. Great Britain was also to end her alliance with Japan, which would be awarded a suitably smaller ration of fleet strength.

Within the officer corps of the Royal Navy, certainly for Admiral of the Fleet Earl Beatty, the First Sea Lord, and Rear-Admiral Chatfield, his naval negotiator at Washington, and his erstwhile flag-captain in the Grand Fleet, the U.S. Navy had supplanted the Imperial Japanese Navy as the Royal Navy's closest foreign service by virtue of the fact that toward the end of the war an American battle squadron had joined Beatty's Grand Fleet, and American destroyers had played an important part in the defeat of the U-boat. The Americans had generated much goodwill by working openhandedly under British command and adapting to British signal books and operational practices. Such cohesion, of NATO standard, between the armed forces of two nations was unprecedented; and it proved, indeed, a transient moment in Anglo-American relations. It is, however, fair to suggest that in this connection the Japanese had missed a trick in refusing to send a couple of *Kongo*s to join the Battle-Cruiser Fleet when asked to do so earlier in the war. For now that Germany's "Risk Fleet" had been disposed of, the British were becoming less sanguine about the benefits of the alliance.

Nonetheless the preponderant view was that its continuation would act as a restraint on Japan's future behavior. And it was held by the Admiralty

> that Britain should tell the Americans to go ahead with building what they liked and good luck to them. No one in Britain contemplated a war with the United States, and if the latter felt inclined to possess the largest fleet in the world, Britain had no cause for apprehension. But for Britain to tie her hands in the all-important matter of sea power, not only in relation to America but other countries too, was a fundamental mistake. There was much to be said for this view.[7]

Had the world not then been "living in an era of dreams [in which it] would take [huge] doses of morphia,"[8] the American remedy could probably have been dismissed on cogently argued rational grounds. But in the atmosphere of moral righteousness prevailing in 1921,

> to challenge the American President's arbitrarily chosen ratios would probably mean wrecking the Conference, and it was thought most inadvisable for Britain, as the American public's hereditary whipping-boy, to risk doing that.[9]

The British naval representatives may also have been unaware of the uncoordinated and private-enterprise nature of policy-making in U.S. government departments, of which skillful use might have been made.

The details of the settlement agreed upon in Washington in 1922 are well known. The British government, beset by war debts and League-of-Nationism, overrode the Admiralty's reasoned objections to the American package and accepted parity in capital ships. Japan was allowed a 60 percent ratio to the big two; France and Italy, 35 percent. Other major warship types were also subjected to limitations for a period of ten years. To make the Far East accessible to the British battlefleet—in compensation for the loss of the alliance—a naval base was permitted at Singapore.[10] The termination of the Anglo-Japanese Alliance "was softened and to some extent disguised by [its] merging in a Four-Power Treaty between the US, Britain, Japan and France."[11]

> Under this pact, they agreed to respect one another's possessions and rights in the Far East, though the necessary machinery for doing so was not created. . . . this device, backed by platitudes regarding friendship and the League of Nations, left no one deceived. The arrangement was manifestly fraudulent and left the Japanese resentful and hurt.[12]

For the Americans, despite ritual protests from their navalists that they had been robbed of their projected battleships, the deal had promoted them "at a stroke into co-equality with the strongest naval power without having to go to the expense of building their way up to that position."[13] For the British Empire, the settlement papered over an insidious strategical flaw, for the alliance with Japan had been worth a squadron of battleships, and Washington made sense only as long as the naval shipyards of continental Europe—which were of no significance to America or Japan—remained idle. Chatfield's throwaway remark to his Japanese opposite at Washington, that "this sort of thing has happened before in our history. It will all be the same in a hundred years' time. Our descendants will soon get it back again,"[14] was sublime gamesmanship. The Japanese regarded the treaties of Washington as a national humiliation.

Admiralty policy in the event of war with Japan was now expressed by the longstanding "Main Fleet to Singapore" plan. The "Main Fleet" was to comprise ten capital ships, and slowly, with stops and starts, a base fit to house it grew out of the mangroves on the Johore Strait side of Singapore island. But the predicament of a global military power trapped in an arms-limitation bargain based on regional mathematics began to disturb the more farsighted almost immediately:

> At the 1923 Imperial Conference . . . that shrewd Boer Jan Smuts, Prime Minister of South Africa, doubted whether the proposed new naval base at Singapore would offer any protection to Australia and New Zealand unless Britain could send the battlefleet—and believed that Japan was unlikely to attack unless she had support in Europe. If this were so, Smuts asked, would it be feasible to divide the Royal Navy, now that Britain no longer enjoyed the old huge superiority? Leo Amery, First Lord of the Admiralty, had admitted in reply: "Of course it is perfectly feasible that, if there were a European combination against us at the same moment as war was declared against us by Japan, we should be in a position of extraordinary difficulty."[15]

The Americans now began to agitate for reductions in the Royal Navy's cruiser strength for the irrelevant reason that they did not need so many. Their campaign strengthened the hands of British economists and pacifists, and they were rewarded, against renewed Admiralty protests, at the 1930 London Naval Conference. But while London also saw Britain, the United States, and Japan extending the Washington restrictions for a further five years, France refused to comply through fear of new German construction, and Italy through alleged fear of France. The dormant naval yards of Europe were beginning to stir. In September 1931 Japan invaded Manchuria. In January 1933 Hitler arrived.

Doubt grew over the assumption that the British "Main Fleet" would be available, whenever needed, to defend the Far East. Washington had thus set the scene for a delayed "game of poker in which the stakes were the Empire itself and the bluff could be called by Japan declaring war concurrently with Germany."[16] Neither of the other two major Pacific powers, the United States and Japan, was compromised in this fashion. The passing of the Anglo-Japanese Alliance was bitterly lamented: Britain had lost the freedom to concentrate her fleet.[17] From this perspective it is unsurprising that pressure for appeasement originated and gathered steam in those ministries responsible for Britain's worldwide strategical balancing act, and that its most dogged advocates were to be found in the Admiralty.[18]

From 1933 Admiral Sir Ernle Chatfield, now First Sea Lord and chief of naval staff—"the dominant personality in the formulation of British strategic policy" before World War II—relentlessly warned that Japan would only (but surely) strike south if the British navy became detained elsewhere.[19]

As early as December 1933 he told the Defence Requirements Sub Committee (DRC) that it was "imperative to do everything possible to keep on good terms with Japan."[20] And in February 1934 he told the commander-in-chief for China, Admiral Sir Frederick Dreyer, that Japan "is unlikely to provoke this country too far until she knows that we have a danger nearer home to worry us." That first preconditional danger would come, he predicted accurately, from Nazi Germany in five years' time.[21]

The next month the Cabinet, prompted by the DRC, discussed the need to get back "at least to our old terms of cordiality and mutual respect with Japan." The discussion shows the essentially naval character of imperial security, the beginnings of appeasement, the central role of Neville Chamberlain, the chancellor of the exchequer, and the lack of dissent in the Cabinet. The secretary of state for India

> pointed out that at present no nation had any influence with Japan who, like Germany, was isolated. It would be a great advantage if we could recover our influence there. The Chancellor of the Exchequer agreed. Everyone must share the anxieties that had been expressed on this possible menace. That anxiety would continue as long as Japan was isolated, but that was an argument for the policy [of rapprochement] which he warmly supported. He recalled that the Japanese were a sensitive people and that the termination of the Anglo-Japanese Alliance had been a great blow to their amour propre. The very fact of our offering to have a fresh discussion

> and some kind of bilateral understanding would tend to restore their ruffled feelings. Turning to the [forthcoming Second London] Naval Conference, he gathered that the Americans wanted us to line up with them in opposing any alteration in the Japanese proportion [of fleet strength]. He could think of nothing more likely to give offence to the Japanese than this, and he thought we should make clear to the Americans that we could not pull the chestnuts out of the fire for them. . . . he put as a basis of discussion the opposite point of view: we should decline to align ourselves with Washington; indicate that we were not prepared to submit ourselves to the limitations of a Treaty and say that we did not mind what the Americans chose to build. At the same time we might go to Japan and say that we had not linked ourselves with America. If this were done Japan would be free of the fear that we might be united with America against her. . . . He therefore suggested that there should be a Pact of Non-Aggression with Japan . . . which would enable us to concentrate on the serious situation that was developing nearer home. The First Lord of the Admiralty strongly supported [Chamberlain]. . . . The Prime Minister [MacDonald] thought that all were agreed that something would have to be done to improve relations with Japan.[22]

Privately, Chamberlain wrote that "I have no doubt we could easily make an agreement with [the Japanese] if the USA were out of the picture. It is the Americans who are the difficulty." [23] And his chief of staff at the Treasury, Sir Warren Fisher, held that "the worst of our deficiencies is our entanglement with the USA" and that Britain should be prepared to sacrifice American friendship to regain the more valuable friendship with Japan.[24]

In comparison, the Admiralty's statements confined themselves to strong support of detente with Japan. For example, the First Sea Lord told Dreyer that

> [w]hile we remain unready we have to do everything that is possible to avoid a conflict with Japan. . . . We [in the Admiralty] have done all we can do at the moment. . . . our foreign policy must do the rest while we are gaining strength . . . the main national policy is keeping out of war with Japan at all costs.[25]

But Chamberlain had been right to suppose that the ending of the alliance at Washington in 1922 had offended the Japanese; they felt discarded and perceived the beginnings of an Anglo-Saxon combination against them. It was very difficult for Britain's reputation in Japan to claw back from this position. There were of course other obstructions, such as growing trade conflicts, tension over China, and the suspicions of the Americans. At the Second London Naval Conference in 1935, the Japanese demanded a common upper limit for the fleet strengths of Japan, Britain, and America, but they let it be known that they were, in the words of the Cabinet minutes, "quite willing that the UK should have a stronger Navy than Japan. This of course gave rise to an almost insoluble problem in as much as the US insisted on naval parity with ourselves."[26]

Impasse. Now Britain found herself caught up in the hostility between France and Germany, in much the same way as between Japan and the United States in the Pacific. Hitler repudiated Versailles in March 1935 and made clear his intention of building a new fleet of capital ships. Another headache therefore hit Britain's naval strategists. The Anglo-German Naval Agreement of June 1935 gets bad press in the history books, for it appeared to legitimize Germany's abrogation of the Treaty of Versailles, and Chatfield was touchy about it in retrospect. A German wish to be allowed a navy of up to 35 percent of the size of the Royal Navy in surface ships, 45 percent in submarines, was granted. The Admiralty was clearly leading Whitehall in appeasement at this time, but its purpose was to forestall the development in European waters of a threat so serious as to preclude the fleet's deployment elsewhere, and indeed Germany's senior naval officers considered the 35 percent limit to rule out Britain as a future adversary.[27]

Then came Italy's attack on Abyssinia. Owing to the lack of commitment of other powers, it fell to Britain alone to provide the forces of so called "collective security" for the League of Nations, and she nearly found herself at war in the Mediterranean. The headache was becoming a migraine. Those responsible for imperial defense knew that "the demands made on the Navy by a war against Germany might threaten the whole basis of the planned Far Eastern strategy,"[28] and foresaw that "[i]n the event of our being embroiled in a European war, Japan might well consider the opportunity favourable for attempting to remove the power of Great Britain to interfere with the policy of Japan."[29] Fences must be mended with Italy to leave the Armed Forces free "to deal with the Far Eastern menace."[30] Chatfield privately took the view that if Italy had a stake in Abyssinia the tables would be turned: Her communications would then be hostage to British sea power, a state of affairs which should favor peace.[31]

By this stage the 'appeasers' had become directionally impartial.

> The dominant feature of the situation was the increasing probability that war would spread from one theatre to another. It was simply not possible to foresee a time when Britain, even allowing for help from France and

> perhaps other allies, would be strong enough to protect herself against Germany, Italy and Japan simultaneously.[32]

In January 1936 Britain's senior general, the chief of the Imperial General Staff, added his voice to the rising litany when he drew the Cabinet's attention

> to the recent occasions on which Japanese statesmen and soldiers had hinted that they would welcome closer relations with this country. It was recognised that there were formidable political obstacles in the way, but it was urged that our weak military situation in the Far East made every effort necessary to overcome those obstacles.

The First Lord of the Admiralty added that "[t]he real danger was lest Germany and Japan should be driven together. Already they were interchanging information on naval matters."[33]

In January 1937 the First Sea Lord petitioned the professional head of the Foreign Office:

> as we cannot fight simultaneously in the East and the West, can we make an agreement in one area or the other, not necessarily a permanent agreement, but one which will give us greater security than we have now during our slow period of rearmament? It appears impossible that we should make an agreement with Japan that would be of the same value as the old alliance. We might placate her by recognising Manchukuo.[34]

And a few weeks later the chiefs of staff hammered away that

> the difficulties and dangers of conducting a war against Japan in the Far East, particularly if we were simultaneously engaged in Europe, are so great that it is manifest that no effort must be spared to establish such good relations with our former allies, the Japanese, as will obviate, as far as possible, the chances of their being aligned against us.[35]

The Foreign Office had understood the Achilles' heel of Britain's Far Eastern policy as long ago as 1925,[36] but obtusely continued to imagine that Britain was capable of responding to the dictators through weight of armaments production alone—if the government so wished. The almost emotional attachment of some historians, such as Correlli Barnett, Martin Gilbert, and Williamson Murray, to the Churchillian myth that the scale of rearmament was constrained by Treasury meanness, and that appeasement was therefore avoidable, persists to this day. In fact, as was painfully obvious to Treasury and Admiralty only a few months into rearmament, existing naval programs had taken up all available specialized industrial capacity.[37] The Admiralty's lobbying for the adoption of the vaunted two-power standard as a policy goal was really a matter of only "academical interest since we shall already be working towards that standard at our best speed and cannot attain it for several years to come."[38] And by the time Chamberlain moved from No. 11 to No. 10 Downing Street, appeasement offered the only accessible escape from the British Commonwealth's strategical nightmare. In his words: "a political adjustment with one or more of our potential enemies was absolutely vital."[39]

And so it went on. In November 1937 the secretary of the Committee of Imperial Defence, Sir Maurice Hankey, joined the First Sea Lord in a strident call for

> something [to be done] in the field of foreign policy to reduce our defensive commitments. With the greatest sense of responsibility I must add my considered endorsement to the repeated warnings of the Chiefs of Staff that action ought to be taken to effect a permanent improvement in our relations with Italy. . . . I wish to urge with all the strength at my command that nothing but national interest of the gravest importance should be allowed to stand in the way of a whole-hearted effort to secure better relations with Italy.

And Chatfield doggedly "pointed out that an improvement in our relations with Germany or Japan is urgent."[40] He had become desperately worried about the likelihood (as he perceived it) "that shortly after the commencement of a war [in Europe] we might have to send a fleet to the Far East, where we now have an enemy instead of an ally."[41]

That same month the Admiralty's director of plans, Captain Tom Phillips, painted the stark strategical urgency of rapprochement: "If we could reach a satisfactory agreement with Germany, our other defence commitments would largely solve themselves, as Italy would never dare attack alone and even if Japan did not moderate her policies we should at least be in a position to deal with her." Chatfield considered Phillips's summary of the situation "very able" and sent it up to his minister with the following covering remarks:

> [T]he main proposal of this paper is that we should make an agreement with Germany because, in view of our Imperial responsibilities, we cannot afford to prolong our enmity. . . . If we have to fight her it will probably also mean war with Japan and possibly Italy—a world war which may last for years with enormous loss of lives and money, and general misery in the world.

He also added his analysis—which did less than justice to his influence as chairman of the Chiefs of Staff Committee—that "[t]he Navy have greater interest, perhaps, in such an agreement because our naval responsibilities are more world-wide than those of the other Services. I feel therefore that Admiralty pressure alone can be used among the three Services to obtain the desired settlement."[42]

After March 1938 only Europe appeared to offer scope for detente, for in that month Japanese intransigence obliged Britain and the United States to cut themselves free from the remnants of the Washington restrictions. Only now, six months before Munich, did Britain accept that friendly relations with Japan were irrecoverable.

The import of this parting of the ways was plain enough to Captain Phillips and the planning chiefs of the other services. In a paper titled "The Military Implications of German Aggression Against Czechoslovakia," they connected the Japanese threat with Britain's options vis-à-vis Hitler:

> [B]y no pressure that we can bring to bear, either by sea, on land or in the air, is it possible for us forcibly to prevent Germany from invading and overrunning Bohemia, and from inflicting a decisive defeat on the Czechoslovakian Army. We should then be faced with the necessity of undertaking a war with Germany, for the purpose of restoring Czechoslovakia's lost integrity and this object would only be achieved by the defeat of Germany and as the outcome of a prolonged struggle. . . . [Meanwhile] the advent of Japan on the side of Germany and Italy would produce a situation which neither the present nor the projected strength of our defence forces is designed to meet. The British Empire would be threatened simultaneously in Western Europe, in the Mediterranean and in the Far East, by an immense aggregate of armed strength and would be faced with the gravest danger. . . . We are therefore of the opinion that Great Britain should not risk the possibility of war except in the defence of interests that are vital to her [which obviously did not include Czechoslovakia].[43]

In February 1939 Lord Chatfield, now Minister for the Coordination of Defence, warned his Cabinet colleagues yet again that in the event of war with Germany, "Japan could embarrass us, not [even] by active intervention, but [merely] by making a strategic disposition of her forces which would constitute a severe threat to Australia and India."[44]

On the 15th of March Hitler occupied Prague and tossed away both the Munich peace promises and the Anglo-German naval agreement. Appeasement had run its course. The Australian government immediately pressed for reaffirmation of Britain's post-1922 commitment to send the Main Fleet to Singapore in the event of Japanese aggression. It was Chamberlain's miserable task to frame an evasive reply, which, as Marder has written, came as a "bombshell" to the Australians. "It struck them as a retreat from previous assurances, referring as it did to 'a combination never envisaged in our earlier plans,' namely, the possibility of Britain having to fight Germany, Italy and Japan at the same time."[45]

A few days later the Cabinet met to consider whether Britain should offer a guarantee of military aid to Poland. The Admiralty, which had spent six years burdened with imperial safety, said wearily that "if Poland were attacked, it [would be] politically impossible for us to stand aside."[46] For Britain's Far Eastern Empire, those resigned words marked the beginning of what an Australian historian has called—with some bitterness—"The Great Betrayal."

Historians have sought to tarnish those who favored appeasement with the smear of "sympathy for the goals of Hitler's Germany."[47] To ascribe such motives to Chatfield and his naval staff would be fatuous. To the Admiralty, which feared that peace, once broken somewhere, would prove to be hemispherically indivisible, appeasement was as obvious as any damage-limitation precaution before a collision at sea. It was simple strategic seamanship. It may also be mentioned that in 1939, after appeasement was seen to have failed, Chatfield was to advocate alliance with Soviet Russia as a means of containing Germany.

To Churchill, the arch-opposer of appeasement, from his backseat position outside government, the vulnerability of the Far East—the "Catch 1922" of British strategy—was inconvenient. And so he belittled the threat from Japan and even disavowed the importance of the colonies, and was to carry this expedient, tendentious, and even wishful perspective into Downing Street in May 1940.

Obviously "a general war in Europe might well provide [Japan] with the same opportunities as in 1914-18 for advancing her own interests without meddlesome intervention by other powers."[48] But while the First World War had offered Japan easy colonial toeholds here and there, this present war could end with Japan sweeping the board in the Western Pacific. However, if the Japanese were to contemplate war against the European colonial powers, and even the Americans, they must be absolutely certain that Germany was going to win the war in Europe, for otherwise, however extensive their short-term military gains, retribution would follow as sure as night follows day. For this reason, and because of all their own internal factions, they waited and watched. And before a year was up the German manifesto was looking plausible.

The catalog of Britain's strategical setbacks makes grim reading, from the point of view of her dependents. First, the demands of new construction for the Battle of the Atlantic caused work to be suspended on the four battleships of the *Lion* class, which the Admiralty had visualized playing a key role in a future conflict with Japan. The flame of renewed battleship programs flickered on in the hearts of the naval staff for some time, but in a symbolic and spiritual sense this was the beginning of the letting-go of the Far East.

Japan's early restraint lulled the British into believing it safe to redeploy forces stationed in the Far East. The cruiser complement of the China Fleet was pillaged for reinforcements elsewhere. And by June 1940 the 4th and 8th Submarine Flotillas were withdrawn from Singapore and Colombo, respectively, and sent to the Mediterranean. The former was an elite force of 15 vessels that had practiced the wolf-pack interception of an invasion convoy in the South China Sea.[49] In November 1941 the British in Singapore would be reduced to inventing submarines for the benefit of Japanese intelligence.

With the entry of Italy into the war and the fall of France in the midsummer of 1940, Britain's strategic assumptions collapsed like a house of cards. It had been mainly from the Mediterranean that most of the capital ships for the Main Fleet to Singapore were to have been drawn, leaving the French fleet to counterbalance the Italian. Now to leave the Mediterranean would be to lose it, while units from home waters being sent to the Far East would have to take the long-haul route around the Cape of Good Hope, thus extending the lead time of response to Japanese attack.

At the same time the orphaning of French colonies in Indochina, combined with Britain's life-or-death struggle in Europe, "offered all sorts of glittering opportunities to Japan,"[50] and the chiefs of staff met at the end of July to reassess the situation in the Far East.

The paper placed before them,[51] its amendments,[52] and the comments added by the War Cabinet on the eighth of August[53] depict exactly the strategical overstretch that the Admiralty had dreaded since 1922:

> [U]ntil we have defeated Germany and Italy or have drastically reduced their naval strength, we are faced with the problem of attempting to defend our Far East interests in the absence of an adequate fleet. . . . the collapse of France, the development of a direct threat to the UK and the necessity for retaining in European waters a fleet of sufficient strength to match both the German and Italian fleets have made it temporarily impossible for us to despatch a fleet to the Far East should the occasion arise. . . . Committed as we are in Europe . . . we must avoid an open clash with Japan. A general settlement, including economic concessions to Japan,

> should be concluded as soon as possible. Failing this settlement, our general policy must be to play for time, cede nothing until we must, and build up our defences as soon as we can.

For information of the commander in chief for the Far East, this dismal material was packed off by surface mail in the Blue Funnel cargo-liner *Automedon.*

On November 11 the *Automedon* was stopped in the Indian Ocean by the armed-merchant raider *Atlantis.* When the British steamer started sending a raider report, she was shelled by the German ship and several officers were killed or wounded, including those whose task it was to throw overboard certain weighted mailbags that now fell into the possession of the German boarding party. The contents duly reached the German Embassy in Tokyo on December 5, where they were perused by Admiral Paul Wenneker, the German naval attaché, and passed to Vice Admiral Kondo.

> At first he could not believe that the documents were genuine, suspecting that they had been deliberately allowed to fall into enemy hands in order to mislead both the Germans and the Japanese. However, when Wenneker explained how they had come to be captured, and the loss of life involved, Kondo accepted the authenticity of this almost incredible windfall. [54]

James Rusbridger believes that this intelligence windfall was the catalyst that pointed Japan southward. His evidence is largely circumstantial. Apart from the presentation of a Samurai sword to Captain Rogge of the *Atlantis* (Goering and Rommel being the only other two Germans so honored), it mainly concerns the timing of subsequent Japanese moves that could be described as preparatory to a strike south—allowing for the fact that the captured intelligence probably took three or four weeks to percolate down to the relatively junior policy-drafting levels of the Japanese military and naval staffs. But the "coincidences" are nonetheless impressive.

In January 1941 Japan took advantage of a clash between Siamese and French troops and intervened. "In return for negotiating a cease-fire, Tokyo demanded the right to station troops in Indochina's southern provinces, to use her airfield and construct others, and to make use of Camranh Bay in the South China Sea."[55] In this month also, Japanese troops began intensive training for warfare in jungle conditions.[56] And, in February, Japan covered her back by signing a secret agreement with Moscow to limit her military commitment in Manchuria.

The implication of all this is that, until the *Automedon* revelations, the Japanese had yet to grasp the full extent of Britain's weakness in the Far East—in which case Willmott's comment, that by the summer of 1940 "[i]t was obvious [to Japan] that not one of the European empires in the Far East was capable of defending itself,"[57] is premature. Britain's desperate and dishonest policy of trying to tiptoe her way past the two or three years of crisis, hoping that her period of greatest vulnerability in the Far East would pass before any rumblings were felt from the enemy-in-waiting, came astonishingly close to success. Plausibly, in Japanese eyes, the aura of supremacy surrounding the Western colonial powers still lingered. Wenneker's diary, at any rate, recalls that "[Admiral] Kondo repeatedly expressed to me how valuable the information contained in the War Cabinet memorandum was for the navy. Such a significant weakening of the British Empire could not have been identified from outward appearances."[58]

If, as Rusbridger considers, the *Automedon* saga was one of the greatest intelligence disasters in history, then by the same token, for Britain to have conned her way past the danger—had she done so—would surely have been the greatest strategical bluff of all time.

The War Cabinet's covering remarks to the COS report included the bold-print observation, which had the unmistakable touch of Churchill, that "our best hope of being able to supply naval forces for the Far East in the near future lies in the possibility of early and successful actions against Italian naval forces in the Mediterranean." By coincidence the interception of *Automedon* took place on the day of the Royal Navy's night attack on Taranto, when a handful of biplanes torpedoed three Italian battleships at their moorings. But when the Australian prime minister asked if ships could now be spared for Singapore, Churchill made further excuses.[59] In July France's Vichy leaders conceded to Japan's demands for airfields and harbors in southern Indochina.

> [R]ealising that this southward move by Japan was likely to be followed by the occupation of Siam as well as the rest of IndoChina, Vice-Admiral Sir Geoffrey Layton [and his service opposites] advised their Chiefs of Staff that, for lack of a Far East Fleet, Malaya now needed 31 squadrons totalling 566 first-line aircraft.[60]

As the officially understood requirement had been 336 aircraft, this caused a prevaricating row about interservice uncoordination, to which London attributed the new, inflated figure. Since there were only 158 "front-line" aircraft in Malaya and Singapore anyway, and most of them were obsolescent, the Air Ministry might have supplied 178 modern fighters and then had the row. They could well have spared them. The Battle of Britain, the Blitz, and the fear of imminent invasion had all passed; the most effective units of the Luftwaffe were in Russia; no escort-intensive bombing campaign worthy of the name had yet begun. But there were more than a hundred fighter squadrons in southern England with little but sweeps over occupied France to pass the time. Ten percent of their number, in Spitfire and Hurricane squadrons, could have made a critical difference to Malaya and no difference to England. But long after MI6 had reported that the Germans had hijacked the *Automedon* mail and presumably given it to the Japanese, leaving no one for the British to fool but themselves and their dependents, the mentality of bluff went on.

The Royal Navy, too, could have spared forces but was forbidden to do so. It is untrue that in the late summer and early autumn of 1941 there was a desperate shortage of operational capital ships.[61] At no other time during the entire war, except in the closing stages when the last three *King George V*s had reached the fleet, were there so many available. The Home Fleet at Scapa Flow had to watch for *Tirpitz*, and the battle-worthiness of the two Scharnhorsts was never clear. But Cunningham had got the measure of the Italian battlefleet, and owing to the steady elimination of German supply ships, as a result of code-breaking successes, the need was passing for Atlantic convoys to be escorted by battleships in case of attack by surface raiders.

Royal Oak and *Hood* had been sunk. *Rodney* was desperately overdue for refit. *Nelson* had been torpedoed in September. *Warspite* was in refit in America; and so too, until September, was *Resolution*. But *Barhnam* (newly repaired), *Malaya, Queen Elizabeth, Valiant, Ramillies, Royal Sovereign, Renown, Repulse, Revenge, King George V,* and *Prince of Wales* were all serviceable, although the *Prince of Wales* workup had been repeatedly interrupted. There were thus at any one time up to 11 assorted capital ships of which any five or six could have been sent at short notice to the East.

In carriers the story was not so good. *Courageous* and *Glorious* had been sunk. The elderly *Furious* soldiered on but was unfit for front-line service. *Illustrious* and *Formidable* had both been bombed and were repairing in Norfolk, Virginia. *Indomitable* was not yet operational. Of first-class units only *Victorious* and *Ark Royal* were fully fit. The slower and smaller-capacity *Hermes* and *Eagle* were serviceable. Thus, one modern fleet carrier could soon be spared (two by early 1942) and one older one.

The air warfare-related equipment of these ships left much to be desired, but they represented a not inconsiderable force—roughly equal to the American ships shortly to be knocked out at Pearl Harbor and Coral Sea, or (very notionally) to the military value of the old Anglo-Japanese Alliance.

The naval staff and the chiefs of staff wanted such a fleet to assemble without delay in the Indian Ocean. Churchill, however, was fixated on the Middle East, where he had invested 500,000 men and 1,000 aircraft, and where he was reliant on Australian troops—to obtain which he had consistently to belittle Australia's own danger from Japan.[62] He promised that if Australia were threatened with invasion, Britain would "then cut our losses in the Mediterranean and sacrifice every interest" to defend the Dominion,[63] but he regarded the likelihood of the debt's being called in as remote.[64]

> This was indeed a tragic issue [he wrote piously after the war], like having to choose whether your son or your daughter should be killed. For my part I did not believe that anything that might happen in Malaya could amount to a fifth part of the loss of Egypt, the Suez Canal and the Middle East. I would not tolerate the idea of abandoning the struggle for Egypt, and was resigned to pay whatever forfeits were extracted in Malaya.[65]

Churchill had been to Egypt: as a young man he had made his name as a maverick war correspondent in the Sudan. He was unfamiliar with the Far East. In reality British interests in the two theaters were interdependent. Vice Admiral Sir Tom Phillips, now vice-chief of naval staff, argued that, whether the prime minister liked it or not, a Japanese fleet in the Indian Ocean would sever the 12,000-mile round Africa supply route to the Middle East.

Churchill considered Naval Intelligence "very much inclined to exaggerate Japanese strength and efficiency,"[66] but now grudgingly agreed to send capital ships to Singapore—although only the minimum that he believed necessary to impress the Malayans and Australians and deter the Japanese. For this force, which he glamorized as "of the highest quality," the battleship *Prince of Wales,* the 25 year-old battle cruiser *Repulse,* and the new carrier *Indomitable* were allocated. And to lead them Churchill chose Tom Phillips—the same officer who, in 1937 and 1938, as director of plans, had warned Churchill's predecessors not to acquire enemies in the East and West simultaneously. Phillips, who would supplant Vice Admiral Sir Geoffrey Layton on arrival in Singapore, embarked in *Prince of Wales* and sailed on October 25.

Hindsight invites comparison of the voyage of Force Z, led by *Prince of Wales,* to that of the Russian fleet on its way to defeat at Tsushima in 1905. Probably Churchill had in mind the precedent of the voyage to meet von Spee, at the Falklands, of the battle cruisers *Invincible* and *Inflexible* in 1914. On that occasion Churchill, as First Lord of the Admiralty, had chosen as task-force leader Vice Admiral Sir Doveton Sturdee, who as chief of war staff at the Admiralty held the equivalent position to Phillips as VCNS in 1941. At any rate, for radio deception purposes, Force Z was allocated the long-vacant call sign of Sturdee's famous ships.[67]

As a man and a staff officer, Tom Phillips had his admirers. But no historian has stood up and said that he was the best choice to lead Force Z, and with good reason. One distinct edge the Royal Navy had over Japanese and Americans alike was a stock of admirals with wartime experience of command at sea—often against considerable odds. Granted that Cunningham was too illustrious to be sent to what was still, and might just remain, a wartime backwater, Somerville, Tovey, Ramsay, or even Layton himself would have been wiser choices; they had all been under fire and none of them had a mind-set about the impotence of airpower.

On November 3, *Indomitable*'s participation in Force Z was canceled when she grounded while working-up in the West Indies. As *Ark Royal* was lost on November 14, she might never have joined anyway. During *Prince of Wales*'s visit, en passant to Capetown, Phillips conferred with Field Marshal Smuts, who warned that the expedition had the makings of a first-class disaster.

Prince of Wales met up with *Repulse* at Colombo and went on to arrive amid much publicity at Singapore. Phillips flew to Manila to confer with General MacArthur and Admiral Hart. Personally, they got on well and they planned to concentrate their naval forces in the event of war, with Force Z being supported by U.S. Navy destroyers and basing itself in the Philippines.[68]

Phillips's visit was interrupted, on December 6, by news of the sighting by the R.A.F. of a heavily escorted Japanese convoy off Indochina, westbound. This reconnaissance patrol was part of a grid set up by the Admiral Layton as recently as November 29, in coordination with the Americans and the Dutch—which circumstance, added to the pooling of naval forces discussed in Manila, would make it surprising if intelligence was not also being shared (if only sotto voce) between the British and the Americans. These issues—coordination and intelligence—have been highlighted in 1991 by James Rusbridger and Eric Nave in their book *Betrayal at Pearl Harbour.*

Nave was an Australian officer working in code-breaking with the Royal Navy, but was in Australia in 1941. Rusbridger's regret is that he was unable to interview the ideal witness, Commander Malcolm Burnett of the British Far East Combined Bureau, who died in 1984. Rusbridger and Nave's thesis is that the British had been reading Japanese navy code JN-25 for some two years without telling the Americans, and knew in advance about the attack on Pearl Harbor but did not tell the Americans—hence the "betrayal."

No one can doubt Churchill's capacity for work in the bushes, but Nave and Rusbridger's account is partly discordant with statements made to me by Commander Burnett, a family friend, in 1980. He stated that his people had broken the Japanese navy code, that they knew an attack on Hawaii was imminent, and that they told the Americans. He would not be pressed over details.

The convergence and divergence of Burnett's account and Nave and Rusbridger's prompted me in November 1991 to contact Burnett's wife. Mary

Burnett worked with her husband in FECB during those dramatic days. She confirms that they had been reading JN-25. She says that Burnett was so sure about a Japanese attack against Pearl that, with Layton's approval, he sent, or caused to be sent, a signal to the Americans, which they expected would reach the president. Graphically she recalls his disbelief and fury when it became apparent on Monday, December 8 (as it was in Singapore), that the message had somehow not gotten through. Subsequently, she says, he and Layton made a fuss, although with whom is unclear. And the plausibility of Royal Air Force scouts finding a convoy without being told where to look adds to the likelihood that Japanese naval "sigint" (signals intelligence) played a part in the vectoring of the reconnaissance patrol. Phillips returned to Singapore, where *Prince of Wales* now had her condensers in pieces. *Repulse,* which had set out on a flying visit to Darwin, was recalled.

Some historians have suggested that when it became clear that the deterrence had failed to deter, it should have been withdrawn at once, and the War Cabinet's deliberations on December 9 seem to recognize this logic. But such a view is incompatible with a typically prodding signal from Churchill asking Phillips what he was going to do about the convoy, which was known to both London and Washington, and "it was inconceivable that the force sent to secure Malaya from attack should not give battle when that attack materialized."[69] Therefore when reports came through of landings in northeastern Malaya, "his duty seemed clear."[70]

> Phillips knew that the bulk of Japan's aircraft-carriers were several thousand miles away . . . and he could reasonably assume that they were accompanied by most of her capital ships. No enemy fleet substantially superior to the *Prince of Wales* and *Repulse* could, therefore, appear in the South China Sea for at least a week. [71]

Force Z left Singapore on December 9 (December 8, Hawaii time) and proceeded northeast into the South China Sea as fast as reassembling condenser tubes allowed. However uncertain the immediate future, morale in the two ships was high. Finding nothing to sink on their northward sweep and knowing that they had been sighted by aircraft, they turned west after dark toward the reported landing areas.

Had they continued north for another 15 minutes,[72] they would have run into Admiral Kurita's eight-inch gunned cruisers. Both British capital ships had Type 284 surface gunnery control radar; the Japanese had none. One can question whether another Matapan (as Marder styles it) might have happened that night. But certainly Force Z might have justified its sortie, if not its sinking the next day.

Where Phillips planned to take Force Z, had they got back safely to Singapore, is unknown. The War Cabinet, on the 9th, had more or less settled for Pearl Harbor, as a sort of consolation prize to the Americans, but decided to sleep on it. When they awoke in London on December 10, it was too late. At around midday, in the Gulf of Siam, Japanese naval aircraft fell upon Force Z and overwhelmed both capital ships with torpedoes and bombs. By 1:20 P.M. all that remained of Churchill's Far Eastern deterrent strategy were several hundred sailors swimming for their lives and a few acres of floating wreckage.

To sum up, at the end of 1941 the U.S. Navy lost five ships of capital value; the Royal Navy lost six: *Ark Royal* and *Barham* to U-boats in the Western and Eastern Mediterranean respectively, *Queen Elizabeth* and *Valiant* to mining by frogmen in Alexandria harbor, and Force Z. Many of the American battleships were refloated and fought again. Moreover, given America's huge industrial resources and her capital ship construction program, and the Royal Navy's near-total commitment to the protection of merchant-shipping stocks through convoying and antisubmarine warfare, this was the end, for what it mattered, of the British navy's centuries-old position in the front rank of fleet powers. In terms of each country's status as the prime mover in world affairs, the losses in the Far East were a blood red dawn for America but sunset for Great Britain.

It has been said that "[i]t is unnecessary to search any further for the causes of the loss of Malaya than the lack of means to defend it."[73] This is untrue. The failure of defense was preceded by the failure of deterrence, and "a policy of deterrence from a position of military inferiority is never likely to prove effective."[74] You cannot then defend your command of the sea with a small, fast squadron best suited for raiding operations: Such a force betrays the mentality of having already lost command.

It could be suggested that if Churchill really hoped the United States might come into the war to defend British interests in the Far East, only a losing battle there could convincingly demonstrate need of help. What was going on in the somber recesses of his mind remains unknown. But the forces to present a credible defensive stance in Malaya were physically available, in terms of aircraft, manpower, and ships. Within a week of the loss of Force Z, five of Britain's nine available capital ships, plus three carriers, began to be brought together in the Indian Ocean, which shows what Churchill could do when he tried—and this in spite of the severe losses discussed above.

In the last analysis, the strategic choices belonged to the politicians and not to the admirals. But part of Churchill's problem with the Japanese threat is that he had simply worked himself into a mind-set about bluff and deterrence working indefinitely. His opposition to appeasement, in the 1930s, had locked him in a set of strategic priorities that were essentially postimperial in outlook. The fact that his wartime premiership saw the birth, by cesarian section, of the post imperial age, is not entirely unconnected.

Notes

1. Correlli Barnett, *Engage the Enemy More Closely* (New York: Norton, 1991), 382.
2. A. J. Marder, *British Naval Policy, 1880-1905* (London: Oxford University Press, 1941), 427.
3. Ibid., 428.
4. Geoffrey Bennett, *Loss of Prince of Wales and Repulse* (Annapolis: Naval Institute Press, 1973), 15.
5. H. P. Willmott, *Empires in the Balance* (Annapolis: Naval Institute Press, 1982), 26.
6. Ibid., 32.
7. Russell Grenfell, *Main Fleet to Singapore* (London: Faber and Faber, 1951), 37.
8. Lord Chatfield, *It Might Happen Again* (London: Heinemann, 1946), 5.
9. Ibid., 41.
10. See Stephen W. Roskill, *Naval Policy Between the Wars,* vol. 1 (Annapolis: Naval Institute Press, 1968); M. D. Kennedy, *The Estrangement of Great Britain and Japan 1917-35* (Berkeley: University of California Press, 1969); and J. R. Ferris, *Men, Money, and Diplomacy: The Evolution of British Strategic Policy 1919-26* (Ithaca, New York: Cornell University Press, 1989).
11. Ibid., 38.
12. Willmott, *Empires,* 36.
13. Grenfell, *Main Fleet,* 40.
14. Toda Ishimaru, *Japan Must Fight Britain* (London: Paternoster Press, 1936), 126.
15. Barnett, *Engage,* 379.
16. David Day, *The Great Betrayal* (New York: Norton, 1988), 10.
17. See, among others: N. H. Gibbs, *Grand Strategy,* vol. 1 (London: Her Majesty's Stationary Office, 1976); and C. G. L. Hall, *Britain, America & Arms Control 1921-37* (New York: St. Martin's Press, 1987).
18. Part of what follows, on the link between the Admiralty's strategic concerns and Britain's prewar policy of appeasement of the European dictators, appeared in my article in *Naval History* (Summer 1991); see also G. A. H. Gordon, *British Seapower and Procurement Between the Wars* (Annapolis: Naval Institute Press, 1988), chapter 17.
19. A. J. Marder, *Old Friends, New Enemies,* vol. 1 (Oxford: Clarendon Press, 1981), 30.
20. 3rd DRC, December 14, 1933, CAB 16/109, PRO.
21. February 2, 1934, CHT 4/4/30, PRO.
22. 9(34), March 14, 1934, CAB 23/78, PRO.
23. Gibbs, *Grand Strategy,* 394-95.

24. Ibid., p. 94; see also C. A. MacDonald, *The United States, Britain and Appeasement, 1936-1939* (1981).
25. August 7, 1934, CHT 4/4/38, PRO. See also 3rd DRC Op. cit.
26. 37(34), October 29, 1934, CAB 23/80, PRO.
27. C. Bekker, *Hitler's Naval War,* 27.
28. Gibbs, *Grand Strategy,* 420.
29. JP Paper 105: "Defence Plans for War Against Germany," October 31, 1935, CAB 55/7, PRO.
30. Roskill, *Naval Policy,* II (1976), 354.
31. Chatfield to Dreyer, September 16, 1935, CHT 4/4/72, PRO.
32. Gibbs, *Grand Strategy,* 400.
33. 3(36), January 29, 1936, CAB 23/83, PRO.
34. CHT 3/2/192-200, PRO.
35. Gibbs, *Grand Strategy,* 398.
36. 193rd CID, June 5, 1925, CAB 2/4, PRO.
37. See Gordon, *British Seapower*; and G. C. Peden, *British Rearmament and the Treasury* (1979).
38. Board of Admiralty memo of April 26, 1937, ADM 1/9081, PRO.
39. Gibbs, *Grand Strategy,* 4O1.
40. "Defence Expenditure 1937-9," CAB 21/534, PRO.
41. Chatfield to Admiral Drax, November 5, 1937, CHT 3/1/224, PRO.
42. November 10, 1937, ADM 116/3631, PRO.
43. JP 279, April 16, 1938, CAB 55/12, PRO.
44. 6(39), February 8, 1939, CAB 23/97, PRO.
45. Marder, *Old Friends,* 40.
46. 16(39), March 30, 1939, CAB 23/98, PRO.
47. M. George, *The Warped Vision* (1965), 115-16.
48. Grenfell, *Main Fleet,* 57.
49. Alastair Mars, *British Submarines at War* (1971).
50. Willmott, *Empires,* 58.
51. COS(4O)592, CAB 79/6, PRO.
52. COS(4O)614, CAB 79/6, PRO.
53. Cab 65/8, PRO.
54. James Rusbridger, "The Sinking of the *Automedon,*" *Encounter* (May 1985), 9-12.
55. Bennett, *Loss,* 25-26.
56. The writer thanks Ned Willmott.
57. Willmott, *Empires,* 58.
58. James Rusbridger, *Betrayal at Pearl Harbour* (New York: Summit Books, 1991), 103n.
59. Churchill to Menzies, December 23, 1940, *Their Finest Hour,* 554.

60. Bennett, *Loss,* 25.
61. The writer thanks David Brown for this angle.
62. Menzies to Churchill, October 4, 1940, *Finest Hour,* 571.
63. Churchill, *Finest Hour,* 351.
64. Winston Churchill, *The Grand Alliance,* 461.
65. Ibid., 341.
66. Churchill, *Finest Hour,* 526.
67. Bennett, *Loss,* 33.
68. Marder, *Old Friends,* 400.
69. Willmott, *Empires,* 166.
70. Bennett, *Loss,* 43.
71. Ibid.
72. Marder, *Old Friends,* 465.
73. Grenfell, *Main Fleet,* 144.
74. Willmott, *Empires,* 107.

3.

Prelude to Pearl Harbor: The Diplomatic Dress Rehearsal

Frederick W. Marks III

For half a century historians have sought to explain the breakdown of the Hull-Nomura talks, last of a series of fateful milestones along the road to Pearl Harbor. Some have focused on Admiral Nomura's imperfect command of English. Others have concentrated on the improbable role of a pair of Maryknoll missionary priests chosen by Tokyo and Washington to act as intermediaries.[1] Still others have put the case that Franklin Roosevelt's war-inducing oil embargo resulted from a bureaucratic short-circuiting of presidential intent.[2] Lately, one hears the argument that Roosevelt's embargo derived from the fear of a Japanese attack on Russia, and it has long been customary to attribute to Japan's so-called militarist leaders a sinister appetite for empire.[3]

The challenge thrown up by each of these theses is two fold. First, there appears to be a lack of unambiguous supporting evidence. Nowhere, for example, did FDR ever say, in so many words, that Germany's invasion of Russia made an oil embargo imperative or that less drastic steps would have entailed an unacceptable risk of Chinese surrender on the mainland. But a second, and probably more serious, reason for suspending judgment is that every discernible pattern of executive thought and action from 1933 on indicates that Roosevelt would have resorted to an oil embargo and refused meaningful compromise on the diplomatic level regardless of circumstance. To put it another way, I would submit that FDR placed the United States on a collision course with Japan as early as 1934 and that what followed was nothing more than the logical outcome of events and attitudes observable from the outset. Even if there had been no Maryknoll priests, no Admiral Nomura, and no German invasion of Russia, Japan would still have been forced into a corner. It would still, in my view, have felt impelled to strike at Pearl Harbor.

To be sure, Nippon might have withdrawn from North China and sacrificed its stake in Manchuria. But such a course would have been excruciatingly painful. More than this, it would have been virtually impossible from a political standpoint since, contrary to the conventional wisdom, Japanese policy was driven not by a militaristic elite but rather by a powerful national consensus.[4] Moreover, such a withdrawal would have confounded norms of equity, as well as prudence, in the Japanese mind. It is true that war with the United States risked serious consequences, but so did withdrawal from the mainland, which would have opened the door to Russian expansion, an age-old Japanese bugbear. Tokyo did not wish to fight for a second time in Korea in order to halt the spread of Kremlin-sponsored aggression. If, therefore, the statesmen of the 1930s were to find a way out of the Far East bramble bush, if they were to reconcile competing ideas of justice and iron out sharp conflicts of interest involving national security, there had to be a spirit of compromise on both sides of the bargaining table.

Yet here is the rub, for what one finds is a president who, from start to finish, was willing, if not anxious, to go to extremes with his adversary, one who was contemptuous of Nippon and who proved unwilling to prepare American defenses to the point where they might have served as a credible deterrent. This was a chief executive who, while biased in favor of China, labored under the illusion that economic sanctions would bring Tokyo to heel without firing a shot. He was therefore opposed to any form of accommodation, appearances notwithstanding. In short, if one views FDR and his approach to Japan as all of a piece, what is remarkable is not so much that war came in 1941 as that it did not come earlier.

Long before Tokyo became the threat it is alleged to have been by mid-1941, Roosevelt had been laying the groundwork for diplomatic stalemate. Years before the American people were sufficiently roused by Hitler's course in Europe to accept hostilities with Tokyo and thus to throw America's weight into the scales against the Axis, the president was disregarding advice that might have averted World War II, and if not world war then a nearly suicidal encounter with the combined forces of Germany and Japan. Roosevelt did more than set aside the advice of dissident counselors. In the cases of Raymond Moley and Rexford Tugwell, he let them go. Francis B. Sayre and J. Pierrepont Moffat he demoted from positions of power on the assistant secretary and division chief level, while Colonel House, an influential figure behind the scenes pleading the wisdom of meeting Japan halfway, had his lips sealed by death in 1938.[5]

Let us focus for a moment on the term collision course. One of the factors at work in 1941 was a widespread perception of American weakness. Japan struck at Pearl Harbor because she thought she could get away with it. It was a calculated risk taken at a time when foreign observers were incredulous at how little Washington had done to rearm. Analysts at Berlin's Washington embassy noted in September 1938 that there were "still no military preparations whatever nor any measures for setting industrial mobilization in motion."[6] German intelligence gathered in late 1940 indicated that America was so feeble militarily that it could not be expected to play a significant part in any overseas conflict until 1945 at the earliest.[7]

Another way of putting it is that the attack on Pearl Harbor occurred after a long period of executive inaction beginning early in Roosevelt's first term. FDR backed the Vinson Naval Parity Act of 1934, but in signing it he stressed limitation, not expansion, as his aim, and subsequently he never requested the financial wherewithal to carry out provisions calling for a treaty-strength fleet.[8] President Hoover had allowed the navy to dwindle to 65 percent of treaty capacity while Japanese naval power mounted to 95 percent, and FDR did little, if anything, to rectify the situation before it deteriorated further. By 1936, Tokyo had reached a ratio of 8:10 vis-à-vis the United States as compared with the 6:10 figure stipulated by treaties signed at Washington and London. Furthermore, when American naval construction began to gather steam in 1939, it was outpaced by overseas competition. FDR finally recommended increases in defense expenditures in January 1938, but when he did so he pared down Hull's proposal for the building of three battleships and two aircraft carriers to two battleships and no carriers.[9]

Other services fared even less well. At a time when German tanks were smashing into Poland, the U.S. Army ranked ninteenth in the world, ahead of Bulgaria but behind Portugal, at less than two-thirds of the peacetime strength authorized by Congress. According to FDR's trusted advisor, William Bullitt, the president delayed his request for Army Air Corps appropriations so long that when France fell and London came under siege, he had only 53 modern bombers and 187 modern pursuit planes at his disposal, a minuscule figure relative to the arsenal of other nations.[10] An army plan for coordination of the military with the private economic sector to facilitate transition to a war footing if and when necessary received strong backing from Bernard Baruch and other industrial leaders, only to die at the hands of FDR.[11]

It may be objected that the task of a president is to bring his nation out on the winning side of whatever wars may be fought during his term of office, and in this area of endeavor FDR is certainly accomplished. Nevertheless, it is equally true that the gravest responsibility resting upon the shoulders of a statesman is that of avoiding war altogether without doing violence to the national interest; and not only avoiding the tragedy of war but helping others to avoid it.

Some may be inclined to reject any and all criticism of Roosevelt because America emerged from World War II as a global colossus. It is hard to argue with success, especially success on this scale. Nonetheless, it should not be forgotten that the margin of Allied victory was slender. How would FDR stand in history, one wonders, if Russian troops had surrendered at Stalingrad, as they almost did, or if Chiang had not sustained a remarkable holding action on the Chinese mainland? What if the British had lost at El Alamein or American Marines had floundered at Tulagi or Guadalcanal, as almost happened? But even assuming victory to have been a foregone conclusion, what kind of success do Americans desire for their country? Military glory and the role of world policeman? At a cost of 50 million lives, along with a holocaust of bestial proportions, when such losses might well have been avoided? And what kind of victory is it that results in a total destruction of the balance of power in both Europe and the Far East, tempting Congress or, as some would argue, *forcing* Congress to vote enormous Cold War defense appropriations? What kind of victory is it that is characterized by crippling trade and budget deficits, not to mention a huge network of overseas military bases along with dozens of alliances and police actions?

My point is that if Roosevelt's America had been strong militarily it might have given Hitler pause and possibly forestalled the attack on Poland. FDR would almost surely have influenced the outcome of the critical debate as to whether or not Japan should risk war with the United States. With respectable force behind it, presidential rhetoric would have commanded far more influence in the parliaments and council chambers of East and West.

But to return to the subject at hand, the irony regarding New Deal stalling on fleet construction is that the Navy Department is said to have been particularly close to FDR's heart.[12] Not only had FDR been assistant secretary under Woodrow Wilson, he had been an active assistant secretary. As president, he drafted a design for landing craft that Admiral Leahy submitted to the Bureau of Ships.[13] The first letter he ever wrote to his mother was hand-illustrated with sailboats, and he is said to have amassed the finest collection of naval books, prints, and paintings outside the Library of Congress.[14]

Scion of a big navy man and himself a defense enthusiast down to the death of cousin Theodore in 1919, he seems to have shifted in the late 1920s when he assailed the Republican Party for having too much of a naval program and fussing overly about Japan.[15] In December 1934, he told William E. Dodd, Jr., his envoy to Germany, that any keels the United States might decide to lay down would be obsolete within ten years.[16] Two years later, he warned Jesse Straus, his ambassador to France, that the armaments race meant "bankruptcy or war. Heavens only knows I do not want to spend more money on our Army and Navy."[17] Having installed the unenthusiastic and complacent Charles Edison as secretary of the navy, he set the tone of his administration by slashing naval and marine requests into 1938 and continuing to discourage rearmament by some of the things he said in 1939. At a press conference on September 8, 1939, he stated, "There is no intention and no need of doing all those things that could be done. There is no thought in any shape, manner or form, of putting the Nation, either in its defenses or in its internal economy on a war basis. That is the one thing we want to avoid. We are going to keep the Nation on a peace basis."[18]

Judging from public opinion analyses, the decade of the 1930s was typical of the decades to come inasmuch as most Americans would have heeded an executive call for increased military appropriations had such a call been forthcoming.[19] Newspaper czars William Randolph Hearst and Roy Howard were favorably disposed, and according to George Gallup, the public in 1935 was "overwhelmingly in favor of building up our defenses . . . ninety per cent of the people wanted to build up our Air Force."[20] In December 1936, polls showed a full 70 percent desirous of a larger navy.[21]

Significantly, mainline pressure to fortify America's Pacific possessions came not from the executive branch but from the legislature. In the spring of 1938, Congress ordered the secretary of the navy to appoint a commission of inquiry, the Hepburn Board, to conduct a survey of Pacific defense installations. Board members recommended the improvement of 25 bases on an overall budget of $326 million. The upshot is that Roosevelt's Budget Bureau cut this to 12 bases at $94 million while FDR saw to it personally that the figure was further reduced to $65 million. Emphasis in one section of the report fell on the need to fortify Guam, but the president made light of the situation, requesting only $5 million for minor engineering projects. By May 1938, he was instructing his acting budget director, Daniel Bell, in regard to the navy's recommendation for greater peacetime preparedness, that "the increase of 9,900 men for the Navy can be cut by nearly

4,000—in other words, I think the total increase for the Navy of 6,000 men is enough. In regard to increase of Marine Corps by 4,000 men, I suggest that this figure be cut—1,000 men." In 1940, Roosevelt's request for $1 billion in army and navy appropriations and his rejection of the concept of a two-ocean navy ricocheted off an independent-minded Congress. Popular opinion continued to outstrip presidential leadership as lawmakers insisted on voting $5 billion for defense along with a two-ocean navy.[22] Parenthetically, the $5 million was too little too late, for Admiral Nagano, chief of the Japanese Naval General Staff, after carefully weighing the combined strength of the American and British fleets, announced at an Imperial Conference on November 5, 1941, that such a grouping could be defeated: "the ratio of our fleet to that of the United States is 7.5 to 10; but 40 percent of the American fleet is in the Atlantic . . . the United States would need considerable time [to] . . . withdraw ships from the Atlantic. . . . We are therefore confident of victory. We can destroy their fleet if they want a decisive battle."[23]

It should be emphasized that throughout the period, Roosevelt's principal advisors, including Joseph Grew, Stanley Hornbeck, Norman Davis, and Bernard Baruch, along with his politically astute secretary of state, Cordell Hull, counseled greater emphasis on rearmament.[24] Hull even offered to help jog Congress for the necessary funds.[25] It was thus FDR, and FDR alone, who is responsible for procrastination. In 1937, not content to drag his feet at home, he went so far as to chide the British for what he termed a "rearmament complex."[26]

Undoubtedly, one of the reasons for this cavalier attitude toward preparedness was a misplaced faith in the power of economic sanctions. Roosevelt was supremely confident that he could bring aggressor nations to heel without firing a shot. In 1938, he is reported by Lord Halifax to have made a case for economic coercion on the basis of depleted Japanese gold reserves which, having stood at 800 million yen in 1937, were down to 300 million and expected to fall to 100 million by 1939. But regardless of the argument adduced at any given point, his basic philosophy, which ran counter to the opinion of such men as Grew and John Foster Dulles, never changed.[27] He and his principal aides believed in 1933 what they believed in 1941. During his first months in office, Roosevelt lobbied British and French leaders on behalf of a sanctionist policy involving an embargo on loans and arms, and by the summer of 1940, he was anxious to go the distance. With Hull away on a trip to Cuba and in connivance with Treasury Secretary Henry Morgenthau, Jr., he signed a proclamation embargoing scrap iron and oil. Intervention by Under Secretary of State Sumner Welles the very next day resulted in the substitution of aviation gasoline for oil, but the writing was on the wall.[28] In the final months before

Pearl Harbor, Roosevelt continued to press for the same basic approach with no holds barred.

To be sure, American sanctions were stepped up gradually beginning with a moral embargo in 1938 on the shipment of aircraft to Japan. But Congress, once aroused and enamored of a myth, went on to vote more and more stringent measures until the country had to choose between losing an economic tug of war and pushing Tokyo beyond the brink. As every student of history knows, sanctions have never succeeded in coercing a powerful nation. They could not even bring Noriega's Panama or Saddam Hussein's Iraq to account in the 1980s, much less Hitler's Germany, Mussolini's Italy, or Tojo's Japan, as Hornbeck later admitted.[29]

From a variety of different angles, the American attitude all along had been one of disdain. Roosevelt subscribed to the notion that the Japanese suffered from underdeveloped skulls.[30] In 1937, he declared that it would take about a generation for Tokyo to build a formidable army in China, assuming they ever attempted it.[31] Nor was he alone. Freda Utley, author of the best-selling *Feet of Clay,* viewed the Japanese as ignorant upstarts.[32] Joseph Grew, American ambassador to Japan, and Henry L. Stimson, Roosevelt's secretary of war, were of like mind in the belief that "when the United States indicates by clear language and bold actions that she intends to carry out a clear and affirmative policy in the Far East, Japan will yield."[33] *Time* magazine, referring to a race of "little yellow men," informed its readers that there was nothing to fear from the Japanese; all it would take to bring them to their knees would be a naval blockade.[34] This was the prevailing ethos.

When a Japanese cruiser capsized in the early 1930s, the theory gained credence that Tokyo's vessels were top-heavy. Similarly, a cliché about the Japanese having bad eyesight is said to have caused American engineers to discount their naval gunnery. According to Professor Neumann, Roosevelt made no effort to apprise himself of Japan's effort to improve its fleet. When queried about this by Stimson in early 1940, he said he did not know and told Stimson to check with Navy Secretary Frank Knox or FBI Director J. Edgar Hoover. Meanwhile, U.S. Army intelligence on Japan's crack fighter plane, the Zero, fell short as to its speed, range, and maneuverability, and Japanese aircraft production, assumed to be 200 per month in December 1941, was actually twice that number. In addition, Secretary of the Navy Frank Knox, as well as Secretary of War Stimson and the army chief of staff, General George C. Marshall, doubtless in the company of Roosevelt himself, regarded Pearl Harbor as well-nigh impregnable.[35]

Now, if contempt had been the sole ingredient of New Deal intransigence, it would have made for a fairly toxic product. But there were other components, such as ignorance and bias, that contributed to the end product as well. Franklin Roosevelt, in contrast to cousin Theodore, viewed the Japanese as "Prussians of the Far East, and just as drunk with their dream of dominion." On one occasion, he recalled that a fellow student at Harvard who was Japanese had spoken to him of the father country's designs on Hawaii, Australia, and New Zealand.[36] Needless to say, Franklin did not share the first President Roosevelt's tolerance for a Japanese Monroe Doctrine. On the contrary, his attitude toward Tokyo was tinged with contentiousness and bellicosity. At his second cabinet meeting, he was already discussing strategy for a military campaign in the Pacific.[37] To advisors Raymond Moley and Rexford Tugwell, who tried to persuade him of the wisdom of a policy of detente, FDR countered that although a hard-line policy could lead to war, "it might be better to have it now than later."[38] Grew and others, including John van Antwerp MacMurray, the former American ambassador to Peking and sometime head of the Far East Division at the State Department, noted China's violations of treaty obligations to Japan, along with a state of general chaos in Manchuria, as justifications for Japanese policy. Yet this was a side of the story with which Roosevelt seemed unfamiliar. He returned to his own version time and time again, especially during his first year in office, so much so that British Prime Minister Ramsay MacDonald, who met Roosevelt in 1933, characterized the president's animus against Japan as his "great preoccupation."[39]

If *preoccupation* is the correct word, it may be traced in part to FDR's maternal forebears, the Delanos, who, along with America's leading trading firm, Russell and Company, had been heavily involved in the development of China—telegraph lines, steamship travel, American consular representation, and the like.[40] When, therefore, the future president wrote home from Groton as a youngster about how a certain lecturer had run down the "poor Chinamen" and "thought too much of the Japs," he was simply reflecting family sentiment.[41]

Of course, if he had not reached the White House at a time when its occupant was obliged to make crucial decisions involving China and Japan, the effect of such sentiment might have been negligible. But given the scenario of 1933, the complexity of events as they unfolded, and the magnitude of the stakes, personal feeling could and did weigh heavily. It seems to have blinded him to the substance of reports from envoys and other overseas observers indicating three things: first, that Japan was morally justified in fighting for its treaty rights; second, that the movement leading to the independence of Manchukuo was legitimate (Manchuria's corrupt ruler had called upon Japan in 1926 to help put down a nationalist revolt and Tokyo had responded, whereas this time Tokyo had sided with the nationalists); third, that the people of Manchukuo were better off than they had been and generally content with the new order sponsored by Tokyo.[42]

Some argued at the time, just as they continue to argue, that the Japanese presence in Manchuria and North China posed a grave threat to western trade. But the evidence for such an assertion is scanty at best. We have only a handful of conflicting reports and prognoses. A commercial attaché stationed at the U.S. embassy in Tokyo after hostilities with China resumed in 1937 was uncertain as to whether his country's trade had been helped or hindered by the war. But he could point to the fact that he was confident that American exports to Manchukuo had increased dramatically in the period from 1936 to 1938, and prospects in the long run were good.[43] American firms never expected, nor had they any right to expect, to compete on equal terms with the Japanese, who were not only physically closer to Far Eastern markets but also psychologically resentful of Roosevelt's policy of unneutral aid to China. Moreover, on the question of whether Japan aimed at a trade monopoly, observers tended initially to be on the sanguine side. In 1935, the report of the National Foreign Trade Council projected a bright future for the China trade even though Japanese hegemony could be more or less taken for granted. Likewise in the case of the British. Neville Chamberlain viewed the emergence of Manchukuo as a net plus for British policy.[44]

Ignorance of diplomatic reality seems to have been the order of the day as FDR declined throughout the period to recognize Manchukuo. It is not clear, in the first instance, that anyone close to the president realized just how separate a people the Manchus had been, with their own army, ministries, flag, and tax collection, not to mention distinctive ponytail. To the Manchus belonged a proud past. They had ruled all of China from 1644 the end of the Ming dynasty in 1911.[45] And during this period, their homeland had flourished as a semi-independent state that discouraged immigration from South China. Recalling, too, that it had been to keep the Manchus out of China proper that the southerners had originally built the Great Wall, one would gather that little love was lost between the two groups.

It is interesting to recall too that the Mongols—Genghis, Kublai, and their descendants—were another people who had ruled all of China for a hundred years and North China for several hundred more. Unlike the Manchus, though, who appealed to Japan when faced with a takeover by south Chinese troops, the Mongols made a successful bid for Soviet aid, and in 1921 Moscow sent troops to secure the independence of the Mongolian Peoples' Manchu Republic. The parallel between the two nationalist movements was as graphic as it is telling. However, it was lost not only on Roosevelt and his entourage but also on most latter-day commentators who continue to cling to the image of

Manchukuo as little more than a Japanese puppet state born of a revolution "made in Tokyo."

Granted, Japanese armies sought to erect buffer states along the border of Manchukuo by supporting local Mongolian and Chinese governments.[46] But this should not come as any surprise, owing to the history of North Chinese separatism and the many pockets of anti-Chiang sentiment.[47] Manchuria's warlord, Chiang Tso-lin, had governed North China from Peking for a time.[48] It was thus comparatively easy for Japan, by means of the Ho-Umezu and Chin-Doihara agreements of 1935, to exclude the military and political arm of Chiang's government from North China. Chinese Vice Minister for Foreign Affairs Tang Yu-jen admitted that Japan had no need to send troops to effect a rupture; it needed only to "supply arms to discontented elements."[49]

But to return to Roosevelt, it seems fair to say that the same mind-set shaping decisions on North China and Manchuria determined the American stance on other issues as well. For instance, Japan never viewed the Nine-Power Treaty as applicable to Manchuria or Inner Mongolia.[50] Yet such application was regarded by New Deal spokesmen as axiomatic and morally binding. Or take Japanese occupation of French Indochina, another case in point. Understandably, Tokyo feared occupation by a non-Asian power, something akin to American hegemonic fears in the Western Hemisphere. Japan was really doing nothing more when she occupied Indochina, Hainan, and the Spratly Islands than the United States and Britain did when they occupied Greenland, Iceland, Curaçoa, and Aruba. Where Indochina was concerned, though, Japan had an added interest in cutting supply lines to Chiang, whose forces continued to hold down more than of a million Japanese troops on the mainland. Indochina was also a vital source for rice and other food commodities that were in short supply due to western embargoes and the squeezing off of the Burma trade. Maxwell Hamilton, chief of the Far East Division at State, recognized that "it would be very difficult to convince Japanese leaders that they were not in danger at this time as a result of political and military developments in the Far East which some of them [have] viewed as steps directed toward the encirclement of Japan." Such notions do not appear to have taken root at the White House.[51]

Perhaps Roosevelt's approach would seem less hidebound and illogical in retrospect were it not for the fact that it went against the grain of world opinion. The Court of St. James's, for example, and even the Kremlin, were prepared to recognize Manchukuo, but because Roosevelt stood resolutely in the way, they held back.[52] In the same vein, London was anxious to sign a nonaggression pact with Tokyo in 1934, along with a liberal naval accord, but British authorities allowed themselves to be dissuaded by a fiercely determined president who instructed roving ambassador Norman Davis to let it be known that if they were "even suspected of preferring to play with Japan to playing with us," he would appeal over their heads to Canada and the Dominions.[53] Time and again, whether in 1934, 1938, 1939, or 1940, it was FDR who squelched Whitehall's effort at rapprochement.[54] In 1937, when 10 Downing Street suggested "an exchange of views on the possibility of putting Anglo-American-Japanese relations on a harmonious footing," the word from Lafayette Square was no.[55] London wanted to withdraw its armed forces from China so as to minimize friction with Tokyo, and again Washington flashed the red light.[56] Later, the British would have followed Tokyo's lead in recognizing the Wang government of China, but they abandoned the idea in order to keep in step with Washington.[57] Early in 1940, the leaders of both Britain and France urged Roosevelt to renew his commercial treaty with Japan. They also solicited American help in negotiating a settlement of the China incident.[58] Again, such pleas came to nothing. By late 1941, Churchill favored a modus vivendi with Tokyo allowing for the limited export of oil as long as this did not jeopardize the lifeline to China. War on two fronts was the last thing he wanted. London also believed that given sufficient encouragement, Japan would part company with the Axis.[59] But this was not the view either of Stanley Hornbeck, still Roosevelt's closest advisor on Asian affairs, or of the president himself.

One of the patterns that stands out most vividly is a recurring sequence of positive feelers on the part of Washington followed by retraction and withdrawal, in effect a dousing of cold water. Roosevelt began in 1933 by paying lip service to the idea of a nonaggression pact. Yet talks with the Japanese went nowhere, because of inexplicable stalling on the American side.[60] FDR next offered Tokyo a summit meeting at Hawaii. The year was 1934. No sooner did Japanese officials commit themselves and their prestige by accepting his offer than he denied the idea had ever crossed his mind, with the result that a highly embarrassed cabinet headed by Admiral Saito was forced to step down.[61] From the earliest days, therefore, it is abundantly clear that rhetoric on the American side was simply that, rhetoric.

Was FDR constrained by the sentiment of John Q. Public? It is worth noting at this juncture that, from all indications, important sectors of public opinion would have been as pleased with a policy of detente as they were with the idea of preparing the nation's defenses. Roy Howard of the powerful Scripps Howard chain of 1,200 newspapers took the position in 1933 that the United States should welcome Japanese immigration and review its stand on Manchukuo. The following year, William Randolph Hearst printed a public letter in all his papers declaring that Manchuria was no concern of the United States.[62]

There were, in other words, viable options. Nonetheless, Roosevelt's tactics remained the same. The circumstances of American duplicity attending the fall of the governments of General Nobuyuki Abe and Prince Konoye in 1940-41 were practically a carbon copy of those surrounding the fall of Saito. In fact, the first performance may almost be viewed as a dress rehearsal for those that followed, so striking is the resemblance.

Again, let me illustrate. In the fall of 1939, Ambassador Grew engaged Foreign Minister Kichisaburo Nomura in a series of talks concerned with renegotiation of the Japanese-American commercial treaty that had recently been denounced by Washington. Grew aimed at a reopening of the Yangtze River as well as the settlement of war claims. Tokyo yielded on both issues until it became obvious that Grew did not have the power to conclude a treaty. Grew himself chafed at instructions confining him in the final stages of a critical negotiation to vacuous statements leading nowhere. But there was nothing to be done, and the Abe ministry came to an untimely end.[63]

Six months later, in May 1940, FDR tapped his commissioner to the Philippines, Francis B. Sayre, to commence another round of talks. Sayre was instructed to sound out Tokyo on the possibility of a nonaggression pact hinging on American mediation of the Sino-Japanese dispute. Once more, Japanese leaders responded positively, even though they preferred bilateral talks with the Chinese. It was agreed that a parley would take place in Hong Kong at which American, as well as British, representatives would participate. No sooner had Japan's government taken a step forward, though, than FDR unaccountably slammed the door. Sayre was directed to revert to generalities and the talks went into a cul de sac. To be sure, Roosevelt covered himself by labeling the initiative "unauthorized," and Sayre followed suit by characterizing his effort as "personal."[64] But this did not alter the end result.

It was not long before Germany crushed France and began its aerial assault on England. In July, Grew was authorized to return to the charge by offering to reconsider the possibility of a nonaggression pact. On July 6, while Grew was engaged in talks with Foreign Minister Hachiro Arita, Roosevelt made a stunning announcement through his press secretary, Steve Early. It was to the effect that he envisioned a world of three Monroe Doctrines—one for the Western Hemisphere, one for Europe presumably with Nazi Germany as arbiter, and one for the Far East (implying Japanese hegemony). Nor was this all. He pledged further that Washington would refrain from interference in the territorial affairs of Asia and Europe. Heady stuff. The following day, however, an irate Hull rushed to the White House to expostulate and FDR executed a typical about-face. Thus did the Grew-Arita talks end without apparent rhyme or reason.[65]

Events now followed in swift succession. As noted above, Roosevelt moved to embargo scrap iron and oil, at which point Welles intervened to substitute aviation gasoline. Tokyo occupied northern Indochina, and the Axis Pact was concluded on September 27. Throughout 1941, the same inconsistency, contradiction, and all-around confusion that marked the American posture from 1933 to 1940 continued unabated. Roosevelt encouraged Tokyo to believe that he was interested in the Hull-Nomura talks, as well as in a summit conference cum modus vivendi, only to dash each of these hopes in turn. American negotiators piled demand upon demand at a time when Tokyo, for its part, manifested more and more of a willingness to compromise. Having begun by saying they were prepared to recognize Manchukuo, the Americans ended by denying it. After insisting on the withdrawal of Japanese troops from China in one year's time, they shifted to a requirement for partial withdrawal in advance of a treaty. After agreeing to accept private assurances of Axis Pact repudiation, they insisted on a public declaration. In addition to going back on their word regarding peace terms, the Americans insulted their opposite numbers by refusing to see them on occasion, delaying the formulation of counterproposals, and suggesting changes in the Japanese cabinet.[66]

Hull's advisors, including Hornbeck and Hamilton, had instructed him to stall—that is, to guard against offering Nomura any genuine basis for negotiation—and he acted accordingly. Plainly, Hornbeck believed what he had always believed, namely that one could not, and need not, trust the Japanese.[67] White House strategy is clear. Welles admitted to the British on August 9, 1941, that Roosevelt was "dragging out" the talks "to the utmost" much as the president promised Churchill at Argentia the same month that his babying of the Japanese would continue.[68]

Not that any of this demonstrates conclusively that Roosevelt erred in putting Japan off and refusing to compromise over a stretch of nearly nine years. The concern here is more with what happened and why it happened than with what should have happened. Is it possible that Japan would have been content to consolidate its position in Manchuria if permitted to station a certain number of troops in North China for a stated interval in order to bolster one or more buffer states? Perhaps. Perhaps not. Who can say, as the opportunity never arose? Would Tokyo have agreed, in return for American acquiescence in the occupation, or at least protectorate, of orphaned French and Dutch possessions in the Far East, to stand aside from its Axis partners and forswear a campaign against the Soviet Union?[69] Again, who can pronounce with certainty? Would the Japanese have agreed to recognize Chiang Kai-shek and withdraw from the remaining portions of China in return for Chiang's acceptance of the status quo in North China and Manchuria? Another good question.

Without a doubt, the strategic picture in late 1941, with Russia reeling from German hammer blows, was fundamentally different from what it had been six months earlier. Hence it is perfectly possible that changed circumstances contributed to the movement toward war. Conversely, pre-1941 patterns do not in themselves furnish a complete picture of how and why the United States came under attack. The sphinx remains. One may safely conclude, however, that the unique historical backdrop of 1941, instead of propelling Roosevelt willy-nilly into war, merely furnished him with the ammunition needed to take his country down a road he had long wanted to travel, that of radical economic sanctions. All of which brings us full circle to the idea that the momentum of the nation since 1933 had been in the direction of a war that FDR neither feared, nor expected, nor tried very hard to avoid.

By way of conclusion, one cannot entirely sidestep the question of policy options. If one were to venture a step or two beyond the intent of the present essay, which has been to draw a bead on circumstances surrounding the collapse of the Hull-Nomura talks, it would be to suggest that FDR had two realistic choices. On the one hand, he could have tried to come to terms with Japan in order to reestablish a Far Eastern balance of power. The Gaimusho, Japan's foreign office, never forgot Woodrow Wilson's admission of its "special interests" in China, just as it believed that the principle of the Lansing-Ishii Treaty carried over into the Nine-Power Treaty. Such a compromise would have meant recognizing Manchukuo, pressing China for cooperation, and perhaps signing a new Root-Takahira Agreement. This was the course recommended by House, Sayre, Moffat, and MacMurray. Others to whom it appealed included Moley, Tugwell, State Department counselor Walton R. Moore, and the historian Samuel Flagg Bemis, not to mention John Foster Dulles, William R. Castle, and Yale professor Edwin M. Borchard. Interestingly enough, Moffat, Grew, and journalist Walter Lippmann, along with Senator Arthur Vandenberg and ambassadors Hugh Wilson and Nelson Johnson, the envoys to Germany and China respectively, all advocated a trade treaty with Japan in 1940 or, at the very least, a nonconfrontational policy. The major consideration would have been to protect America's economic stake on the mainland, foster naval disarmament, and steer Japan away from Hitler.

A second policy, the one championed by Stimson, would have been to contest Japanese control of Manchuria by bringing maximum moral and economic pressure to bear from the beginning. This implied an early effort to educate public opinion along the line of intervention. It also presupposed the building and maintenance of a navy powerful enough to command respect, and perhaps, too, the forging of a naval understanding or tacit entente with Britain as urged by House, Dodd, and the Chinese.

What Roosevelt did was to straddle. He adopted Stimson's moral imperative while declining to build his navy to treaty strength despite clear signs of congressional support and the insistent prodding of nearly all his advisors. In sum, he enraged the Japanese while inviting their scorn, which was tantamount to setting the stage for war.[70]

Notes

1. For criticism of Nomura's command of English, see, for example, Lewis L. Strauss, *Men and Decisions* (Garden City, N.Y.: Doubleday, 1962), 124-25. For criticism of the Maryknoll priests, see ibid., 123-25; John H. Boyle, "The Drought-Walsh Mission to Japan," *Pacific Historical Review* 34 (May 1965): 151; Robert J. C. Butow, *The John Doe Associates: Backdoor Diplomacy for Peace, 1941* (Stanford: Stanford University Press, 1974), 45, 103, 110, 140, 315-16.
2. Jonathan Utley, *Going to War with Japan, 1937-1941* (Knoxville: University of Tennessee Press, 1985), 153-56; Irvine H. Anderson, Jr., "The 1941 De Facto Embargo on Oil to Japan: A Bureaucratic Reflex," *Pacific Historical Review* 44 (May 1975): 203. Anderson points out that at a cabinet meeting on July 18, FDR expressed fear that an oil embargo might lead to war in the Pacific and cut Britain off from Australia and New Zealand (for Japan to secure her trade routes to Java, source of Dutch East Indies oil, she had to knock out Singapore). See ibid., 219. This squares with a letter he had written to Eleanor on November 13, 1940. See Elliott Roosevelt, ed., *F.D.R.: His Personal Letters,* 4 vols. (New York: Duell, Sloane and Pearce, 1947-50), 4:1077. But it does not jibe with what we know of Roosevelt's leanings and what he let Morgenthau get away with during the summer of 1940 while Hull was in Havana. See Julius W. Pratt, *Cordell Hull, 1933-44,* 2 vols. (New York: Cooper Square, 1964), 2:469; James H. Herzog, "Influence of the United States Navy in the Embargo of Oil to Japan, 1940-1941," *Pacific Historical Review* 35 (August 1966): 318-19. For a good analysis of weaknesses in the Anderson-Utley argument, see Waldo Heinrichs, "The Russian Factor in Japanese-American Relations, 1941" in Hilary Conroy and Harry Wray, eds., *Pearl Harbor Reexamined: Prologue to the Pacific War* (Honolulu: University of Hawaii Press, 1990), 165-66. It should be noted in addition that, according to Anderson, Japan was not committed to a southward thrust until Washington gave signs of moving to cut off her oil.
3. Heinrichs, "Russian Factor" (on the threat to Moscow).
4. Frederick W. Marks III, *Wind over Sand: The Diplomacy of Franklin Roosevelt* (Athens: University of Georgia Press, 1988), 266-68; Joseph Grew, *The Turbulent Era,* 2 vols. (Boston: Houghton Mifflin, 1952), 2:1038; Grew

Personal Note, November 1939, vol. 94, Grew Diary, Joseph Grew Papers, Houghton Library, Harvard University; James B. Crowley, *Japan's Quest for Autonomy: National Security and Foreign Policy, 1930-1938* (Princeton: Princeton University Press, 1966), 126, 129; Dorothy Borg, *The United States and the Far Eastern Crisis of 1933-1938* (Cambridge: Harvard University Press, 1964), 452-53; Shigenori Togo, *The Cause of Japan,* trans. by Fumihiko Togo and Ben Bruce Blakeney (New York: Simon and Schuster, 1956), 184; Nobutaka Ike, trans. and ed., *Japan's Decision for War: Records of the 1941 Policy Conferences* (Stanford: Stanford University Press- 1967), xxiii. On politics in the Japanese army, see Crowley, *Japan's Quest,* 135, 172-73, 231.

5. Marks, *Wind over Sand,* 49-52, 278, 283. See also Moffat Diplomatic Journal, October 10, 1937, J. Pierrepont Moffat Papers, Houghton Library, Harvard University.
6. For the state of American preparedness, see Pershing to FDR, November 25, 1938, Roosevelt, ed., *Letters,* 4:837-38; Robert E. Sherwood, *Roosevelt and Hopkins: An Intimate History* (New York: Harper, 1948), 113; Dwight D. Eisenhower, *Crusade in Europe* (Garden City, N.Y.: Doubleday, 1948), 2-3, 7-8; Barbara Tuchman, *Stilwell and the American Experience in China, 1911-1945* (New York: Bantam, 1972), 259: William W. Kaufmann, "Two American Ambassadors: Bullitt and Kennedy" in Gordon A. Craig and Felix Gilbert, eds., *The Diplomats, 1919-1939* (Princeton: Princeton University Press, 1953), 653; Thomsen and Bodtticher to German Foreign Ministry, September 12, 1938, U. S. Department of State, *Documents on German Foreign Policy, 1918-1945, Series D* (Washington, D.C.: Department of State, 1959-64), 2:923. See also Marks, *Wind over Sand,* 149-50.
7. Gerhard L. Weinberg, "Hitler's Image of the United States," *American Historical Review* 69 (July 1964): 1014-15.
8. Borg, *Far Eastern Crisis,* 102; John Van Antwerp MacMurray, "Developments Affecting American Policy in the Far East" (known as the MacMurray Memorandum), 86, Houghton Library, Harvard University; Thomas A. Bailey, *A Diplomatic History of the American People,* 9th ed. (Englewood Cliffs, N.J.: Prentice-Hall, 1974), 653.
9. Fred Greene, "The Military View of American National Policy, 1904-1940," *American Historical Review* 66 (January 1961): 360; William L. Neumann, *America Encounters Japan: From Perry to MacArthur* (Baltimore: Johns Hopkins University, 1963), 233 (for the 8:10 figure); MacMurray Memorandum, 86; Tuchman, *Stilwell,* 219; William R. Emerson, "F.D.R. (1941-1945)" in Ernest R. May, ed., *The Ultimate Decision: The President as Commander-in-Chief* (New York: Braziller, 1960), 142; Henry L. Stimson and McGeorge Bundy, *On Active Service in Peace and War* (New York: Harper, 1947), 173;

Cordell Hull, *The Memoirs of Cordell Hull,* 2 vols. (New York: Macmillan, 1948), 1:287 (on the 65 percent and 95 percent figures), 459 (on battleships and carriers).

10. Tuchman, *Stilwell,* 259; William C. Bullitt, "How We Won the War and Lost the Peace," *Life* 25 (August 30, 1948): 88.
11. Harold W. Stein, ed., *Civil-Military Decisions* (Tuscaloosa: University of Alabama Press, 1963), 96; William L. Langer and S. Everett Gleason, *The Undeclared War, 1940-41* (New York: Harper, 1953), 182, 197. Baruch chaired the War Industries Board under Wilson.
12. Roosevelt, ed., *Letters,* 4:784.
13. William D. Leahy, *I Was There* (New York: Whittlesey House, 1950), 128.
14. Roosevelt, ed., *Letters,* 1:xviii; Rita Hal le Kleeman, *Gracious Lady: The Life of Sara Delano Roosevelt* (New York: D. Appleton-Century, 1935), 223. FDR's collection included some 7,000 books, 10,000 pamphlets, and about 600 paintings, lithographs, and etchings, according to Kleeman.
15. Franklin D. Roosevelt, "Our Foreign Policy: A Democratic View," *Foreign Affairs* 6 (July 1928): 579; Marks, *Wind over Sand,* 8.
16. William E. Dodd, Jr., and Martha Dodd, eds., *Ambassador Dodd's Diary: 1933-1938* (New York: Harcourt, Brace and Co., 1941), 208 (entry for December 29).
17. FDR to Straus, February 13, 1936, Roosevelt, ed., *Letters,* 3:555-56.
18. Sherwood, *Roosevelt and Hopkins,* 134.
19. Samuel P. Huntington, *The Common Defense* (New York: Columbia University Press, 1961), 235-47 (especially 235, 246); Neumann, *America Encounters Japan,* 232.
20. Travis Beal Jacobs, "Roosevelt's Quarantine Speech," *The Historian* 24 (August 1962): 501n. (on 90 percent and public opinion generally); Martell to Paul-Boncour, July 17, 1933, and report of French naval attache in Washington, September 2, 1933, Ministère des Affaires Etrangères, *Documents diplomatiques français, 1932-1939* (Paris, 1964-), Ser. 1, 4:22-23, 289-90 (on Hearst and Howard). Hereafter *Documents diplomatiques français.*
21. Neumann, *America Encounters Japan,* 232.
22. Borg, *Far Eastern Crisis,* 249-50; George Morgenstern, Pearl Harbor: the *Secret War* (New York: Devin-Adair, 1947), 52-53 (on one billion vs. five billion and two-ocean navy); FDR to Bell, May 13, 1938, Roosevelt, ed., *Letters,* 4:784. Langer and Gleason termed Roosevelt's leadership in the area of rearmament during 1940 a "notorious failure." *Undeclared War,* 181. See also ibid., 182, 569.
23. For a Japanese attitude of contempt dating back to 1934, see Grew to Hill, December 23, 1934, United States Department of State, *Papers Relating to the*

Foreign Relations of the United States, 1933-1941 (Washington, D.C., 1950-69), 1934, 3:689-90 (hereafter *FRUS*). Admiral Nagano was even more confident in December than he had been in July. See also Herbert Feis, *The Road to Pearl Harbor: The Coming of the War Between the United States and Japan* (New York: Atheneum, 1966 reprint), 294; Ike, ed., *Japan's Decision,* 233. (Nagano's words belie Ike's opening statement concerning the futility of preparedness). See also ibid., 280.

24. Stimson was of course anxious to see the fleet built up to treaty strength. See Stimson and Bundy, *On Active Service,* 173; also Stimson's diary of a trip to Britain in 1933, Stimson Papers, Yale University. For Grew, see Grew to Hull, December 27, 1934, *FRUS,* 1935, 3:827. For Baruch, see Sherwood, *Hopkins,* 113. For Hornbeck, see memo, January 3, 1935, *FRUS,* 1935, 3:837. For Davis, see Davis to Hull, November 10, 1937, ibid., 1937, 4:177.
25. Hull, *Memoirs,* 1:457, 459, and Hull to FDR, January 22, 1935, *FRUS,* 1935, 3:842-43.
26. Roosevelt to Dodd, August 30, 1937, President's Personal File (hereafter PPF) 1043, Franklin Delano Roosevelt Papers, Franklin Delano Roosevelt Library, Hyde Park, N.Y. (hereafter FDRL). For Roosevelt's general line of thought, for example his notion that arms were more apt to provoke than to deter, see Marks, *Wind over Sand,* 279.
27. See, for example, Lothian to Halifax, December 14, 1939, FO 800/324, Public Record Office, Kew, England (hereafter PRO); Stimson Diary, January 9, 1933, May 17, 1934, Stimson Papers, Yale University; Halifax to Kerr, October 17, 1938, E. L. Woodward and Rohan Butler, eds., *Documents on British Foreign Policy, 1919-1939,* Series 3 (London: H. M. Stationery Office, 1949-55), 8:146 (regarding 800 and 300 million yen). See also Norman Graebner, "Japan: Unanswered Challenge, 1931-1941," in Margaret F. Morris and Sandra L. Myres, eds., *Essays on American Foreign Policy* (Austin: University of Texas Press, 1974), 144. Hornbeck, in contrast with Grew, insisted on September 5, 1941, that Japan would not go to war with the United States. For Hornbeck's view in 1938, see Hornbeck Memorandum, December 22, 1938, *FRUS,* 1938, 3:426. For Grew's view of the consequence of sanctions, see Anderson, "The 1941 De Facto Embargo," 203-4.
28. Bullitt to FDR, January 23 and 26, 1933, PPF 1124, FDRL (on British and French willingness to withhold loans at American urging); Lindsay to Simon, March 8, 1933, Woodward and Butler, eds., *Documents on British Foreign Policy,* Ser. 2, 5:778 (U.S. pressing Britain to halt arms sales to Japan). On FDR's signing of a proclamation announcing the oil embargo on July 25, 1940, see Pratt, *Hull,* 2:469; Herzog, "The 1941 De Facto Embargo," 318-19. Professor Utley argues that FDR's action on July 25, 1940 was as unintentional as what happened a year

later with reference to the same commodity, oil (Utley, *Going to War,* 98-99). But this is by no means clear from the documentation. Here, as elsewhere, Roosevelt's intentions and motivation are far from transparent, as he had a penchant for leading with someone else's chin. See Marks, *Wind over Sand,* 20-21, 85-86, 141, 143-45, 149, 304-5. All one can say is that his subordinates generally did what he wanted them to do in situations such as this. Under pressure, he would deny that this was so and take one or two backward steps only to advance with renewed vigor at a later date. In any case, it is hard to imagine a person as close to FDR as Morgenthau committing the president to something as serious as an oil embargo without the latter's knowledge and approval.

29. *London Times Literary Supplement,* June 13, 1975 (for Hornbeck's admission of error).
30. Christopher G. Thorne, *Allies of a Kind: the United States, Britain, and the War Against Japan, 1941-1945* (New York: Oxford University Press, 1978), 158-59; Stimson Diary, May 17, 1934, Stimson Papers, Yale University.
31. Harold L. Ickes, *The Secret Diary of Harold L. Ickes,* 3 vols. (New York: Simon and Schuster, 1953-54), 2:226.
32. Frederick Moore, *With Japan's Leaders: An Intimate Record of Fourteen Years as Counsellor to the Japanese Government, Ending December 7, 1941* (New York: Scribner's, 1942), 303 (on Utley).
33. Grew Diary, vol. 94 (1939), Speech to American Groups, June-September 1939, p. 10, Grew Papers, Houghton Library, Harvard University; Thorne, *Allies,* 3 (the quote is Stimson's).
34. *Time,* October 14, 1940, p. 40 ("little yellow men" appears twice on a single page) and October 21, 1940, 25.
35. Neumann, *America Encounters Japan,* 285-86, 288.
36. Willard Range, *Franklin D. Roosevelt's World Order* (Athens: University of Georgia Press, 1959), 81; Daniel M. Smith, "Authoritarianism and American Policy Makers in Two World Wars," *Pacific Historical Review* 43 (August 1974): 314 (on "Prussians"); Stimson Diary, May 17, 1934, Stimson Papers, Yale University. For Hull's mind-set on Japanese imperialism, see Hull, *Memoirs,* 1:274 (one of many instances).
37. William L. Neumann, "Franklin D. Roosevelt and Japan, 1913-1933," *Pacific Historical Review* 22 (May 1953): 153; Range, *Roosevelt's World Order,* 81.
38. Robert Dallek, *Franklin D. Roosevelt and American Foreign Relations, 1933-1945* (New York: Oxford University Press, 1979), 29. As Roosevelt put it, he had always felt "the deepest sympathy for the Chinese" (ibid.).
39. MacDonald Report, May 5, 1933, CAB 23/76, PRO, Kew, England. MacDonald's impression was shared by Premier Edouard Herriot of France on a similar visit in 1933. Herriot found the president "deeply preoccupied."

See Herriot to Paul-Boncour, April 27, 1933, *Documents diplomatiques français,* Ser. l, 3:334. For the Japanese side, see Grew, *Turbulent Era,* 2:929 (on MacMurray's views), 939 (Grew's views); also Mamoru Shigemitsu, *Japan and Her Destiny: My Struggle for Peace* (New York: E. P. Dutton, 1958), 59-60.

40. Tuchman, *Stilwell,* 219.
41. FDR to his parents, May 16, 1899, Roosevelt, ed., *Letters,* 1:310.
42. Walsh Diary, November 10, 1938, Visitation Diaries, Bishop James Walsh Papers, Maryknoll Archives, Maryknoll, N. Y.; Russell D. Buhite, *Nelson T. Johnson and American Policy Toward China, 1925-1941* (East Lansing: Michigan State University Press, 1968), 66-67; Johnson to Hull, March 6, 1933 ("Chinese population of Jehol . . . welcomed Japanese"); Grew to Hull, March 24, 1933; Lockhard to Hull, April 7, 1933 ("Chinese officials and volunteers . . . are said to have gone over to Manchukuo during Jehol campaign"); Lockhart to Hull, April 19, 1933 ("there are increasing signs that this new 'anti-Chiang Kaishek army' or 'pro-Manchukuo army' [of North China] is preparing [to] extend its operations to territory west of the Lwan River in which case change of government [in] this area may be expected. It is significant that [the] general in command of so-called Fifth National Salvation Army . . . in occupation of Changli and some other towns east of the Lwan River is Li Chi-chun who is alleged to have taken a prominent part in the plan to spirit Pu Yi to Manchuria"); Grew to Hull, April 22, 1933; Myers to Johnson, February 3, 1934; Grew to Hull, February 8, 1934 ("the inhabitants of Manchuria have apparently accepted the 'new deal' with a considerable degree of contentment at their comparatively well-ordered existence. If, in future, disturbances should break out in North China . . . it seems not beyond reason that incorporation within the protecting fold of the new empire might eventually be brought about without force of arms"). See *FRUS,* 1933, 3:224, 247, 269, 280, 285; *FRUS,* 1934, 3:24-25, 30-31. Chiang Tso-lin, Manchuria's warlord until a few years before the establishment of the Manchukuan state, taxed the peasants at exorbitant levels, and his son was a playboy. By contrast, the government of Manchukuo reduced taxes, reformed the currency, suppressed banditry, supported road-building and other public works, and increased the gross national product dramatically.
43. Frederick C. Adams, "The Road to Pearl Harbor: A Reexamination of American Far Eastern Policy, July 1937—December 1938," *Journal of American History,* 58 (June 1971): 77-80; Errol MacGregor Clauss, "The Roosevelt Administration and Manchukuo, 1933-1941," *The Historian* 32 (August 1970): 608. Tyler Dennett warned in 1932 that the United States had two alternatives: an open door closed by Japan or an open door closed by China (Clauss, 610). American exports to Japanese-held areas of North China were

not seriously affected in the years 1938-39 (despite the concern voiced by various American chambers of commerce in Chinese ports) and in some areas they even showed an increase (Neumann, *American Encounters Japan,* 226).

44. Chamberlain Memo, September 1934, NC/8/19/1, Neville Chamberlain Papers, Birmingham University Library (England); John W. Masland, "Commercial Influence upon American Far Eastern Policy, 1937-1941," *Pacific Historical Review* 11 (September 1942): 294.
45. O. O'Nara, *Manchukuo: The World's Newest Nation* (Mukden: *Manchuria Daily News,* 1932), 63; Christopher G. Thorne, *The Limits of Foreign Policy: The West, the League, and the Far Eastern Crisis of 1931-1933* (London: Hamish Hamilton, 1972), 33.
46. James B. Crowley, "A Reconsideration of the Marco Polo Bridge Incident," *Journal of Asian Studies* 22 (May 1963): 278.
47. Two months after Grew wrote Hull that North China, if subjected to disturbances, might be brought into Manchukuo "without force of arms," Nelson Johnson, American ambassador to China, alerted Hull to the fact that the North Chinese provinces no longer had any real connection (or even nominal union) with Nanking and that if there were fighting on behalf of independence it would most likely pit Chinese against Chinese. See Johnson to Hull, April 11, 1934, *FRUS,* 1934, 3:107.
48. MacMurray Memorandum, 77.
49. Crowley, "Marco Polo," 278; Marks, *Wind over Sand,* 45.
50. Grew, *Turbulent Era,* 2:934; Sadao Asada, "Japan's 'Special Interests' and the Washington Conferences 1921-22," *American Historical Review* 67 (October 1961): 69-70.
51. For Hamilton's views, see Butow, *John Doe,* 227. On Burma and the availability of rice, see Ballantine Memorandum, July 25, 1941, *FRUS (Japan),* 1941, 2:531. On Indochina's supply route to Chiang, see Bullitt to Hull, May 9, 1938; Grew to Hull, June 28, 1938, *FRUS,* 1938, 3:164, 207. On Japanese occupation of southern Indochina as a means of maximizing the chance for a successful strike at Singapore (in the event of war), see Winston S. Churchill, *The Grand Alliance* (Boston: Houghton Mifflin, 1950), 617 (by implication, since it was from Saigon that the actual strike was launched).
52. Lothian to House, November 20, 1934, #200, GD 40/17, Lothian Papers, Scottish Record Office, Edinburgh, Scotland; Bullitt to Hull, March 21, 1934, *FRUS,* 1934, 3:83 (on Russian recognition of Manchukuo); Cadogan to Hornbeck, February 14, 1938; Hornbeck to Cadogan, April 13, 1938, *FRUS,* 1938 3:93, 141, 148-49. See also Grew to Hull, April 19, 1935, *FRUS,* 1935, 3:115 ("the Soviet Union has given virtual recognition [to Manchukuo] through the sale of the Chinese Eastern Railway").

53. Neville Chamberlain Diary, October 9, 25, and 30, 1934, NC 2/23, Neville Chamberlain Papers, Birmingham University Library (England); Neumann, *American Encounters Japan,* 207.
54. See, for example, Carruthers to Murray, December 6, 1935, vol. 68, Gilbert Murray Papers, Oxford University; Halifax to Cecil, January 30, 1940, vol. 14, Cecil of Chelwood Papers, British Library (London); Neville Chamberlain to Ida Chamberlain, October 27, 1934, NC 18, Neville Chamberlain Papers, Birmingham University Library (Chamberlain wanted rapprochement with Japan, but "it is the Americans who are the difficulty and I don't know how we can get over it"); Neumann, *America Encounters Japan,* 207; Donald F. Drummond, *The Passing of American Neutrality, 1937-1941* (Ann Arbor: University of Michigan Press, 1955), 135; undated Drought Memorandum, Box 1, James Drought Papers, Maryknoll Archives, Maryknoll, N.Y.; Dallek, *Roosevelt,* 89, 237; Woodward and Butler, eds., *Documents on British Foreign Policy,* Ser. 2, 13: 2-3.
55. Pratt, *Hull,* 1:241.
56. British Embassy to Department of State, October 20, 1939; Hornbeck Memorandum, October 20, 1939, FRUS, (1939), 3:292-93; Hull, *Memoirs,* 1:717-24.
57. Grew Diary, October 21, 1939, vol. 94 (1939), Joseph Grew Papers, Houghton Library, Harvard University; Grew Memorandum, October 21, 1939; Welles Memorandum, November 21, 1939, *FRUS,* 1939, 3:299-300, 322; K. K. Kawakami, "Far Eastern Triangle," *Foreign Affairs* 18 (July 1940): 643. Wang Ching-wei was a leading Kuomintang figure for a generation, a trusted lieutenant and political heir of Sun Yat-sen, and between 1931 and 1938 foreign minister and premier of Nationalist China.
58. Dallek, *Roosevelt,* 237.
59. Churchill, *Grand Alliance,* 595; Craigie to Foreign Office, November 1, 1941, FO 371/27911; Foreign Office to Lothian, October 18, 1941, CAB 65/23 ("we should still prefer if possible to keep Japan out of the world conflict and to detach her from the Axis"), PRO. See also Cadogan to Craigie (draft), November 8, 1941, FO 371/27911; C. E. Scott Minute, October 7, 1941 ("war, of course, is the last thing we want"); and Halifax to Washington, October 17, 1941, FO 371/27910.
60. Howell to FDR, December 19, 1933, January 20, February 2 and 16, 1934, PPF, FDRL; Hull Memoranda, May 16 and 29, 1934, *FRUS,* 1934 3:651-61.
61. Hull to Grew, June 11, 1934; Grew to Hull, June 13 and 18, 1934; Hull to Grew, June 15, 1934, *FRUS,* 1934, 3:662-64; Pila to Barthau, July 4, 1934, *Documents diplomatiques français,* Ser. 1, 6:869 (for a French commentary on Tokyo's "humiliation" at the hands of FDR).

62. On Hearst and Howard (through the eyes of French observers), see Martel to Paul-Boncour, July 17, 1933; Report of French naval attaché in Washington, September 2, 1933, *Documents diplomatiques français,* Ser. 1, 4:22-23, 289-90. See also Marks, *Wind over Sand,* 62. For a shift in American opinion, coming in late 1937 as indicated by an article in England's *Contemporary Review,* see ibid., 47, 312 (n. 15).
63. Marks, *Wind over Sand,* 84-85.
64. Ibid., 85-86.
65. Hull to Grew, July 7, 1940, *FRUS, 1940,* 4:389; Marks, *Wind over Sand,* 86-87.
66. Marks, *Wind over Sand,* 96-109.
67. Hornbeck to Hull, March 7, 1941; Hornbeck Memoranda, May 23 and August 15, 1941, *FRUS,* 1941, 4:62-63, 212-13, 365; Marks, *Wind over Sand,* 104.
68. Welles Memoranda, August 9 and 11, 1941, *FRUS,* 1941, 1:348, 360. FDR told Churchill he thought the Japanese could be stalled for at least thirty more days. For orders given to Hull to avoid specifics and thus to stall in the final round of talks, see Hamilton Memorandum, April 11, 1941; Hornbeck to Hull, March 7 and June 10, 1941 (in which Hornbeck lamented the fact that Drought had succeeded in bringing Tokyo and Washington to a negotiation "no matter how it may be otherwise be described"); Far East Division Memoranda for Hull, April 10 and 15, 1941, *FRUS,* 1941, 4:62-63, 136, 146, 152-53, 263. For Hornbeck's opposition to any and all attempts at genuine negotiation with Japan, see Hornbeck Memoranda, May 23, August 15 and 19, 1941, *FRUS,* 1941, 4:62-63, 212-13, 365, 399. For Hornbeck's doubt that economic sanctions entailed any serious risk of war, see Graebner, "Japan," 144.
69. Churchill seems to have felt that this was a strong possibility at the time. See Churchill, *Grand Alliance,* 595.
70. Marks, *Wind over Sand,* 277-78. For Stimson's advocacy of preparedness, see his diary, May 17, 1934, Yale University.

4.

Japanese Wartime Rhetoric in the Traditional Philosophical Context

Marleen Kassel

Material written by Americans in the Second World War period incorporates both an overall attitude of derision toward Japan and an almost hysterical fear of Japan's goal of establishing a Greater East Asian Co-Prosperity Sphere.[1] Japan was ascribed with the goals of conquering the world, infusing it with Japanese morality, and reigning supreme. However, to appraise Japanese wartime rhetoric without considering the framework from which it develops results in misunderstandings. While tracing the ideological continuity linking Japanese government documents promulgated between 1940 and 1942 with that of the Meiji period (1868-87) Emperor System ideology (*Tennsei ideorogii*),[2] and the Tokugawa period (1603-1868) Neo-Confucian ideology[3] does not defuse the Japanese wartime threat, it provides a context in which to understand better the wartime Japanese philosophical construct.

The purpose of this chapter, therefore, is to ferret out salient philosophical terminology and constructs and interpret these in the traditional Japanese philosophical context. Four documents promulgated by the Japanese government to its own people between 1940 and 1942 have been selected as illustrative examples. These documents, "The Way of Subjects,"[4] "Read This and the War Is Won,"[5] "The Imperial Rescript (Declaring War),"[6] and "The Great Shinto Purification Ritual and the Divine Mission of Nippon: A Prophecy of the Dawn of a New Age"[7] will be described in brief, and the main philosophical concepts contained in all with be analyzed together vis-à-vis the traditional Confucian, Buddhist, and Shinto Japanese traditions.[8]

"The Way of Subjects" was promulgated to the Japanese public by the Ministry of Education in August of 1941. Purporting to contain the new moral code of the Japanese people, this document was distributed to all schools and adult educational organizations for study and guidance. The stated purpose of "The Way of Subjects" was to guard the imperial throne and bolster the empire that had been wavering in strength since the Meiji Restoration of 1868.

The document begins by distinguishing between an old and new world order. In the old world order, characterized by individualism, liberalism, and materialism, the weak and small countries of the world were exploited by the great powers. Japan's victory in the Russo-Japanese War of 1904-05 was a pivotal event that both elevated Japan's status in the world and ushered in the new world order based on Japanese moral principles. According to "The Way of Subjects," under the new order, all nations will seek their proper place in the fixed hierarchy of the nations of the world, East Asia will be emancipated and stabilized, and lasting peace and harmony will ensue throughout the world.

Section two of the document, "Japan's Ethical Code," analyzes the implication of contemporary political events for Japan. It posits that international meetings such as the Versailles Treaty, the Washington Conference of 1921-22, and the London Conference of 1930 illustrate that certain European nations and the United States are jealous of Japan's recent success and themselves desire to annex East Asia for their own purposes. In moving to curb Japan's power in the Pacific, they have created a tense situation that threatens to cut off Japan's lifeline. The Manchurian Affair of September 1931 resulted from this threat to Japan, and with it a new page in world history began. In 1937 Japan founded the State of Manchuria (Manchukuo) in order to consolidate Japan-Manchuria unity and established the state ideals of bliss and racial concordia, also known as the Kingly Way, for the 30 million people who lived there.

The document next describes Japan's ultimate mission in the world as follows: Japan's national structure has been marked by increasing national strength, because Japan has been absorbing western science and technology from the time of the Meiji Restoration to the present. This national structure accounts for Japan's victories in the Sino-Japanese and Russo-Japanese Wars, and her economic prosperity during the First World War. So-called frivolous Western ideas such as individualism, liberalism, utilitarianism, and communism have been absorbed by the Japanese along with the very science and technology that help to account for Japan's success. These frivolous ideas have distracted some Japanese people temporarily from the substance of Japan's polity and the spirit of the founding of the empire. Natural disasters such as the Great Kant Earthquake of 1923 marked the beginning of the "back to Japan spirit" under which Japan embarked on a program of reestablishing a unified Japanese national spirit in all realms of Japanese life—political, economic, cultural, and educational.

The first call to action is for Japan to perfect this national structure in order to defy foreign aggression. The second call to action is to enhance justice in all directions and place the whole universe under one roof *(hakko ichi)*. As stated in the Imperial Rescript granted to the nation by the Emperor upon completion of the Tripartite Treaty among Japan, Germany, and Italy, when all nations seek their proper place in the hierarchical structure of the world, lasting peace will ensue.

Japan's role in this is the following: Her political mission is to rescue nations in the Greater East Asia Co-Prosperity Sphere from their quasi-colonial status with regard to Europe and America; her economic mission is to eradicate the evils of their exploitation and help them establish an economic structure for coexistence and coprosperity; and her cultural mission is assist East Asian nations in developing their collective oriental culture and teach them not to fashion themselves after European and American culture.

One concrete objective of perfecting the unification of Japan's national spirit is to create a highly geared and centralized mechanism for defense both in wartime, defined as times of actual battle, and in peacetime, defined as times when nations of the world speak of peace but actually wage economic and cultural war.

The cardinal objective of strengthening the total war organism is solely to support the imperial throne. This is accomplished when each person fulfills his duty in his respective status in life.

Japan's ultimate mission is to make manifest her ideals throughout the entire world. Because Japan has been under the rule of a line of Emperors unbroken for ages eternal, it has grown and developed in harmony as a nation just as though it were one large family. However diverse the empire may have been throughout history, its ideals have always been unified under the dignity and glory of the Emperor, the center of the nation. No other country in the world merits such a superb and lofty mission.

"The Way of Subjects" traces Japan's mission, constructing the world based on Japan's moral foundation, to the founding of the empire itself. Izanagi and Izanami, Japan's divine parents, gave birth to Amaterasu, the Sun Goddess.

Amaterasu's grandson, Ninigi, descended to reign over Japan with the three emblems of his rule, the curved jewel, the mirror, and the sword. Three generations later when Emperor Jimmu expanded eastward and established the Japanese Empire in Yamato Province in the present-day Kant area, he established the principle of the "imperial spirit of expanding the empire." The wartime attempt to unify the world under one roof is nothing more than a continuation of Emperor Jimmu's principle of expansion.

The imperial family is the source of all things national and private in Japan. It is the duty of the Japanese people to manifest loyalty and filial piety, virtues inseparable one from the other, toward the Emperor. These virtues are the source of Japan's strength and are unmatched by virtues of other countries. Japan embarked upon the China Affair as a holy task by which to propagate the ideals of Japan's empire-founding throughout East Asia and the world over. Japan is the fountain source of the Yamato [Japanese] race, Manchukuo is its reservoir, and East Asia its paddy field. The way or duty of the people of Japan, the imperial subjects, is none other than to strive toward this goal. This is the central message of "The Way of Subjects."

The second document under consideration, the "Imperial Rescript (Declaring War)," was promulgated by Tojo Hideki as prime minister of war, at 11:00 A.M. Tokyo time on the eighth day of the twelfth month of the sixteenth year of Showa, or December 8, 1941. This was several hours after the attack on Pearl Harbor. While this document is an official declaration of war, albeit somewhat belated, it is couched in ideological terminology similar to that of the documents issued by the government for popular consumption.

The "Imperial Rescript" is a one-page declaration of war on the United States of America and the British Empire for their involvement with Chiang Kai Shek. According to this document, their actions have aggravated disturbances in East Asia and obstructed Japan's attempts to ensure stability in East Asia and world peace. The "Rescript" invokes both the hallowed spirits of Japan's imperial ancestors and the loyalty and courage of the Japanese people in carrying forward the mission bequeathed by Japan's forefathers: eradicating evil, establishing immutable, enduring peace in East Asia, and preserving the glory of the empire of Japan.

"Read This and the War Is Won," the third document, is a pamphlet first discovered by the U.S. Fifty-fifth Infantry Division in the Southwest Pacific in November of 1943. This document is much more of a practical "how-to" manual for soldiers and sailors than the others under consideration here. It includes the following material:

What sort of place is the Southern field of operation? It is a place where 100 million Orientals are being oppressed by 300,000 white men. Its terrain ranges from a warm-weather paradise with bananas and pineapples to the misery of year-round swamps and jungles infested with malaria.

Why must we fight? It is the Imperial Will [toward which the people owe loyalty and filial piety] that we fight. We fight in this present Showa Restoration toward the goal of peace in the Orient just as we did during the Meiji Restoration. Japan's spiritual unity compensates for what Japan lacks in caliber and number of airplanes, tanks, and guns.

What course will the war follow? It will begin with a long sea voyage and be followed by landing operations. Act as though you are part of the gang of Forty-seven Masterless Warriors.[9] Utmost secrecy and care must be maintained aboard ship. Never be without your gas mask. The Europeans are dandies, not soldiers, so it is best to do battle in times they most dislike—during squalls, mist, or night.

Japan's very existence is at stake in the present war. America has tried to strangle Japan slowly through economic means. Over one million Japanese comrades have been killed though American and European guns sold to Chiang Kai Shek. America is aiding Europe in the war against our allies, Germany and Italy. If Japan waits any longer, her war machine will be unable to do combat effectively.

Japan is presently confronted with a great mission: As representatives of the Oriental race, Japan must bravely deal the finishing blow to the American and European invasion that began several hundred years ago in the Meiji Restoration. Japan's navy and national spirit is ready. Japan owes victory to those comrades who have died, and to His Majesty the Emperor who, pursuant to the 2,600 years of Japan's glorious history, has bestowed this important mission upon us. Our soldiers in the ranks must exhibit solidarity and uniformity in order to complete this Showa Restoration and realize the Imperial Will.

The fourth document, "The Great Shinto Purification Ritual and the Divine Mission of Nippon: A Prophecy of the Dawn of a New Age" was written by Chikao Fujisawa and published in English in the *Herald Press* in Azabu, Tokyo, in 1942. Chikao Fujisawa was one of Japan's leading conservative intellectuals and was instrumental in shaping the political ideology of the war years. He served as professor of political science at Kyoto Imperial University from 1924 until 1930, and went on to become the director of the research station of the Imperial Rule Assistance Association (IRAA). This quasigovernmental political organization was created by Premier Konoe in the autumn of 1940 and effectively absorbed all of Japan's legal political parties. Fujisawa's convoluted treatise evolves a concept of cosmic unity based on his sense of Japan as a nation *(kokutai)*. This cosmic unity, known as the "one-is-many-and-many-is-one principle" *(musubi)*, is one and the same as the Japanese

Way of the Gods (Shinto), and is embodied by the Japanese Emperor *(Tenn)*. Fujisawa develops the concept that Japan is a self-generating spiritual theocracy. Japan's exemplary morality, unsurpassed by that of any other nation, is manifest in the fact that her imperial line has ruled uninterrupted since its establishment by Amaterasu, the Sun Goddess. This fundamental character of Japan accounts for her unassailability and mystical invulnerability to invasion. Fujisawa further presents unconvincing evidence that all disparate areas of the world originated from Japan. Japan's current attempt to reunite the world is simply an attempt to return it to its original, correct state, which was fractured by the unbridled ego and capitalist individualism of enemy countries such as the United States.

He states that Japan's mission is to permeate the whole world with her cosmic vitality so that all separate nations will abandon their individualistic attitudes and unite in a bond of brotherhood. Japan will reunite the nations of the world into one single household and take her place as the head of this all-embracing universal family. By restoring the absolute cosmic life-center of the world and reconstructing the fundamental vertical order prevalent among nations in remote antiquity, Japan will enable all nations to secure their due places and transform the present lawless and chaotic world into a world of accord and consummate harmony.

Fujisawa further extends this cosmic theory by grounding it in Shinto[10] terminology and ceremony, and in the traditional theory of the Five Elements.[11] He begins by linking the five elements of earth, wood, fire, metal, and water with the five prehistoric human races—yellow, blue, red, white, and black.[12] Each race wore colored robes to illustrate his racial traits, and each paid homage in hierarchical order to Japan.

Next, Fujisawa expands traditional Shinto purification ceremonies into a grand Shinto purification of the world, which can effectively be construed as a holy war. In this tangled passage, he develops the traditional Shinto purification by sweeping *(harai)* into the cosmic theory of "sweeping away the impurities heaped upon one's life," and the traditional purification by water *(misogi)*, into "cutting off filth from the body and injecting new life." Once these purification rites are carried out, all nations will be able to comprehend the cosmic truth: All nations have issued forth from the one absolute life-center embodied by Japan and must restore themselves to their proper places in the hierarchy of nations.

The common aim of each of these four documents is to further the Japanese wartime goal of establishing the Greater East Asia Co-Prosperity Sphere and to create a unified world with Japan at its helm. Each document seeks for validation within the rich and variegated Japanese tradition. The specific elements each chooses to elevate from within this tradition, however, vary. While the majority of the terminology follows the Neo-Confucian tradition, Shinto and Buddhist influences are also very much evident.

All of Japan was united and embarked upon a mission. This concept of mission *(mei)* derives from the Confucian concept of the Mandate of Heaven, and the Neo-Confucian concept of the Way of Heaven and the Way of Man. The Mandate of Heaven theory dates from the earliest dynasties of Chinese history and forms the bedrock upon which Confucian and Neo-Confucian statecraft is built. On the highest level the Mandate of Heaven is a theory in which statecraft is linked inextricably to the moral character of those who rule. It states that society functions harmoniously under the leadership of a ruler who rules virtuously. As long as the ruler maintains correct morality as defined by the Confucian virtues, all under his rule will be moral. When the ruler strays from illustrious virtue, natural disasters such as earthquakes, floods, and famine will ensue. The people will become discontented and the Mandate of Heaven will be shifted to another whose rule will be virtuous. This is the Way of Heaven, or the way in which Heaven provides for governance on earth.

In China, the Mandate of Heaven theory gave rise to the theory of dynastic succession as rule shifted throughout Chinese history. The Mandate was said to be bestowed and revoked dynasty by dynasty according to the virtue of the ruler. This was not the case, however, in Japan. The virtue of Japan's ruler was evident from the very fact that the imperial line has ruled unbroken since its divine establishment by Amaterasu. To the Japanese, this fact in and of itself validates the exemplary morality of the Japanese emperor and singles Japan out as a nation among nations.

By the time this concept of the Mandate of Heaven had become integrated into the Japanese Neo-Confucian philosophical framework, the Mandate existed on three different levels: the Way of Heaven, the Way of the Ruler, and the Way of Man. The Way of Heaven establishes the ideal for correct governance on earth as detailed by the Confucian sages.[13] The Way of the Ruler is the mandate that Heaven accords the ruler, the mandate to govern with exemplary virtue. The Way of Man is the mandate, more appropriately translated as a mission, that Heaven, via the emperor, accords each individual person. Each person's specific mission is dictated by two things: first, his place in the five traditional Confucian relationships, and second, his timeliness, or specific place in society.

The five reciprocal Confucian relationships make up the sole workings of society, outside of which (with the exception of Chinese eunuchs and religious people in both China and Japan) there exists no legitimate place in society for a person to interact. These five relationships state: 1) between parent and child there is affection; 2) between subject and ruler there is righteousness; 3) between husband and wife there is differentiation; 4) between elder brother and younger brother there is precedence; and 5) between friends there is trust.

The concept of timeliness[14] establishes that the basic principles underlying life are the same for all men regardless of their stations in life. Differentiation arises from the specific historical time, geographical place, and social position that characterize an individual's life. In addition, each person is imbued with basic talent, the potential enabling him to perform certain tasks, such as governance. For a person without the correct basic talent to undertake a task would be like a blind man walking on a dark night without a light. Further, each person has the obligation to cultivate and realize the potential of his talent through proper learning. For a man to attempt a task without proper learning would be like a blind man who cannot make his own way but walks only where he is directed. These two basic philosophical constructs, the five Confucian relations, and the concept of timeliness result in a rigid social structure with little flexibility outside of the prescribed hierarchical order.

Unlike the Western world, in which the husband-wife relationship forms the core of the home, in Japan the parent-child relationship reigns supreme, both in the home and the nation. Japan's national structure is none other than this parent-child relationship writ large. The emperor is the parent of all and the countrymen are his children. Specific virtues characterize the nature of the ruler vis-à-vis his subjects and the subject vis-à-vis his ruler. The ruler is to rule benevolently or human-heartedly, as stated in the *Analects* of Confucius: "What I do not want others to do to me, I have no desire to do to others."[15] In this way the emperor fulfills his duty to protect and nurture the people. In return the individual must fulfill his duty to the emperor to behave with loyalty and filial piety. While the specific criteria of one's duty are dictated by his respective place in society, the overarching virtues of loyalty and filial piety apply to all.

Insofar as Heaven is embodied by the emperor, the Imperial Will is one and the same as the Will of Heaven. The Will of Heaven lies in the emperor's call to action, the stated wartime objective of strengthening the total war organism of the nation. Each person's first and foremost duty is to recapture his proper place in society. When all people know and seek their proper place, the nation will be strengthened, and the Will of the Emperor and the Will of Heaven will be realized. But Japan's call to action did not stop at national borders.

Japan's mission was construed both as a divine mission and a holy war. The divine mission, to establish peace and harmony on earth, emanated from Heaven as embodied by the emperor. It was to be accomplished first by restoring proper morality among the Japanese people and second by establishing proper morality throughout the world using Japan as the platform from which virtue would radiate forth in concentric circles. Such a messianic endeavor is reminiscent of the religious fervor and political message of Nichiren Buddhism.[16]

Nichiren (1222-82), a prominent but contentious Buddhist leader, lived during the Kamakura period (1192-1338), a time when Japan experienced her first serious threat of impending foreign invasion. In 1274 and again in 1281 the Mongols sent fleets of ships from China toward Japan. These were destroyed by what the Japanese called "divine winds," or *kami-kaze*. This is the locus classicus of this term. Nichiren urgently warned of the imminent danger of invasion and of Japan's need to combat this threat aggressively and militantly. He was disregarded, discredited, and finally banished by the government, although he was immortalized by his followers.

It is Nichiren's political teachings more than his religious teachings that concern the present discussion. While his focus on Buddhism as the vehicle to protect the country had been an integral part of Japanese Buddhist rhetoric from the Nara period (710-794) forward, Nichiren imbued his Buddhist message with a sense of urgency, militancy, and self-sacrifice that had not previously existed in Japanese Buddhism. He took his name from the symbols of the sun *(nichi)* and the lotus *(ren)*. The sun represents the Light of Truth and the Land of the Rising Sun, and the *Lotus Sutra* represents the vehicle that can best preserve Japan in her present threat against foreign powers.[17] In addition, Nichiren assumes for himself the task assigned to the Bodhisattva of Superb Action. He was prepared to sacrifice his life for his mission and taught his disciples to act accordingly. In this Nichiren laid the foundation for the thought that suffering for a grand cause is glorious and that self-sacrifice is only part of one's noble mission. Finally, Nichiren centered on Japan as the land in which the true teachings of the Buddha would be revived and subsequently the platform from which these teachings would be propagated throughout the world.

Japan's wartime sense of mission required a nationwide fighting spirit reminiscent of the fighting spirit cultivated through Zen Buddhist practices by the warriors of the Kamakura period.[18] Essentially Zen is a spiritual training that is focused on transcending the mundane world and realizing one's internal Buddha-nature. Various religious techniques were used toward this end, but one of the most popular, that of sitting in meditation or concentration, helped to nurture the inner strength required of warriors. Through Zen, warriors were able to focus their inner strength and maintain equanimity and serenity in times of battle.

In order to curry such a fighting spirit nationwide, the ideologues of the war years offered to all members of society that which only the elite had previously been entitled. The *samurai* warrior, the highest social rank, had carried the most prestige in Japanese society from the Kamakura period to modern times. To encourage the rank and file of the nation, who could not claim such a pedigree for themselves, to muster such valiant and honored martial zeal, these ideologues turned to one of the most popular historical events in Japan, the incident of the Forty-seven Masterless Warriors.[19]

Although the incident of the Forty-seven Masterless Warriors posed no particular threat to the workings of government, it is significant in that it opened up the theme of feudal virtue beyond the ranks of the elite warrior class to popular discussion on all levels of Japanese society. The details of the incident are as follows: In 1703 a lower-ranking member of the warrior class was provoked to draw his sword and wound a higher-ranking member of the warrior class in Edo (present-day Tokyo) castle. Because the act of drawing a sword within the castle grounds itself was an impropriety punishable by death, the lower-ranking warrior was ordered to commit suicide by ritual disembowelment *(hara kiri)* and forfeit his domain. Upon his death, his retainers were reduced to the status of masterless samurai *(rnin)*. For two years they plotted to avenge their master, and they did so finally by killing the official who had caused his death. In turn they were ordered to commit ritual suicide as punishment. The consensus of public opinion at the time of the incident was to praise these righteous warriors for their resurrection of the samurai ideals of loyalty and resolute action. Numerous poems and essays were immediately written in their honor and the incident became the theme of much popular drama. For ideologues of the wartime years to offer such a legacy to those even of commoner origins was quite an inducement and rallying point in the war effort.

It is very much a part of Neo-Confucian historiography to harken back to a Golden Age in history, regardless of whether or not the interpretation of that Golden Age is historically accurate or utopian, and apply perceived lessons to contemporary times. During the war years, certain extremists harkened back to the Meiji Restoration for guidance in what they designated the contemporary Showa Restoration. Their longing references to the Meiji Restoration imply that the Meiji Restoration was a time when the foreign presence was handled well by loyalists to the throne. The slogans[20] developed during the late Tokugawa period leading into the Meiji Restoration illustrate the foundation upon which later wartime attitudes toward foreigners were developed. Perhaps the most well-known slogan is "Revere the Emperor and Expel the Barbarians" *(sonn-ji)*. Two things are implicit in this slogan. The first is a hierarchical understanding of the nations of the world, with Japan, the embodiment of civilization, at the core. The second is the call to armed action which Restorationists during the Meiji Period took as a sort of battle cry. While Meiji Restoration slogans per se were not invoked in the materials distributed during the war years, these allusions were not lost on the general population.

Finally, a concept very much evident in these documents but not a part of the traditional Japanese philosophical tradition is the element of race. This is a complex issue at best, one that cannot be explored except incidentally in this chapter. Basically Japan developed a sense of self and a heightened sense of nation *(kokutai)* in order to counterbalance the idea of racial inferiority imposed on Japan by western standards, to which Japan did not and could not fully measure up. Social Darwinism and unequal treaties are two fundamental elements in the Japanese issue of race during this period. The topic of race in Japan necessitates more detailed attention.[21]

By concentrating here on prominent philosophical constructs of selected wartime documents, this paper illustrated the continuity in certain terminology, philosophical constructs, and ideology from the premodern through modern Japanese rhetoric. Concepts such as the Mandate of Heaven, the Will of Heaven, the Imperial Will, the Way of Heaven, the Way of the Subject, loyalty and filial piety, exemplary morality, mission, call to action, Golden Age, and hierarchical place in society and in the world all derive from the Neo-Confucian framework that formed the basis of statecraft in Japan from the Tokugawa period. The sense of militancy and urgency encompassed by the fighting spirit derives from Buddhism, both Nichiren and Zen. The great emphasis on the emperor and his exemplary virtue leading the world as a household united derives from the Neo-Confucian–Shinto amalgamation that was manifested in the Meiji period Emperor ideology. Reasserting the context from which these concepts derive possibly would have made Japan's rhetoric less fearful to her enemies living and writing during the war years, even if it would not have lessened her political threat.

Notes

1. Examples of such literature are Otto D. Tolischus, *Tokyo Record,* (London: Hamish Hamilton, 1943); Peter de Mendelssohn, *Japan's Political Warfare* (London: George Allen & Unwin, Ltd., 1944); and Walter Smith, *Japan at the Crossroads* (London: Lawrence & Wishart, 1936), among others.
2. On Meiji Period ideology see Carol Gluck, *Japan's Modern Myths* (Princeton: Princeton University Press, 1985); Marlene J. Mayo, "Attitudes Toward Asia and the Beginnings of Japanese Empire," in Grant K. Goodman, comp., *Imperial Japan and Asia: A Reassessment* (New York: East Asian Institute, Columbia University, 1967); and Shunsuke Tsurumi, *An Intellectual History of Wartime Japan 1931-1945* (London: KPT Limited, 1986, translated edition), especially p. 1-33.

3. I distinguish between Confucianism, the basic formulation of the statesman-philosopher Confucius (551-479 B.C.), and Neo-Confucianism, the amalgamation of philosophical traditions that evolved during the Song Dynasty (979-1279) in China and was naturalized during the Tokugawa Period (1603-1868) in Japan. On Tokugawa ideology see Herman Ooms's *Tokugawa Ideology: Early Constructs, 1570-1680* (Princeton: Princeton University Press, 1985). On Neo-Confucianism see Wm. Theodore de Bary, *Neo-Confucian Orthodoxy and the Learning of the Mind-and-Heart* (New York: Columbia University Press, 1981); Wm. Theodore de Bary, "Some Common Tendencies in Neo-Confucianism," in David Nivison, ed., *Confucianism in Action* (Stanford: Stanford University Press, 1958); Wm. Theodore de Bary and Irene Bloom, eds., *Principle and Practicality: Essays in Neo-Confucianism and Practical Learning* (New York: Columbia University Press, 1979), among others.
4. "The Way of Subjects" (*Shinmin no michi)* is found in translation in Tolischus, *Tokyo Record,* 405-27.
5. "Read This and the War Is Won" *(Kore dake yomeba ware wa kateru)* is found in translation in the Supreme Commander for the Allied Powers, *Reports of General MacArthur,* vol. 2 *(Japanese Operations in the Southwest Pacific Area),* part 1:9-12.
6. The "Imperial Rescript (Declaring War)" is found in translation in the Supreme Commander for the Allied Powers, *Reports of General MacArthur,* vol. 2 (*Japanese Operations in the Southwest Pacific Area),* part 1:7.
7. "The Great Shinto Purification Ritual and Divine Mission of Nippon: A Prophecy of the Dawn of a New Age," is found in translation in Tolischus, *Tokyo Record,* 429-49.
8. In describing the contents of these selected documents, I have intentionally stayed as close as possible to the rhetoric used in the translations of the documents themselves. It is important to maintain the wartime choice of English terms rendered from Japanese, so as not to lose more than already has been lost in the translation.
9. I elaborate on the details of the incident of the Forty-seven Masterless Warriors below.
10. In its earliest form, Shinto, the indigenous religion of Japan, was preliterate and animistic. Its religiosity was centered on reverence for localized awe-inspiring natural phenomena and on physical cleanliness and purification. See Sokyo Ono, *Shinto the Kami Way* (Vermont and Japan: Charles E. Tuttle and Company, 1962); and Joseph M. Kitagawa, *Religion in Japanese History* (New York: Columbia University Press, 1966).
11. The Theory of the Five Elements is a pseudo-scientific Chinese construct that developed as early as 300 B.C. in China. One basic concept is that the dualistic

forces in nature, *yin* and *yang*, are mutually complementary and balancing. Another is that nature is composed of varying combinations of the five elements, wood, metal, fire, water, and earth. Extensive and all-encompassing cosmic correlations and historiological theories were developed based on these basic concepts. The Japanese adopted this as part of their Neo-Confucian system, and at times placed more stress on the aspect of mystical cosmic ordering than did the Chinese. On the Five Elements, see Wing-tsit Chan, *A Source Book in Chinese Philosophy* (Princeton: Princeton University Press, 1963); and Wm. Theodore de Bary et al., comps., *Sources of Chinese Tradition*, vol. 1 (New York: Columbia University Press, 1960).

12. The only race other than the Japanese that Fujisawa describes specifically is the red: "the representative of the red race, consanguineous with the Jews, was dressed in a scarlet gown decorated with beautiful embroideries. . . . That the British king wears a scarlet robe on the occasion of his coronation and offers a prayer to the sacred *pillow stone* [stone of Scone from Scotland] brought over to England from Palestine reveals its close relation to the prehistoric usage of [Japan]. It is said that the Jewish blood runs in the veins of the English kings and for this reason the former Edward VIII enjoys a great popularity among the Jewish people of the United States." (Fujisawa, in Tolischus, *Tokyo Record*, 444).
13. The words of the Confucian sages are embodied in the Confucian classics. Exactly which classics were extolled varied from historical period to historical period and from China to Japan. The core classics include: *Book of Changes, Book of Documents, Classic of Filial Piety, Book of Ritual, Book of Songs, Spring and Autumn Annals, Analects, Mencius, Doctrine of the Mean,* and *Greater Learning.*
14. For more on the concept of timeliness, see *Kumazawa Banzan* in *Nihon shis taikei* 30:213-14, as cited by Minamoto Ryen in "'Jitsugaku' and Empirical Rationalism," in de Bary and Bloom, *Principle and Practicality*, 407.
15. Arthur Waley, trans., *the Analects of Confucius* (New York: Vintage Books, 1938), 110.
16. On Nichiren see Anesaki Masaharu, *Nichiren, the Buddhist Prophet* (Cambridge: Harvard University Press, 1916); and Tsunoda et al., comps., *Sources in Japanese Tradition*, vol. 1, (New York: Columbia University Press, 1958), 213-25.
17. Nichiren articulates his politico-religious philosophy in his various treatises, "Treatise on the Establishment of Righteousness for the Protection of the Country" *(Shugo kokka ron)*, and "The Establishment of the Legitimate Teaching for the Security of the Country" *(Rissh ankoku ron)*. See Tsunoda et al., *Sources in Japanese Tradition*,: 213-25.
18. On Zen, see Anesaki Masaharu, *History of Japanese Religion* (Vermont and Tokyo: Charles E. Tuttle and Company, 1963), 206-39; and Furukawa

Tetsushi, "The Principle of Self-Sacrifice and Zen," in *Philosophical Studies of Japan 1,* (1957): 74-84.

19. I am indebted to Donald Keene's analysis of this affair. See his introduction and translation in Donald Keene, *Chshingura: The Treasure of Loyal Retainers* (New York: Columbia University Press, 1971).

20. This so-called End of Shogunate period *(bakumatsu)* includes the last years of the Tokugawa period until the Meiji Restoration, and is usually designated as 1853-68.

    A cogent analysis of these *bakumatsu* period slogans is offered by Bob Tadashi Wakabayashi in *Anti-Foreignism and Western Learning in Early-Modern Japan* (Cambridge: Harvard University Press, 1986), an excellent account of the writings of the prominent Neo-Confucian scholar and statesman, Aizawa Seishisai; and in Carol Gluck, *Japan's Modern Myths: Ideology in the Late Meiji Period,* (Princeton: Princeton University Press, 1985).

21. An extremely interesting and informative work on this topic is John Dower, *War Without Mercy: Race and Power in the Pacific War* (New York: Pantheon Books, 1986).

5.

Moscow on the Pacific: Soviet Historians and the War in the Pacific, 1941–1945

J. Thomas Sanders[1]

According to an anonymous wag, the Soviet Union was the only country in the world with an unpredictable past. Insofar as it concerned prominent individuals, the witticism was accurate enough. An individual's historical treatment varied with his political fortunes. Beria, for example, was purged and had his entry in the encyclopedia replaced by one on the Bering Strait. In one satirical Soviet short story a ship travels the length of the Volga. At each of its stops, the old name of the ship is painted over and a new one stencilled on, as, one after another, the individuals for which it was named fall into disfavor. Most valid for the Stalinist era, this process of prominence, purge, rehabilitation, "dehabilitation," and so on continued under Khrushchev and Brezhnev, and on up through Gorbachev. It was this pattern that led someone to observe that in the Soviet Union "you never know what's going to happen yesterday." Judged from this perspective, the only element of predictability in Soviet history was its unpredictability.

But if one could not be certain based on past historical coverage how a prominent individual would fare when placed in the Russian/Soviet historical scales, for many Western historians there was a mind-numbing predictability to the interpretation given to major historical events in Soviet historiography. According to Western assessments, rooted in a more pluralist historical culture, once events were nested in the overall Soviet analysis of the past, they were bound in place by the unyielding rigidity of the structural framework. This subordination of specific historical judgements to overall political purposes rendered Soviet historical writing, as far as most non-Marxist Western historians were concerned, "so supine and so devoid of redeeming qualities that they long tended to ignore it."[2] As far as they could tell, this determined, if not determinist, historical schema allowed practically no room for interpretive disagreement or for nuanced explanations.

Perhaps it is true that all the historical cats were gray in the historiographical dusk that prevailed in the Soviet Union, but as one's eyes became adjusted to such light as existed, one could discern differences in them. In point of fact, it was never true of any area of Soviet historiography that countervailing currents did not exist at all, but the generally monotonic character of much of what they saw, combined with the enormous language barrier, discouraged most Western scholars from studying the phenomenon long enough for significant variations of quality and tone to emerge. Moreover, it was precisely where attention was most heavily concentrated—on the explanation of major events of the recent, especially Soviet, past—that the Soviet historical community showed itself in the worst possible light. Most likely, the powerful mentality of the Cold War worked its influence as well, subconsciously predisposing western scholars to accept as a given the existence of a "monolithic" Soviet view. This was most unfortunate, since in those vast spaces of the historical past practically devoid of contemporary political relevance, and hence of wide popular interest, Soviet historians were less constrained and offered up more challenging and subtle explanatory schema. Indeed, a great deal of worthwhile and even outstanding historical literature was produced in the Soviet Union.[3]

In considering aspects of the Soviet views of the war in the Pacific, we touch on an issue, which, while not the most sensitive in absolute terms, is nonetheless very highly politicized. One's interpretation of the Pacific campaigns carries implications for a variety of questions, ranging from overall Soviet conduct at the time to the current international context in Asia. In approaching this problem, then, it seemed valid to ask to what degree the relative autonomy and professionalism characteristic of Soviet historiography as a whole prevailed here, and to what extent ideologically oriented party history was the norm. In order to address that larger question, it was necessary to analyze the evolution of the historical discipline in the postwar Soviet context, the dominant Soviet interpretation of the war in the Pacific, any internal tensions within that interpretation, and how they were reconciled. The next step involved an exploration of Soviet historical output under glasnost, what it has provided, and why. Finally, it might prove interesting in a brief descriptive codicil to examine the new historical materials that are beginning to emerge in some volume.

Soviet Historical Analysis, 1945–85

However surprising it may be, the topic of World War II was virtually neglected, or rather suppressed, in the immediate postwar era. Although there were early indications that the war would be a central *topos* of the postwar period, that trend was very quickly halted and reversed.[4] As a result, "from 1946 until near the end of Stalin's life, the history of World War II was virtually a forbidden topic for Soviet professional historians."[5] It may strike us as odd that, although "the war experience was undoubtedly crucial in forming what is today the political, economic, scientific, cultural, and military elite in the Soviet Union," World War II remained "virtually untouched by scholars and participants alike" until the late 1950s.[6] Indicative of this is the fact that the periodical *Voenno-istoricheskii zhurnal,* which had been in existence for scarcely two years when it was suspended owing to the war in July 1941, was not published again until July 1958.[7] Clearly, from Stalin's perspective there were too many danger zones in the Soviet wartime experience to allow for open treatment by scholars, despite the fact that the historical community had been weaned of most of its feral proclivities.[8]

It was only with the death of Stalin and the de-Stalinization drive (the most important manifestations of which were the so-called secret speech by Khrushchev at the Twentieth Party Congress in 1956 and his further actions at the Twenty-first Congress in 1961) that a significant body of literature, both scholarly analysis and memoir material, began to emerge. Not only did new material begin to appear, but the type of history produced was vastly better than the literature (one hesitates to call it history) turned out under Stalin—repetitive, hyperbolic, and characterized by a fetishistic use of quotations from the "Great Helmsman."[9] Nonetheless, while the worst aspects of Stalinist mutilation of the historical record ended, the political use of history did not. The limits of experimentation in history were established as a result of the well-known "Burdzhalov affair," during which the leaders of revisionist history still well within a Party context were sharply reined in.[10] What occurred was the replacement of the "cult of personality" *(kul't lichnosti)* with the cult of the Party and of the system.[11] With individual exceptions, particularly Marshal Zhukov, this meant the rehabilitation of the professional military at the expense of Stalin. This trend can be said to have continued until the fall of Khrushchev, after which a gradual recrudescence of conservatism led to an end to attacks on Stalin and his partial rehabilitation.[12]

The transition from the more critical approach to the war characteristic of the Khrushchev era back to a more patriotic and triumphant tone occurred in 1965-67. The linchpin of this rightward swing in history was the so-called Nekrich affair, revolving around Alexsandr Nekrich's highly critical *1941, 22 iiunia,* its initially positive reception, and the subsequent virulent rejection of both author and text.[13] This coincided roughly with the articulation of policies against the emerging movement that came to be known as dissidence, the intervention in Czechoslovakia, and the overall conservative shift of the Soviet government. Although countercurrents existed and much worthwhile historical literature was produced, the overall conservative, party-oriented, anticritical trend continued and deepened in the 1970s. The graying of the "Brezhnev generation," the disastrous decision to intervene in Afghanistan, the surprisingly (to the Brezhnev leadership group) negative reaction on the part of the West to the Afghanistan adventure, and the further worsening of Soviet-Western relations during the first Reagan administration with its confrontational style could only serve to intensify the politicization of historical study in the Soviet Union, especially where such vital issues as World War II were concerned.[14]

The overall Soviet interpretation of World War II and of the Pacific component is clearly established and easily summarized. The starting point for any understanding of World War II is the Bolshevik Revolution of 1917, which, by founding a socialist form of government, fundamentally altered the world political order. The Soviet Union became the center of global progressive forces and the source of unceasing torment to the capitalist powers.[15] The outbreak of war in 1939 was not a sudden, chance occurrence; rather it grew out of the structural contradictions of "imperialism as a social system."[16] Blame for the war rests on the inequities, dominant classes, and major governments of that system.[17] As the internal contradictions (expressed in the global economic depression) were ratcheted upward, the pressure generated sought release through increased state capitalism, militarism, fascism, and expansionism, breaking the major capitalist powers into two antagonistic camps. This situation was complicated, however, by the existence of the Soviet Union, which united the entire capitalist world around the cause of liquidating this standing challenge and reproach to their unjust system. This prevented the Western powers from joining with the USSR in a "unified front to safeguard peace," because they hoped that by providing "political, diplomatic, and financial assistance" to Hitler that they would enable Germany to extinguish the USSR and thus "to resolve in favor of capitalism the main contradictions of the epoch."[18] Thus, the "real possibility" of peace based on "the constant strengthening of the economic and military might of the USSR, its peace-loving policies," and the general growth of revolutionary national liberation and working class movements was passed over by the "governing circles" of the United States, Britain, and France, whose attempt to incite Germany against the USSR was papered over only by the fig leaf of the Munich treaty. As a result, the Soviet Union was "compelled" to sign a nonaggression pact with Germany to preempt the coalescing of a unified antagonistic capitalist front.[19] The case of Japan is subsumed under this interpretive umbrella, with the United States hoping vainly for a "Pacific Munich" that would turn Japan against the Soviet Union.[20]

Eventually, owing to the barbarism of the Axis powers and the entry of the Soviet Union into the ranks of the combatants, the war was transformed from an imperialist war into an antifascist, liberationist war.

While this is the interpretation that came to dominate in the Soviet Union, it did not hold immediate, exclusive sway. In connection with the Pacific war, Matthew Gallagher cites a number of nondogmatic, nearly sympathetic works on prewar Japanese-American diplomacy and even on aspects of the war itself. "A number of historians," in Gallagher's words, " . . . continued to show considerable scholarly objectivity despite the hardening of the official line and showed a notable laggardness in keeping abreast of the ideological demands of the times."[21] One article "presented a detailed, virtually nonideological exposition of international events in the prewar years," abstaining from utilizing "the obvious openings for moralizations or ideological sermons," and seeming at times to take "pains to blunt the ideological edge of the events described."[22] Other works treat the assault on Pearl Harbor "in a way that was not unsympathetic to the U.S."; elsewhere Gallagher finds "not a single really derogatory word about the U.S. in the article, or even a typical Communist formula."[23] He cites works noteworthy for their "considerable objectivity, or at least minimal ideological distortion."[24]

Wartime exigencies had led the Stalinist leadership to change the tenor of its rhetoric regarding the United States and Britain and to relax social controls. It is to be expected that some Soviets, as was the case with some Americans, would have trouble transitioning in short order from the wartime spirit of cooperation and allied collegiality to the harshness and acerbity of the Cold War. In the late 1940s and early 1950s, however, books reflecting this transition were criticized, withdrawn from circulation, and even refuted by their authors in new books.[25] Gallagher's assertion that once the limited heterodoxy had been replaced by a new standard interpretation, "there was very little development or change in the Soviet interpretation of the Japanese surrender during the postwar period" is undoubtedly correct overall.[26] It is necessary to note only two qualifications: 1) that without sacrificing its main points there was an expansion and elaboration of the general Soviet interpretation, and 2) the tenor of Soviet historians' discussions was strongly influenced by the climate of contemporary Soviet foreign relations.

As regards the decisive contribution to the capitulation of the Japanese, the Soviet reading has never strayed from the assertion that it was neither the Anglo-American military efforts up to August 1945 nor the nuclear devices dropped on Hiroshima and Nagasaki that led the Japanese leadership to surrender, but rather the defeat of the Kwantung forces by the Soviet military. According to Gallagher, this interpretation had three primary components: "(1) that the Allies had achieved no significant military successes against the Japanese during the course of the Pacific war; (2) that, in Manchuria, the main military strength of Japan remained throughout the war untouched; and (3) that, in 1945, Japan was still capable of continuing the war for another two years at least."[27] The arguments that need to be added to this equation are the following: 1) that the Soviet Union had already contributed greatly to the Pacific war effort by its heroic victories in Europe, which forced the Japanese to keep significant forces oriented toward the Soviet Far East, and 2) that the USSR was the inspiration for indigenous resistance forces throughout East Asia, forces that added greatly to the demands on Japanese energies.[28]

Without entering into specific weaknesses in the analysis and documentation of Soviet historians, a number of problems in this interpretation present themselves. First of all, a primary assumption of the Soviet interpretation is that the Second World War comprises a unified whole, almost a centralized conspiracy coordinated from Berlin. The shakiness of that assertion, problematic enough in isolation, is compounded by the fact that on the basis of it they criticize "bourgeois" historians for treating the Pacific war in isolation from the European effort. Yet they themselves are guilty of the same thing, when they deprecate the significance of the contributions of the Anglo-American forces in North Africa and the Mediterranean, in the Pacific, and through the lend-lease program. Furthermore, they disparage the idea of the decisive American contribution, either through the strategic bombing program or as a result of the addition of vast American industrial-agricultural resources and manpower to the Allied effort. Soviet assertions that the entry of the Soviet Union on the antifascist side (because of its progressive socialist system) and the Soviet campaigns in the Far East (despite their duration of a scant two weeks) were decisive rest on no more foundation than the fact that they involved the Soviet Union. Despite the scorn of Soviet analysts for anything not deemed "objective," this is the most subjective of epistemological bases.

Above and beyond this contradiction, there is the Soviets' difficulty reconciling the special and separate treatment they render to the so-called Great Fatherland War with the role they reserve for themselves in World War II taken as a whole. If we consider, for example, the periodization of World War II, they identify five main phases to the war: 1) September 1939–June 1941; 2) June 1941–November 1942; 3) November 1942–December 1943; 4) January 1944–May 1945; and 5) May–September 1945.[29] Except for December 1943/January 1944, which seems to be a somewhat arbitrary halfway point between Stalingrad and Berlin, all other dates connect to significant Soviet-related developments in the European theater. Certainly, there is nothing in this periodization to indicate the significance of December 1941 or, for that matter, August 1945. Furthermore, despite their claims to decisive significance in the Pacific theater, only the final period, or five of 72 months that passed from the German invasion of Poland to the Japanese signature of the articles of surrender, concerns the Pacific war. This points to the "historiographical shoals" Soviet historians have to skirt, since "[n]either the Great Patriotic War nor World War II provides a completely satisfactory framework for Soviet historians dealing with Soviet entry into hostilities in the Far East."[30] The way they reconcile the overwhelming importance they attribute to the European war (and within it to the Nazi-Soviet battles in the forests and plains of eastern Europe) with the decisive role of Soviet forces in the war against Japan is by emphasizing the interrelated nature of the war. In this scenario, the USSR kept substantial Japanese forces in check (despite the nonaggression pact) while contributing the lion's share to the defeat of Hitler and then, after the fall of Berlin, shifted its unmatched land forces to the Far East and destroyed the largest standing Japanese army. Despite the supposed structural strength of such a rationale, this is a pretty thin reed on which to base an argument.

Soviet Historiography under Gorbachev

The type of argumentation discussed above was tepid at best, and one would think it would have become stale with the passage of time. To be sure, Brezhnev-era historiography emphasized the positive elements of the Soviet Union's experience in World War II,[31] but could this not be reconciled with a less ideological approach to Anglo-American participation in the collective defeat of the Axis powers? The answer is that it could until "peaceful coexistence" and detente began to sour in the late 1970s and 1980s, at which time a renewed stream of politicized history appeared. The periodical *Voenno-istoricheskii zhurnal* even ran a regular section entitled "Against the Bourgeois Falsification of History." Such inspirational pieces as "Criticism of the Basic Trends of the Bourgeois Falsification of the Heroism of Soviet Soldiers"[32] and "Criticism of the Bourgeois Falsification of the Role of the USSR in the Crushing Defeat of Militarist Japan"[33] enriched our understanding of world historical processes. Moreover, the fact that, as the publication dates of these articles—1985 and 1987, respectively—indicate, such historiography continued to appear well into the Gorbachev era raises fundamental questions about the impact of glasnost on Soviet society. In fact, for very good reasons the new openness affected the historical discipline only very slowly and superficially, and—whatever the longterm impact of glasnost might have been had it run a more peaceful course—no fundamental reorientation of the discipline, either as a whole or in the area of military history (at least as revealed in an analysis of coverage of the war in the Pacific) was forthcoming by the time the Soviet system as a whole collapsed in August 1991.

If we probe the situation further, we discover numerous factors restricting the energetic, multifaceted reexamination of the past. First of all, real support for "openness" was not forthcoming from the political leadership for a couple of years. Gorbachev actually attempted to restrain revisionists from dealing with sensitive subjects, and it was only when he began to realize that he needed public opinion to counteract the recalcitrance of the entrenched conservative forces that he expanded the boundaries of historical inquiry.[34] Even when the traces were removed, Soviet scholars had every reason to go slow, given the long winter freezes that had followed warm spells in the past.[35] Furthermore, the historical profession, especially that involved in the study of the Soviet period, had not attracted the sharpest minds, probably because it was "establishment-oriented, averse to risk-taking, and rather bureaucratic."[36] To embrace revisionism pell-mell, "historians who have made careers out of writing on the Soviet period would have to repudiate not only the official line of the Brezhnev years, but the entire rationale and *modus operandi* of Soviet historiography since at least the time of the *Short Course,* that is, since the mid-1930s."[37] Writing in 1988, Emmons predicted book-length revisionist works no earlier than 1990-91. That same year (1988) the noted military historian and academician Aleksandr Mikhailovich Samsonov was still urging that "[d]ocuments must be declassified. Archives must be made accessible."[38] Indeed, Soviet historians seemed more engaged in reconfiguring the discipline to enable it to produce revisionist history than in actually producing such histories.[39] In these circumstances, it would be asking a great deal to expect historians of the Pacific war to offer up a radical reformulation in short order, especially given their general conservatism and the resistance of much of their constituency to the entire Gorbachev experiment.

Any winds of historiographical change should stir the leaves of major historical journals long before their force reveals itself in monographs. In search of any significant changes in the treatment of the war in the Pacific, I surveyed the contents of three of the most important general historical journals and a major military history journal for the period from 1985 to the present.[40] The picture that emerges is one in which even extremely tentative steps at reconceptualizing the past do not go unchallenged. Furthermore, the tone of "revisionist" pieces indicates that the Soviet historical community as a whole has been unable to break with the dominant didacticism that has characterized the practice of the historian's craft in the Soviet Union for over half a century. Thus, in *Voprosy istorii,* for example, A. M. Samsonov and O. A. Rzheshevskii[41] initiated a discussion focused on the confused use of terms like "turning point of the war," "beginning of the turning point of the war," and other related terms, which are integral parts of much of the Soviet historical literature on "bourgeois falsification."[42] The purpose of this exercise is not, however, to transcend the extremely stale discussion of such issues that characterized much of the Soviets' polemical literature relating to "bourgeois falsificators" but rather to refine them. The piece ends with a reaffirmation of the thesis that the entry of the U.S. into the war was not as significant a turning point as the Battle of Moscow. Similarly restricted is the historiographical debate over the role of England and France in World War II begun in mid-1988 by M. I. Semiriaga.[43] That so much ink and paper should be expended discussing whether England and France fought a just or an imperialist war is almost as disconcerting as the fact that the latest installment in the debate concludes that the overall Soviet interpretation is "basically correct."[44] Yet even this ambiguous and nonsystemic revisionism is beyond the pale for the editors of *Voenno-istoricheskii zhurnal,* who have seen fit to publish excerpts from a "totally discredited," largely ghost-written 1930s biography of Stalin.[45] These excerpts from a book that Laqueur skewers as "probably the most notorious document of the period of the 'cult of the individual'" were published in part to counter the movement resulting in the rehabilitation of Bukharin and other 1930s purge victims.[46] The same journal featured an extended series of articles in 1989 blasting Trotsky as "the greatest coward who had ever disgraced the Russian earth."[47] Although they do not relate to the war in the Pacific, these instances of the historiographical "Vendee" are astonishing demonstrations of the conservative forces resisting revisionism.

More noteworthy, perhaps, are the self-limiting conceptions of even the well intentioned. In an article published at the end of 1987, A. N. Mertsalov subjected Soviet treatment of Western historiography on World War II to what is apparently a thoroughgoing critique in connection with "the demands of new political thinking."[48] Although there is an extensive literature on the subject, Mertsalov writes, it is characterized by an overly simplistic approach. This results in "an indifferent approach to the subject of the criticism, reduction of the task of bourgeois science to [that of] imperialist propaganda, interpretation of any deviation from the truth as conscious distortion, . . . surveying foreign historiography out of context," and so on. Anyone who attempts to criticize this approach is accused of "defending" bourgeois historiography.[49] These deficiencies result from factological ("faktografizm") and stereotyped approaches.[50] He criticizes specific works, including works on which the notorious Rzheshevskii collaborated.

All of these points are valid, but when we consider to what end they were registered we encounter the limits of "new thinking" in the historiography of World War II. To be sure, the author faults these methods for adding nothing to the study of either bourgeois historiography or of history itself, but also for contributing nothing "to the elaboration of [new] means of polemicizing" with bourgeois historiography.[51] The author's objection is methodological, not substantive; he rejects not the effort itself, but the means employed. Lest anyone doubt this, we are told that "[d]eceit comprises an integral trait of the politics and ideology of imperialism. Serving them [i.e., the politics and ideology of imperialism], bourgeois historical science cannot be free of its [imperialism's] influence, but by no means does it [history] always fuse with them. Moreover, the deviation of bourgeois historians from the truth often reveals not only premeditated deceit, but also the involuntary mistakes of subjectively honorable people." The question now is "how can one distinguish error from falsification."[52] The times call for improved means of engaging bourgeois historiography, because

> [i]n the conditions of the revolutionary restructuring of Soviet society and of the unprecedentedly sharp confrontation on the world stage of the forces of progress and social revanchism, the tasks of scientific knowledge and ideology have grown extraordinarily. Criticism can fulfill those tasks only by constantly perfecting its approaches and methods.[53]

But for the reference to perestroika, this could have been written, word for word, in the full glow of Brezhnevism. Again, this is an emendation of the concept, not its repudiation. While its sense of historical practice is much closer to world standards, the understanding of the purposes of history reflected in this article and in the "revisionist" historiography on World War II in the journals reviewed does not differ in any essential way from that which has exercised a deforming influence on Soviet historical writing for decades. Working from the assumption of the politically determined character of all historiography, Soviet as well as Western, the "revisionists" have revised very little and have retained an instrumental approach to history. Rendering history a means rather than an end in itself, the revisionists cannot help but produce a deformed, albeit more liberal, history.

The Shape of Things to Come

If we lift the edge of Clio's mantle and peek tentatively into the future, we see some encouraging signs. For one thing, previously classified materials that were available in the West only on a very restricted basis, if at all (for example, complete runs of *Morskoi sbornik* from 1947 to 1960 and *Voennaia mysl'* from 1947 to 1989), are now accessible.[54] Perhaps more enticing are the numerous internal studies, produced in numbers approaching the high hundreds for internal consumption only and never available in any form until quite recently. The campaign to fill in "blank spots" has been under way long enough and sufficient restrictive forces have been eliminated so that the regular journals that have existed for some time in the erstwhile Soviet Union will begin to publish new memoirs or articles based on newly available materials. We will also begin to see articles written earlier with little or no chance of publication under the conditions then prevailing. Finally, new, more popular journals aimed at the "amateur" historian and the history aficionado are surfacing (e.g., *Naval Historical Journal* and *Gangut,* the latter's name being the Russian form of the famous naval battle against the Swedes in the Great Northern War). Taken together with the collapse of the Soviet historical censorship and the opening up of major archival holdings, these publications and materials signal the dawn of a new day in Soviet naval and military history. The promise of fundamental re-articulation of Russian/Soviet military history has never been greater.

Conclusion

The conclusions emerging from this examination of a discrete problem in Soviet historiography from the end of the war to the present are clear. First of all, the instrumentalism indigenous to Soviet historiography—the subordination of history to political purposes—hamstrings every effort at mature, sophisticated historical treatment, even under the increased liberality of glasnost. The further away one gets from issues of contemporary political importance, the less this factor comes into play. As a result, some very good history has been written in the Soviet period. The discipline as a whole was nonetheless stunted by these external forces; so much so that the brief, carefully supervised flowering under glasnost was not enough to bring forth a crop of new historians. Furthermore, the war in the Pacific, or the Asian-Pacific war as they sometimes refer to it, has been too closely connected with recurring foreign policy considerations to ever break free of the powerful gravitational pull generated by political concerns of the leadership. In particular, the proximity of two important events in American historiography about the war (Pearl Harbor and Midway) to two significant turning points according to the Soviet interpretation of the war (the defense of Moscow and the battle of Stalingrad) clearly influenced Soviet discussions of the former. Similarly, contemporary foreign policy, the question of the use of nuclear weapons, as well as sensitivity concerning the Soviet Far Eastern campaigns, have affected treatments of the defeat of Japan.

Certain qualifications should be noted. First of all, the consideration of Soviet historical coverage of the war in the Pacific has not been balanced by an analogous survey of American and other Western treatments, examples of which no doubt also bear some disfiguring frostbite marks from the Cold War.[55] Secondly, we have focused on the interpretive segments of these books and articles, and Soviet historiography is routinely more ideological in introductory and concluding passages, while it is frequently the case that the historical material forming the meat of this sandwich is a completely unobjectionable, ofttimes interesting, narrative exposition of the problem under consideration. Thirdly, even within the largely politicized historiography on the Pacific theater, there are some almost apolitical works, and there are sharp variations in the degree of historical legitimacy (e.g., Samsonov vs. Rzheshevskii) among the politically correct. And finally, to reiterate, this topic is far more politically sensitive than most and casts and especially harsh light on the physiognomy of the Soviet historical world.

Furthermore, while we are in a position to expect some radical revisionism to emerge from both Russian historians and from historians of other nationalities of the former Soviet polity, we should bear in mind the good possibility that there will also be prominent strands of continuity with Soviet historical interpretations. Most assuredly, the husk of the overall interpretation of the fundamental importance of the 1917 revolutions and the consequent existence of the first "socialist" state, the role of the party as "vanguard" of the masses, and so on, will be shucked and cast aside. But important kernels will remain. It is reasonable to expect a "populist" reinterpretation, for example, that throws out the bathwater of the leading role of the party, but retains the baby: the central significance of the Eastern Front to the overall war effort, the premier role played by Soviet peoples in the defeat of Hitler via enormous human and material sacrifices, related anger over the length of time required for the opening of a second front by the U.S. and Britain. The Soviet interpretation of the war as the outcome of dueling imperialisms does not differ that much from Western interpretations, although the latter are expressed in terms of more traditional geopolitical formulations and not à la Marx. Hence, a (post-Soviet) Russian historical reading that retained the core of this idea seems not unreasonable, and, as a corollary to it, they might also preserve the idea that the bombs were dropped on Hiroshima and Nagasaki for their demonstration effect vis-à-vis the Soviet Union (Russia). Whatever they retain from the historiographical legacy of the Soviet period, it is virtually certain that they will invigorate global historical understanding of World War II with new interpretations and new materials.

The above qualifications notwithstanding, the restraints placed on the practice of history—in effect, on the truth insofar as it can be determined by free inquiry—rendered the Soviet historical community anything but healthy. Academic history was superfluous to many of the efforts to reconstitute the true record under glasnost, and the historical community as a whole is held in low repute by the public, owing to the large number of careerists and time-servers. One is left to wonder what those courageous and intellectually questing historians who produced interesting history despite the systemic constraints might have generated had academic history been less hobbled. As it is, having come to maturity in conditions of theoretical sterility and largely deprived of challenging alternative conceptions of the past against which to whet their own conceptual swords, the best of the older generation seems to find it impossible to cast off completely the ingrained habits of thought of the past. In that regard, Professor Byrnes was probably correct when he maintained recently that the repression and *Gleichschaltung* of academic history from 1928 to 1934 "established a Stalinist spirit that many historians still accept," whether that acceptance is explicit or implicit.[56] As we have indicated, the winds of change are stirring, but a storm of new ideas is still a ways off. Perhaps it is wrong to expect a more rapid transformation. Thomas Kuhn in his enormously influential work *The Structure of Scientific Revolutions* notes Max Planck's contention that "paradigm shifts" emerge as dominant not by winning over opponents, but rather when the opponents die off and are replaced by adherents of the new model. Western historical study will be challenged and stimulated when fresh historical ideas begin to appear in the lands of the former Soviet Union, but it seems clear at this point that those ideas will be forthcoming only when a new generation, weaned on a more open, freer brand of historical study, has come of age.

Notes

1. The author thanks the U.S. Naval Academy, the Hoover Institution, and the State Department, and gratefully acknowledges the assistance of the library staffs of the Hoover Library and Green Library at Stanford University.
2. Samuel H. Baron and Nancy W. Heer, "The Soviet Union: Historiography Since Stalin," in Georg G. Iggers and Harold T. Parker, eds., *International Handbook of Historical Studies: Contemporary Research and Theory* (Westport, CT: Greenwood Press, 1979), 281.
3. Ibid., 283.
4. Matthew P. Gallagher, *The Soviet History of World War II: Myths, Memories, and Realities* (New York: Frederick A. Praeger, 1963), 79-81.
5. Ibid., 81-82.
6. Seweryn Bialer, ed., *Stalin and His Generals: Soviet Military Memoirs of World War II* (New York: Pegasus, 1969), 15-16.
7. Anatole G. Mazour, *The Writing of History in the Soviet Union* (Stanford, CA: Hoover Institution Press, 1971), 356.
8. See John J. Stephan, "The USSR and the Defeat of Japan: Introduction," *Soviet Studies in History,* 24, no. 3 (Winter 1985-86): 6.
9. On the changed spirit and opportunities, see Aleksandr Nekrich, *Forsake Fear: Memoirs of an Historian,* Donald Lineburgh, trans. (Boston: Unwin Hyman, 1991), ch. 5.
10. On the Burdzhalov affair see the "Translator's Introduction," in E. N. Burdzhalov, *Russia's Second Revolution: The February 1917 Uprising in Petrograd,* trans. and ed. Donald J. Raleigh (Bloomington: Indiana University Press, 1987): ix-xxxii. It is significant that Burdzhalov's revisionist history was eventually published in the Soviet Union: *Vtoraia russkia revoliutsiia: Vosstanie v Petrograde* (Moscow, 1987).
11. Ibid., 16-18. Bialer uses the phrase "cult of the Party." (18) See also, Gallagher, *Soviet History,* ch. 6, and Nancy Whittier Heer, *Politics and History in the Soviet Union* (Cambridge: MIT Press, 1971), 246-50.
12. Heer, *Politics and History,* 248-50.
13. R. W. Davies, *Soviet History in the Gorbachev Revolution* (Bloomington: Indiana University Press, 1989), 102-3, and esp. Nekrich, *Forsake Fear,* chs. 7 and 8.
14. Baron and Heer, "The Soviet Union," 290-91.
15. The following discussion is based primarily on the introductory section by the editorial commission for the twelve-volume *Istoriia vtoroi mirovoi voiny 1939-1945* (M., 1973-82), vol. 1, pp. v-xxxviii. See also P. A. Zhilin, "Nauchnye

itogi i opyt razrabotki truda po istorii vtoroi mirovoi voiny," *Voprosy istorii,* no. 9 (1985), 3-19. For this point see *Istoriia vtoroi mirovoi voiny,* vol. 1, p. v.

16. *Istoriia vtoroi mirovoi voiny 1939-1945,* viii.
17. Ibid.
18. Ibid.
19. Ibid., ix-x.
20. See, for example, A. Savin, "Put' k Piorl-Kharboru," *Voenno-istoricheskii zhurnal,* no. 11 (1971): 38-39.
21. Gallagher, *Soviet History,* 83.
22. Ibid.
23. Ibid., 84.
24. Ibid., 84-85.
25. Ibid., 91-102.
26. Ibid., 35.
27. Ibid., 34.
28. See, for example, *Istoriia vtoroi mirovoi voiny,* vol. 12 (Moscow, 1982): 36.
29. *Istoriia vtoroi mirovoi voiny,* vol. 1, p. xxvi.
30. Stephan, "The USSR and the Defeat of Japan," 5, 7.
31. Michael Parrish, "Soviet Historiography of the Great Patriotic War 1970-1985: A Review," *Soviet Studies in History,* vol. 23, no. 3, (Winter 1984-85): iii.
32. V. A. Sekistov, V. M. Gobarev, "Kritika osnovnykh napravlenii burzhuaznykh fal'sifikatsii geroizma sovetskikh voinov," *Voenno-istoricheskii zhurnal,* no. 2 (1987): 52-58.
33. V. A. Sekistov, "Kritika burzhuaznykh fal'sifakatsii roli SSSR v razgrome militaristskoi Iaponii," *Voenno-istoricheskii zhurnal,* no. 8 (1985): 62-66.
34. "What emerged by late 1987 was a *working* consensus . . . that few dramatic developments occurred in Soviet professional history between March 1985 and late 1986, [and] that events moved rapidly since early 1987." William B. Husband, "Glasnost and the Historians: Introduction," *Soviet Studies in History,* 27, no. 1 (Summer 1988): 4. One prominent scholar asserts that by 1988 there "hardly seemed any limits that writers or scholars needed to respect." See Alexander Dallin, "Soviet History," in Alexander Dallin and Bertrand M. Patenaude, eds., *Soviet Scholarship under Gorbachev* (Stanford, CA: Center for Russian and East European Studies, 1988): 8. Anyone interested in tracing developments in the Soviet historical community should consult the journal *Soviet Studies in History* for the last couple of years. Donald J. Raleigh, its editor, and William B. Husband are two of the foremost students of the changing contours of academic history in Russia. See also Donald J. Raleigh, ed., *Soviet Historians and Perestroika: The First Phase* (Armonk, N.Y.: M. E. Sharpe, Inc., 1989).

35. Husband, "Glasnost and the Historians," 3.
36. Dallin, "Soviet History," 9.
37. Terence Emmons, "Comment," [on Dallin's "Soviet History"], in *Soviet Scholarship under Gorbachev*, 14.
38. See the interview reproduced in *The Glasnost Reader,* New York: New American Library, 1990 comp. and ed. Jonathan Eisen, 409.
39. Husband, "Glasnost' and the Historians," 9.
40. The general journals are *Istoriia SSSR, Voprosy istorii, Novaia i noveishaia istoriia;* the military history journal, *Voenno-istoricheskii zhurnal.*
41. By the way, the collaboration of Samsonov and Rzheshevskii may have undetected political ramifications. While Samsonov's writings follow the main Soviet line of interpretation, his work is characterized by a much more balanced approach than that of Rzheshevskii, who is one of the principal timpanists beating the drum of "bourgeois falsification." See, e.g., his *World War II: Myths and Realities* (Moscow: Progress Publishers, 1984) and "Noveishaia burzhuaznaia istoriografiia o korennom perelome v khode vtoroi mirovoi voiny," *Istoriia SSSR,* no. 3 (Winter 1985): 155-68. The latter ends by reasserting "the necessity of the utmost effort on the part of scholarly social scientists in unmasking bourgeois falsifications of the history of the Great Fatherland War." (168) That Rzheshevskii is a doctor of historical science and head of the Section on Problems of Military History of the Institute of World History of the Academy of Sciences (USSR) is a telling indication of the structural impediments to reform of the discipline. For a sampling of Rzheshevskii's style, see O. A. Rzheshevskii, "Bourgeois Assessments of the Soviet Victory over Japan," and especially Dr. Stephan's accompanying notes in *Soviet Studies in History,* 24, no. 3, 69-77 and 77-79, respectively. Professor Stephan has written extensively on Russian and the Soviet Union in the Pacific, and his work is noteworthy for its balanced tone, as well as for his use of Soviet, Japanese, and American sources.
42. A. M. Samsonov and O. A. Rzheshevskii, "O korennom perelome vo vtoroi mirovoi voine," *Voprosy istorii,* no. 4 (1987): 70-81. See also the follow-up piece, A. F. Vasil'ev, "O nachale korennogo pereloma vo vtoroi mirovoi voine," *Voprosy istorii,* no. 5 (1988): 57-74, which far from moving beyond the concept, seeks to demonstrate that the turning point in the economy preceded that at the front.
43. "K voprosu o politicheskom kharaktere vtoroi mirovoi voiny," *Novaia i noveishaia istoriia,* no. 4 (July-August 1988): 90-106. For other contributions to this discussion see the same issue, as well as 1989, nos. 3 and 6, and 1991, no. 3.
44. B. G. Solov'ev, "O politicheskom kharaktere vtoroi mirovoi voiny," *Novaia i noveishaia istoriia,* no. 1 (May-June 1991): 99.

45. The book in question (*Stalin,* New York, 1935) was purportedly written by Henri Barbusse but is apparently the work mostly of others. See Walter Laqueur, *Stalin: The Glasnost Revelations* (New York: Charles Scribner's Sons, 1990), 16-17, and 339, n.5. Excerpts in *Voenno-Istoricheskii Zhurnal,* no. 12 (1989), and no. 1 (1990).
46. See Ibid., 83, and 346, n. 39. Quotation by Laqueur from n. 39.
47. Laqueur's words in ibid., 342, n. 10.
48. A. N. Mertsalov, "O kritike burzhuaznoi istoriografii vtoroi mirovoi voiny," *Voprosy istorii,* no. 12 (1987): 35.
49. Ibid., 35.
50. The former is superficial and lacking in theoretical bases; the latter reveals "an inability to see anything new in world science, an unwillingness to call something by its real name, onesided judgements, apologetics, a desire to avoid 'blank spots' in history, subjective preferences, [and] epidemics of careerism." Ibid., 36.
51. Ibid.
52. Ibid., 37.
53. Ibid., 50.
54. Although the free market has begun to work in the former Soviet Union, at least as far as these materials are concerned, the leading marketer at the present seems to be East View Publications of Minneapolis. At this point, the author would like to express his sincere gratitude to Dr. Kent Lee of East View and to Dr. Jacob Kipp for their generously given collegial support. Dr. Kipp was particularly helpful in the initial stages of this project, and Dr. Lee has been unstinting in his assistance. This paragraph is based on a phone interview with Dr. Lee.
55. Professor Stephan writes of Western histories of the end of the Pacific war that "[d]emonology aside, Rzheshevskii's arguments are not without merit. American historians as a whole do treat the war against Japan as basically an American effort. Ideological propensities and linguistic barriers (how many historians of the Pacific War read Russian?) have led American writers to underestimate the *political* impact of Soviet belligerency on Japan's leaders, who had naively pinned their last hopes for a compromise peace on Stalin." See Stephan, "The USSR and the Defeat of Japan," p. 7. The emphasis is his.
56. Robert F. Byrnes, "Creating the Soviet Historical Profession, 1917-1934," *Slavic Review* 50, no. 2 (Summer 1991): 307.

6.

"Just Dumb Luck": American Entry into World War II

Stephen E. Ambrose

The fiftieth anniversary of American entry into world War II invites rethinking about how and why it happened, using the fresh eyes of a new generation born since the war and growing up with its results. In Russia, for example, young scholars are asking what kind of a victory was it when the Soviet Union lost 20 million people, had most of its European area devastated, and ended up with a worse-than-ever Stalinist dictatorship. To that question older Russian scholars reply: Ask the people of Poland, the Balkans, the Ukraine, or European Russia what life under Nazi occupation was like. To which answer the young scholars respond: We were born during the Khrushchev regime and grew up during the Brezhnev regime and that hardly seems an improvement over a Hitler regime.

In Japan, for another example, some young scholars are asking why the United States opposed the Japanese conquest of China. Had Japan been given a free hand, they say, China today would not be a Communist dictatorship. To the American answer that the Japanese acted as the occupiers of China in a manner brutal beyond description, the Japanese reply: Worse than Tiananmen Square?

In the United States, a question frequently asked by today's college students is: Was there not a way we could have defeated Hitler without supporting Stalin? Considering that eight out of every ten Wehrmacht soldiers killed in the war were killed by the Red Army, the answer is: Certainly not. But considering that the United States was years ahead of the Germans in atomic research and development, the question appears valid.

We can never know what the consequences of different decisions would have been, while we know precisely what the consequences of a decision made and enforced were. But anniversaries lead us to think about what might have been if different paths had been followed, to consider why they were not, and to speculate on the risks involved in setting out on the path that was chosen.

This chapter attempts to deal with some big questions about American entry into the war and begins by disposing of one that many Americans regard as the biggest question of all: Did President Roosevelt know that the Japanese were about to attack Pearl Harbor and deliberately keep that information from the commanders in Hawaii, in order to suffer a humiliating defeat that would unite a badly divided country behind American involvement in the war? Did he take the "Back Door to War"? The answer is unequivocally no. The charge is ridiculous. Although widely made and widely believed, it displays a stunning ignorance of how government works and of Roosevelt's actual policy.

Commonsense questions answer themselves. Could Roosevelt, by himself, have kept information about the attack from the commanders in Hawaii? Of course not. Teams of men were involved in breaking the Japanese code; admirals and generals in Washington got the intelligence and took it to the president. They would have had to have joined him in a conspiracy. Can anyone believe the admirals would have allowed their battleships to go down without protest? In its most extreme form, the conspiracy thesis charges that FDR knew that battleships were obsolete, and therefore was willing to sacrifice them, and that he recognized that the aircraft carriers were the key weapon in the coming war, so he therefore made certain the carriers would be out of port on December 7. That is so silly it leaves one helpless with laughter. FDR loved the navy and he loved battleships, and no more than anyone else did he recognize that they were obsolete.

A more recent charge is that Churchill knew the attack was coming and refused to inform Roosevelt, the idea being that Churchill wanted America to be drawn into the war. The logic of the charge totally escapes me. How can anyone believe that Churchill would want the U.S. Fleet destroyed when the

British fleet was stretched to and beyond its limit? If he knew the attack was coming, he certainly would have wanted the U.S. Navy to meet and defeat it—after all, the United States would be fully into the war the moment the battle began in any event. To the more reasonable charge that Roosevelt maneuvered events in such a way as to leave the Japanese no choice but to strike, the reply is that while he certainly put pressure on them, most of all with his on-again, off-again oil embargo, he did not put a gun to Tojo's head and tell him to attack or die. Nor did he want the Japanese to attack, at least not in December of 1941. His policy was to avoid war in the Pacific.

We now turn from what Roosevelt did not do to what he did do. The central point is that United States did not voluntarily enter either the war in the Pacific or the war in Europe. On December 8, 1941, Roosevelt did not ask Congress to declare war on Japan, but to recognize that a state of war existed between the two countries. Nor did he ask Congress to declare war on Germany until after Hitler, on December 11, declared war on the United States.

These are fundamental facts and they force us to examine Roosevelt's policies from an entirely different angle than the Pearl Harbor conspiracy thesis. Roosevelt's supporters, and they are many and learned, praise him for carefully overcoming the strong isolationist sentiment of the American people and bringing them to recognize their duty and self-interest. Much can be, and has been, said in support of this interpretation, but much can also be said against it.

In rethinking American involvement in the war from the perspective of fifty years later, what stands out is the terrible risks Roosevelt and the United States were taking in the fall of 1941, how close we came to catastrophe—not by edging toward war, but by refusing to prepare for it and failing to provide any significant help to the enemies of fascism and militarism in their hour of greatest need. As a parallel theme, one is struck by how American commentators have concentrated on developments in the Pacific theater while ignoring the really decisive impact of developments in the Nazi-Soviet war inside the Soviet Union. As a third theme, one is also struck by the situation Roosevelt found his nation on December 10, 1941: The United States was not involved in the war he had been determined to enter, against Germany, but was involved in the war he had been determined to put off until later, against Japan. His foreign policy, right up to December 10, was a dismal failure. What saved him and his policy was nothing he did, but Hitler's act of lunacy.

This chapter cannot detail Roosevelt's failure to provide any semblance of world leadership in the crisis years of 1938 to 1941, but must simply note that he recognized the Anschluss of Austria de facto, without a wimper. He was not present at and exerted little influence on the Munich Conference. His response to the invasion of Poland and the outbreak of war in Europe was purely verbal. He failed to respond to desperate French pleas for assistance when the Germans invaded in May 1940. He gave no significant aid to Great Britain during the Battle of Britain in the summer of 1940. In the fall of 1940, during his campaign for a third term, he gave the Axis powers what amounted to a pledge that they had nothing to fear from the United States when he promised American mothers that "your boys are not going to be sent into any foreign wars." His response to the Japanese conquest of Manchuria and much of eastern China was limited to nonrecognition and a trickle of aid to the Chinese. While war raged around the world, he failed to mobilize the United States. In other words, he fully adopted the twin themes of American diplomacy of the 1920s and 1930s: neutrality and unilateral disarmament.

With millions of men under arms around the world in 1940, the American army numbered 375,000 men, with virtually no tanks or airplanes. Although Roosevelt was the leader of the greatest industrial power in the world, a nation that had colonies in the Pacific and worldwide interests to defend, he had no influence on events because he had no armed forces capable of attacking anyone and only the navy with which to defend the United States. The world was in flames, the United States was vulnerable to winds from both directions, and the nation had no firefighters but was only dealing out garden hoses.

Of course Roosevelt and his supporters blame this situation on the isolationists, but it can be said with equal justification that Roosevelt's policy had been to appease the isolationists. Perhaps he could not have done more, but we will never know because he did not try. His hesitancy to act reflected a nineteenth-century isolationist America rather than a world power ready to proclaim that the twentieth would be "the American Century."

So, in the spring of 1941, the situation was as follows: Hitler had either conquered or browbeaten into an alliance the whole of non-Russian Europe, and he commanded the greatest and most successful armed force the world had ever seen. Roosevelt had entered into an economic alliance with the only nation then at war with Hitler, the United Kingdom, through the destroyers-for-bases deal of September 1940, and the Lend-Lease program, enacted in March 1941, leading him to proclaim that the United States had become the "arsenal of democracy." But it was not much of an arsenal, nor was Britain much of a threat to Hitler—the British were absolutely incapable of mounting an offensive against Germany. Hitler was free to do whatever he chose.

In Asia, the initiative was with Japan. Fully mobilized, with a navy that outclassed the American navy in the critical weapon—aircraft carriers—the Japanese were free to strike north, into Asian Russia, or south, against the French, British, and Dutch colonies, whenever they wished. But in Asia,

Roosevelt did have the power to influence events, because of Japanese dependence on American oil.

Roosevelt's policy was clear and sensible. He recognized that Germany was the greater threat, that Germany could not be defeated without full American participation, that America was hardly prepared to fight on two fronts, and that therefore it was critical that he get the nation involved in Europe while stalling the Japanese.

But Roosevelt's implementation of this policy was badly muddled and fraught with grave risks. The aid lend-lease provided to Britain was barely enough to keep her going. His reinforcement of the Philippines by stationing B-17s at Clark Field, starting in the spring of 1941, was designed to deter the Japanese from striking south, but it was a classic case of half-measures. The bombers were insufficient as a deterrent but provoked to the Japanese. His policies left him vulnerable to charges from the isolationists that he was planning for war but left him short of preparing for war.

Consider: in May 1941, the United States had but one combat-ready division, while the Germans had 208 and the Japanese over 100. The United States had a total of 471 military aircraft, while Hitler had 2,700 on his eastern frontier alone. The American army had 200 tanks, while the Wehrmacht was about to invade the Soviet Union with 3,500 tanks. Never in human history has the preparedness gap between potential enemies been greater.

On June 22, Hitler launched Operation Barbarossa. The initial German successes put the world at a deadly peril. A quick German victory—and Hitler came awfully close to achieving it—would have made the Nazis self-sufficient in natural and human resources and rendered Britain's only weapon, the naval blockade of Germany's North Sea ports, useless. We know today that Hitler had made his first major mistake in attacking the Soviet Union, but at the time expert opinion, in the United States and the United Kingdom as well as in Germany, held that the Red Army would be defeated before winter. But what did Roosevelt do to prevent such a catastrophe? It is amazing to look back and realize how limited was his response to Barbarossa. His naval advisor, Admiral Harold Stark, urged him to go to war, by providing escorts for convoys all the way to Britain and to Russia's northern ports, but he would not.

Nor would he mobilize. Through the first three months of the Russo-German war, American industry produced 115 tanks per month, at a time when Stalin was demanding 500 per month to keep the Red Army in the battle. American war production during those critical months, when much of the rest of the world was waging total war, amounted to only 10 percent of the total output of American industry. In July, when the Russians asked for 3,000 fighter airplanes, Roosevelt promised 200—of which 140 came from British stocks.

Stalin wanted 3,000 bombers and got five. He asked for 20,000 anti-aircraft cannon and machine guns and got none, 5,000 anti-tank guns and got none, 25,000 rifles and got 1,000. As Waldo Heinrichs puts it, "For waging a battle he regarded as decisive, the president had painfully little to offer besides tokens and promises."[1]

These paltry figures need to be put beside the latent, capacity of American industry. When Roosevelt—who proved to be a magnificent war leader once the nation was committed—called for the production of 50,000 airplanes a year, people thought he was crazy. But within a year of entering the war the United States was producing 4,000 military airplanes per month; by 1944 it was 8,000 per month, or 96,318 for the year. Altogether, the United States built over 250,000 airplanes during the war. There were similar, all-but-unbelievable great leaps forward in the production of tanks, ships, landing craft, rifles, and other weapons. And all this took place while the United States put its major effort into the greatest industrial feat up to that time, the production of atomic weapons (hardly begun in 1942, completed by mid-1945). Had the United States possessed in the fall of 1941 the power the nation was to have by the fall of 1943, the Axis almost surely would have been deterred.

But as it was, in the fall of 1941 Roosevelt was unable to help Russia, barely able to help Britain, unwilling to try to persuade the American people that their national security was in danger, and thus incapable of mobilizing. He was reduced to attempting to goad Germany into declaring war on the United States. He ordered the navy to become ever more active in the Battle of the Atlantic, culminating in his "shoot on sight" orders in September. He evidently thought that such deliberate provocation would force Hitler to declare war. But to Hitler, the American navy was only an irritant. As his armies drove ever deeper into Russia, Hitler ordered his submarine commanders to avoid incidents in the Atlantic involving the Americans.

As Roosevelt tried desperately to get involved in the European war—without ever once telling the American people that they absolutely had to come to grips with the Nazis, who could not otherwise be defeated; indeed promising them, in the face of all logic, that with American tools the British and Russians could do the job—he was trying desperately to avoid war with the Japanese. They were obviously stirring, eager to take advantage of the weakness of the colonial powers in Asia: the French conquered, the Dutch conquered, the British fully involved with Germany, the Americans preoccupied with Germany. Roosevelt wanted to keep the Japanese from striking out; if they attacked to the north, against Siberia, it could well be disastrous for the Soviet Union and thus for the anti-Axis forces worldwide. If they attacked to the south, neither the Dutch nor the French could do anything about it, the British would have to divide their already hard-pressed fleet, and the United States, as noted, could well be involved in a two-front war when it was not yet ready to fight a one-front war. So Roosevelt played a delicate game with the Japanese, entering into serious negotiations, attempting to use oil as a weapon (by selling them enough to keep them from making a desperate decision to conquer their own sources of oil in the Dutch East Indies, but not enough to allow them to plan for all-out war), buying time.

Roosevelt had gotten himself at cross-purposes with public opinion. He wanted war with Germany, but many Americans felt that Germany had done nothing to the United States and in any case the Germans were killing Communists; he wanted to avoid war with Japan, but many Americans felt Japan had violated a bedrock American principle, the Open Door to China, threatened the American colony in the Philippines, and must be stopped.

We cannot go too far with this public opinion business. Roosevelt's supporters cite the polls that indicated most Americans wished to avoid war. When put that way, however, the question almost answered itself. But the polls also showed that a majority supported the lend-lease bill and that 62 percent supported the "shoot on sight" policy. What the polls could not measure was how attitudes might have changed had presidential leadership been stiffer. Back in May 1941, secretary of war Henry Stimson had warned Roosevelt against relying on incidents instead of leadership to light the path.[2] Roosevelt had nevertheless continued to rely on incidents.

In August 1941, secretary of the treasury Henry Morgenthau responded to a temporary halt in the German advance into Russia by telling Roosevelt, "We will never have a better chance. Somebody has been looking over this country and the good Lord has been with us, but we can't count on the good Lord and just dumb luck forever."[3] Still, Roosevelt refused to attempt to rouse the nation to an all-out effort.

The Roosevelt administration was living in a dream world. The dream was that the Russians would hold out unaided, that the Japanese would wait until the Americans were ready before attacking, and that Hitler would declare war on the United States. That the first and third dreams turned out to be realities does not mean that they were not dreams in late 1941; the second dream, or expectation, that the Japanese would wait until the Americans were ready before attacking, turned out to be a costly mistake.

It was based on faulty intelligence as much as wishful thinking. Of all the areas in which the United States was unprepared in late 1941, intelligence stands out. It was simply terrible. In late October, U. S. Army intelligence told Roosevelt that simultaneous attacks by the Japanese on the Dutch East Indies, Malaya, and the Philippines were beyond Japan's means. The intelligence experts did not even consider the possibility of an attack on Hawaii. In late November, intelligence "lost" the Japanese aircraft carrier fleet. This must rank as one of the great intelligence failures of all time. Consider: the Germans were at the gates of Moscow, the Battle of the Atlantic had reached a critical stage, negotiations with Japan had reached an impasse and the Japanese had mobilized and were on the move. The world crisis had reached a white-hot heat, the potential enemies' main offensive weapon—the aircraft carriers—had sortied from their home port, and American intelligence could only guess in which direction they were sailing.

Under the circumstances, one would have thought that every American base in the Pacific, and on the West Coast, would have been on full alert; and that airplanes from the Philippines, Wake and Midway Islands, Hawaii, Los Angeles, and San Francisco would have been flying round-the-clock reconnaissance flights. But they were not, partly because of complacency, mainly because there were not enough airplanes.

Meanwhile, Roosevelt waited for Hitler to declare war on the United States. This too flew in the face of logic and ignored recent history. By the time America entered World War I, it had long since become a war of attrition. Germany had won that attrition war against Russia only to have victory snatched from her when the American Expeditionary Force tipped the balance to win the battle of attrition on the Western Front. Hitler knew that Germany could not win a war of attrition against the combined forces of the Soviet Union, Britain, and the United States. His policy therefore was blitzkrieg, lightning war. It worked in 1939 in Poland and in 1940 in France, but it came a cropper in Russia in the fall of 1941. By November, when the Wehrmacht was halted short of Moscow— only just, but still halted—the war on the Eastern Front had become a war of attrition. Hitler had every possible motive to avoid war with America, against whom he could launch no offensive operations of any kind in any case. For Roosevelt, under these circumstances, to pursue a policy of goading Hitler into declaring war was to pursue a hope, not a plan. And the hope was that Hitler was a madman.

In a number of ways Roosevelt had already enjoyed more dumb luck than he could ever have counted on. First, in a tactical sense, although Pearl Harbor was a humiliating defeat, the Japanese had failed to follow up their victory with a second strike or a landing aimed at taking Hawaii. Even more important were their political mistakes. Their objectives were Burma, Malaya, and the Dutch East Indies, where the oil was located. But they had attacked the American bases in Hawaii and the Philippines. The nature of the unprovoked sneak attack united the American people as nothing else could have done and ensured Japan's defeat. That Japan attacked the United States at all was surely a major mistake.

The Japanese leaders assumed that the American air force in the Philippines would cut their line of communication to their targets in the south, but this is one of the biggest "what ifs" of modern history. What if they had attacked British and Dutch colonial possessions and bypassed the Philippines and ignored Hawaii? In November, Roosevelt had more or less casually told the British ambassador to the United States that if the Japanese launched such an attack, he would come to the support of the British. But telling that privately to the British was one thing, while persuading Congress to declare war on Japan in defense of European colonialism in Asia quite another. We can never know what might have happened without the attack on Pearl Harbor and the Philippines, but we do know that the American response to the Japanese offensive in China had been mainly verbal; so too the response to the Japanese occupation of the French colonies in Indochina. We can assume that Roosevelt's speech to congress on December 8—the "a day that will live in infamy" speech—would have been much different without Pearl Harbor. The point is, in Stimson's words, Roosevelt was relying on incidents instead of leadership to light the path.

Despite Pearl Harbor, between midday of December 7 (Washington time) to the morning of December 11, the path remained dimly lit. In planning for war, the American military had assumed that American entry would transform the ongoing two regional conflicts—one in Europe pitting Germany and Italy against Britain and the Soviet Union, the other in Asia pitting Japan against China—into a world war. In that war, the United States would go on the defensive in the Pacific while undertaking an offensive against the more dangerous enemy, Germany. But that could not happen so long as America was at war with Japan but not with Germany. What Roosevelt would have done had Hitler not declared war is something else we can never know. He evidently planned to proceed on the assumption that war against Japan also meant war against Germany, but he would have found it exceedingly difficult to persuade the Congress, not to mention the U.S. Navy, to go on the offensive in the Atlantic while maintaining a defensive posture in the Pacific. Once again the point is that the initiative was not his. He could not shape events but could only react to them. His foes charged that he was a dictator pushing the United States into war; actually he was a cautious politician who was taking great risks with national security because of his unwillingness or inability to light the path. So why did Hitler solve Roosevelt's problem for him by declaring war? He was not required to do so by the terms of the Tripartite Alliance between Italy, Germany, and Japan of September 1940, as that was a defensive alliance that required Germany to come to Japan's aid only if Japan were attacked. Japan had not come to Germany's aid in June 1941, when Germany invaded the Soviet Union.

Hitler had little to gain from declaring war on the United States; in no way could he carry out a strategic offensive campaign against American industry or mobilization capacity, nor had he any thought of doing so. On the Eastern Front his armies were engaged in the greatest battle ever fought; that very week the Red Army had launched its counterattack outside Moscow. The United States was making only a minuscule contribution to that conflict. The declaration of war did free German submarines to wage all-out war against American shipping, but Hitler could have done as Ludendorff did in 1917 and launched unrestricted submarine warfare without declaring war, thus putting the onus of declaring war back on Roosevelt. It seems probable that Roosevelt would have responded as Wilson had back in 1917, but had he asked for a declaration of war against Germany, the isolationists would have argued that his policy of supplying Germany's enemies had forced Hitler to sink American ships. Asking for a declaration of war also would have invited intense criticism of going to war to support the Communist dictatorship in the Soviet Union.

That is all speculation. What happened is that Hitler did declare war. It was Roosevelt's biggest break and the most inexplicable decision on Hitler's part. The distinguished German journalist Sebastian Haffner calls it "the most incomprehensible of his mistakes," and points out that it was "the most lonely of his lonely decisions."[4] Amazingly, he consulted no one. He threw away his long-range plan for world conquest, and on the 11th simply announced his intentions to the Reichstag.

Thank God he did. In doing so, he sealed his fate and saved Roosevelt. Morgenthau, it turned out, had been wrong when he warned Roosevelt that "we can't count on the good Lord and just dumb luck forever."

"Enter" is an active verb, implying some positive deed. In that sense, the United States did not "enter" World War II. It was pulled in, despite, rather than because of, the actions of the American president.

Notes

1. Waldo Heinrichs, *Threshold of War: Franklin D. Roosevelt and American Entry into World War II* (New York: Oxford University Press, 1988), 140-41.
2. Ibid., 83.
3. Ibid., 140.
4. Ewald Osers, trans., Sebastian Haffner, *The Meaning of Hitler* (Cambridge: Harvard University Press, 1979), 120.

7.

Pearl Harbor in a Global Context

Waldo Heinrichs

When we remember Pearl Harbor, what do we forget? The Japanese strike at Hawaii was not the only attack of late 1941, nor was every battle a defeat. The same day the Japanese assaulted the Philippines, Hong Kong, and Malaya. On December 1, the Russians recaptured Rostov, saving the Caucasus, and three days later they counterattacked on the Moscow front. On November 18, the British counterattacked in the North African desert, and soon after Pearl Harbor the Chinese inflicted a devastating defeat on a Japanese force at Changsha. Pearl Harbor is of special importance to Americans, but it also needs to be seen as an extension of ongoing wars, indeed as a juncture where existing regional wars in East Asia and Europe expanded into worldwide war. This chapter will dwell on this global context of Pearl Harbor.

To this larger context of American policy Franklin Roosevelt's mind was well attuned. As the president explained to Ambassador Joseph C. Grew, the problems he faced were "so vast and interrelated that any attempt even to state them compels one to think in terms of five continents and seven seas." Roosevelt had a retentive memory and keen intuition, usually working in harness. According to a perceptive observer, Secretary of Labor Francis Perkins, at times

Roosevelt would have "flashes of almost clairvoyant knowledge and understanding of a terrific variety of [unrelated] matters." This ability seemed to Perkins especially valuable during 1940-43; the threat of the Axis pushed his faculties to their highest pitch. Many times, she wrote, Roosevelt "could see it all: men, guns, ships, food, the enemy, the Allies, the war aims and finally the peace."[1]

The threat posed by the Axis was very real. Today we see the expansion of Germany and Japan as much more complex than it was seen in the first postwar histories, but the menace to American security posed by these two powers in the modern analysis was no less great. The Nazi system was essentially acquisitive, depending on ever more space and resources. Hitler concentrated on conquering Europe and Russia, but he dreamed of eventual world domination and had started to build "superbattleships" and a bomber capable of hitting New York from the Azores.

Japanese expansion was less singleminded but no less dynamic. The dominant military sought imperial self-sufficiency in resources for what they took to be an age of total war, but the army and navy had different versions of this resource empire—one was northward toward the Soviet Union, the other toward Southeast Asia—and were fiercely competitive in securing existing war production and determining the direction and pace of advance. The lack of any central authority determining ends and means led to an inchoate expansionism, with each venture creating the need for further steps and violent changes in world politics providing the opportunities.

Germany and Japan pursued separate expansions in the 1930s but these began to merge with Japan's debilitating war in China and the start of the European war in 1939. Then Germany administered two great, successive shocks to the international system, which reshaped it into a simple worldwide confrontation of power. The first of these came in the spring of 1940 with the German conquest of France and mastery of Europe, the second in June 1941 with the German attack on the Soviet Union.

The shock of 1940 interrupted a British trend toward a more permanent association with France. Now Britain desperately sought a special relationship with the United States.[2] Step-by-step Roosevelt moved toward Anglo-American partnership and sponsoring Western resistance to Hitler. The Soviet Union, which had been counting on the survival of France, seemed hypnotized as the German war machine turned east and coiled to strike. Italy joined the war, opening Mediterranean, North African, and Middle Eastern dimensions of conflict. Japan, tempted by British, French, and Dutch weakness, moved south to secure war resources and seal off China. It joined the Axis to hem the United States into the Western Hemisphere and looked hopefully toward a vast entente embracing the Axis powers and the Soviet Union. The United States responded with the first steps of embargo and further aid to China. The shock of 1940 reverberated into all parts of the world.

The shock of 1941 was no less profound. It established the Soviet Union as a potential partner of Britain and the United States in the destruction of Nazi Germany. It encouraged a more active American role in the Battle of the Atlantic. It led Japan to prepare against the Soviet Union and move into southern Indochina from where it could assault Malaya. This brought the United States to total sanctions against Japan, including oil, which in turn forced a Japanese decision either to resolve problems with the United States or engage in war. In short, the shock of 1941 brought the remaining great neutrals to the verge of war.

President Roosevelt responded to the spreading conflict cautiously, weighing his alternatives and taking one step at a time. He had powerful reasons for doing so. In the first place, with world politics undergoing dramatic changes, he could only guess at what might happen next. No American system existed for evaluating intelligence; OSS was in its infancy. MAGIC, the process of decrypting Japanese diplomatic messages, was valuable but with important exceptions not a predictor. So Roosevelt waited on events. "When I don't know how to move," he said, "I stay put."[3]

In the second place, the United States lacked the military forces to risk war. For example, the U.S. Navy had too few destroyers until September 1941 to take any share in the transatlantic convoy circuits. As of April 1941, only two U. S. Army divisions were listed as combat ready, and they were undermanned and underequipped. Third, the United States was in fact deterred by the Axis alliance. It was unable to shift sizable portions of its fleet for fear of a two-front war. Finally, the American people, while more willing to risk war, were not ready to choose it. Roosevelt, for reasons already mentioned, was not far ahead of public opinion. He aimed to stay in touch with it, helping along the emerging international consensus.

At least until the summer of 1941, the U.S. government operated under severe constraints. Constraint did not mean paralysis, however: Rearmament on a huge scale was under way. Critical change was occurring internationally as well in the ever-tightening bonds of cooperation and assistance which the United States was establishing with three enemies of the Axis—China, Great Britain, and eventually the Soviet Union.

Roosevelt was above all a coalitionist diplomat. He was an artist in the formation and maintenance of political groupings in domestic politics and in foreign affairs, and he felt most at home operating in this inclusive and enveloping manner. As early as 1937 he manifested an interest in cooperating with other powers to contain Japan. As the existing world order crumbled, he sought opportunities within his means to forge a counterbalance to Axis power.

The first associate was China. Reading backward the corruption and passivity of the Chinese government during the Pacific war, we tend to underrate the importance of China to the United States in the pre–Pearl Harbor years. In those years of the Sino-Japanese War, the Chinese armies were more effective. Merely by fighting on, China absorbed most of Japan's expansive energy.

Recognizing the benefit of Chinese resistance, Roosevelt began providing aid, small loans at first and then larger amounts. In October 1940, after signature of the Axis pact, with Japan pressing for a peace settlement and Germany mediating, Chiang Kai-shek informed the British and American ambassadors that China could not continue the war without more help. Roosevelt responded with a loan of $100 million. The Sino-Japanese peace talks promptly collapsed and the Japanese recognized the Wang Ching-wei puppet regime. With steadily increasing aid, repeated assurances of American support to China, the establishment of Japanese aggression in China as a fundamental issue in Japanese-American relations, and near universal American public sympathy for China against Japan, the United States had arrived at a deeply etched moral commitment to China by mid-1941. At the same time, half the strength of the Japanese Army, 27 divisions, remained bogged down there.

In the case of Great Britain, no one would underestimate its importance to the United States, but one can overrate the extent of the American commitment to the beleaguered island, at least before the Atlantic Conference. Mounting American aid to Britain is a familiar story, from the sale of surplus arms to destroyers for bases to lend-lease to extended Atlantic patrols. Combined strategic planning, coordinated fleet deployments, and exchange of intelligence and cypher material reflect rapidly growing intimacy. Nevertheless, it is important to recognize the differences. It is notable that Roosevelt rendered little assistance to Britain for six weeks after the fall of France, until he was finally convinced in August that Britain would fight on. Britain and the United States did not agree on how to defend Southeast Asia, on the importance of the Mediterranean, or on peace aims. Roosevelt refused, at least before midyear, to send American naval forces to Britain, to authorize use of force against German submarines and raiders in the Atlantic, and to engage in escort of convoys. He preferred to partition the Atlantic, reserving the western portion as an American security zone.

While Roosevelt unquestionably regarded the survival of Britain as of very great importance to the United States, he nevertheless was not prepared to guarantee it because he could not be sure, at least until late spring 1941, that Germany would not invade and conquer the island. A careful examination of intelligence records shows that the United States was uncertain which direction German aggression would take in 1941 until early June. In the worst case the

United States might still defend itself across the Atlantic as Britain did across the channel after France fell.

The relationship with the Soviet Union was not prefigured or shaped over time. It formed abruptly in the wake of the second shock, the German invasion of the Soviet Union. Soviet-American talks had proceeded for many dreary months before the German attack, without substantial progress. Mistrust and suspicion abounded, reaching back to Brest-Litovsk and then the 1939 partition of Poland. Stalinist appeasement of the Axis infuriated American officials; the difficulty of securing American war materials frustrated the Soviets.

The German attack on the Soviet Union radically altered the circumstances. Washington believed at first that the Soviet Union would not survive the onslaught longer than the summer and that any aid sent would be wasted. Then after a month of dramatic success, the German advance on Moscow stalled, partly from Soviet resistance, partly from the need for replenishment, partly from disagreement over strategy. By the end of July the possibility loomed up that the Soviets might after all survive until winter and thus into 1942, and that realization had an enormous impact on American policy.

The possibility of Soviet survival fundamentally altered the strategic equation. Before, the question had been one of survival in the face of German domination of Europe, even Europe to the Urals. Survival meant the Western Hemisphere and perhaps the British Isles. If Hitler defeated the Soviet Union it was hard to see how to land on the continent and defeat Hitler. Now, against a coalition of Russia, Britain, and America, Hitler could not in the end survive. The president pressed his subordinates imperiously to hasten and enlarge aid to the Soviet Union. He came to an understanding with Churchill about peace aims, ordered the American navy into escort of convoy, and authorized use of force in a greatly enlarged Western Hemisphere. On September 28, he and Churchill responded to a desperate plea from Stalin for aid by promising to send 400 aircraft and 500 tanks a month. The American tanks could only be sent by delaying the formation of American armored divisions and tank battalions. This decision, impinging directly on America's own defense capability, marks the point of American political commitment to the Soviet Union, in effect the date when the Grand Alliance came into being.

The emerging American stake in Russian survival had significant consequences for American East Asian policy. Japan had now not only moved southward to secure bases in southern Indochina but also reinforced its army in Manchuria so that if Russia weakened, it could strike northward.

The American hard line in the Pacific can be better understood by keeping in mind the Soviet connection that was forming at the same time. A vital question was whether Stalin would be able to draw reinforcements from his

Siberian troops facing the Japanese. Thus Japan's aggressive designs became twice linked to Europe: once by way of Britain's resources in Southeast Asia, and again by way of Russia's reinforcement pool in Siberia. Now, in Roosevelt's mind, East Asian problems fitted snugly into a global scheme of politics.

From this perspective he probably concluded that to do nothing would allow Japan a free hand and imperiled his purposes. A diplomatic settlement with Japan would remove the threat to Southeast Asia and perhaps detach Japan from the Axis, but only at the expense of China, where Japan insisted on retaining troops. The United States could hardly urge allies to stand firm while it pursued appeasement. Chiang had threatened a separate peace before and would do so again; Stalin was seeking German terms at that very time. A settlement that extricated Japan from China and provided stability in the south might well encourage Japan to attack northward.

Roosevelt chose the third alternative, the hard line. The Soviet-German war seemed to have intensified Japanese expansionism, opportunism, and unpredictability. Whether Japan went north or south, it threatened the improving balance of world forces. This careening expansionism had to be stopped. Japan had to be contained and immobilized. So, not a drop of oil; let Japan's capacity for military operations anywhere shrink. Reinforce the Philippines with bombers that could reach Japan. Create such uncertainty and concern among Japanese decision makers about the south and relations with the United States that they dare not go north. Support China. Solidify defense arrangements with the British, Dutch, and Australians. Above all, maintain coalitions east and west. This became final policy.

Thus the German attack on Russia reverberated to America and Asia. It had a profoundly clarifying effect on Roosevelt's mind and American policy, leading to decisive action on all fronts after months of uncertainty and constraint. Japan, however, was not deterred. It chose to attack rather than succumb. That outcome had been risked; seemingly worse had been prevented. The Soviet Union survived. China remained at war. The coalitions hung together. What surprised everyone was the weight, extent, and destructiveness of the attack, a surprise arising from pervasive misconceptions about the Japanese, but that is another story.

Notes

1. As quoted in George Martin, *Madam Secretary: Frances Perkins* (Boston: Houghton Mifflin, 1976), 435-36; and Frances Perkins, *The Roosevelt I Knew* (New York: Viking Press, 1946), 153-54 and 161-63.

2. David Reynolds, "1940: Fulcrum of the Twentieth Century?" *International Affairs,* 66, no. 2 (1990): 329-33.
3. As quoted in Waldo Heinrichs, *Threshold of War: Franklin D. Roosevelt and American Entry Into World War II* (New York: Oxford University Press, 1988), 46. This book serves as a basis for this chapter.

8.

The Debacle in the Philippines

Michael Schaller

In March 1942, as Japanese forces consolidated their control of Southeast Asia and the Pacific, President Franklin D. Roosevelt revealed some of his frustration during a private meeting with Admiral Thomas Hart. As commander of the Navy's Asiatic fleet in Manila, Hart had worked closely with General Douglas MacArthur, the officer responsible for defending the Philippine archipelago. Roosevelt recounted his bitterness over the general's abject failure to fulfill his promise that he would easily repulse an invasion. "If I had known the true situation," Roosevelt mused, "I could have babied the Japanese along quite a while longer."[1] Three months later the president told Press Secretary William D. Hasset that while the public might be fooled by MacArthur's heroics, the general's record resembled closely that of Admiral Kimmel and General Short, the commanders who "face court-martial on charges of laxity at Pearl Harbor." Roosevelt characterized MacArthur's behavior in the Philippines as criminal.[2]

Public awareness of events in the Philippines early in the Pacific war focused on the desperate resistance of American forces on the Bataan Peninsula and Corregidor Island, on General MacArthur's escape to Australia, and his dramatic declaration to liberate the islands, "I shall return." These developments obscured the military blunders of December 8, 1941, and the strategic misconceptions of the previous year that made the debacle in the Philippines all but inevitable.

As Roosevelt perceptively noted, destruction on the ground of most of the substantial American air force in the Philippines several hours after the air raid on Hawaii, and the subsequent Japanese sweep over the islands, constituted a second Pearl Harbor. For a variety of military and political reasons, however, no official inquiry ever took place into this disaster and most of those responsible for it escaped professionally unscathed. Douglas MacArthur, above all, parlayed defeat into command of a new theater of war, a Congressional Medal of Honor, and a decadelong string of victories that ended only on China's Yalu River boundary with Korea.

Many puzzles surround the events of December 8, 1941, in the Philippines. Critical records were lost during the Japanese occupation and the recollections of key participants proved contradictory and self-serving. Also, to be sure, successful surprise is not all that uncommon in war and it would be foolish to overlook the role of honest mistakes and chance in what occurred in the Philippines. Nevertheless, the pattern of self-delusion, arrogance, interservice squabbling, confused motives, faulty intelligence, and personal aggrandizement that emerges from this episode helps explain the larger causes of this failure.

American political and military leaders had long recognized that the more than 7,000 Philippine islands were probably indefensible against a Japanese attack. As early as 1907 President Theodore Roosevelt described the colony as America's "Achilles heel" in the Pacific. His successors appropriated minimal funds to defend the island chain and preferred to strike a series of deals with Japan to guarantee Philippine security. Should war erupt, the formal defense plan, War Plan ORANGE, called only for holding Manila Bay while awaiting rescue by a U.S. fleet. A 10,000-man combined force of U.S. Army and Filipino troops were expected to hold out for up to six months against as many as 300,000 Japanese invaders. However, since the navy estimated it might take as long as three years for the fleet to reach Manila, the defense seemed doomed. Small wonder that in 1935 the army's War Plans Division characterized the Philippines as a "military liability of incalculable magnitude."[3]

The perception of the military significance of the Philippines changed gradually between 1935 and 1941, largely because of two developments: Japanese aggression in China and Southeast Asia and the dispatch of General MacArthur as defense adviser to the newly formed commonwealth government in Manila. The Philippines went from being considered a liability to a military asset when strategists decided that it could play a key role in deterring or retaliating against Japanese aggression. MacArthur's grandiose military plans and giddy optimism also swayed planners in Washington.

The general's dispatch to Manila in 1935 served several ends. Following passage of the Tydings-McDufie Act in 1934, the Philippines became a partially self-governing commonwealth. This initiated a decadelong transition to full independence. Since the colony lacked any ability to defend itself, and American protection would probably end with independence, commonwealth president Manuel Quezon urged Roosevelt to help the emerging nation prepare for its own security. FDR approved sending a defense mission to Manila, to be headed by retiring Army Chief of Staff Douglas MacArthur, a close friend of Quezon. This pleased the Filipinos while alleviating the administration of direct responsibility for arranging the future defense of the islands. For political reasons, Roosevelt was pleased to send MacArthur halfway around the world. For his part, the general savored the opportunity to assume a prestigious job in his beloved Philippines. The special assignment also allowed him to double his salary while remaining on active duty. Undoubtedly, all the parties to the agreement hoped Japan would take note of the appointment and draw the appropriate conclusions.[4]

Assisted ably in Manila by Majors Dwight D. Eisenhower and James Ord and Captain T. J. Davis, MacArthur supervised the drafting of an elaborate defense plan for the Philippines. The general left the details to his staff, but suffused the so-called "MacArthur plan" with what Eisenhower called "purple splendor." Despite a budget of only some $8 million and vague promises of surplus American military equipment, MacArthur wanted to build a standing Filipino army of about 1,000 officers and 7,000 enlisted men. Each year an additional 7,000 conscripts would be trained as a reserve. When Ike and Ord questioned how this slender force could possibly resist a Japanese invasion, MacArthur dismissed them as defeatists.

By 1936, MacArthur's plans expanded further. He informed the Philippine legislature that he would turn their emerging nation into a bastion of Pacific economic and military power. He would "forge you a weapon that will spell the safety of your nation from brutal aggression until the end of time."[5]

While this purple prose attracted much attention, a cruder reality belied it. For one thing, the danger to the Philippines was as likely to come from internal rebellion as from a Japanese invasion. MacArthur ignored this completely. As early as December 1935 the Army's War Plans Division dismissed MacArthur's call to build a Philippine Army as "wholly ineffective." Military officials in Washington pressed him, to little avail, to concentrate on developing a mobile constabulary "for the purpose of maintaining internal order."

President Roosevelt, too, questioned the logic of building up substantial American or Filipino forces on the archipelago. In November 1936 he told State

Department officials and members of his Cabinet that if war came with Japan, the Philippines would quickly fall. After a few years, he predicted, U.S. naval forces "would gradually move westward in an island-hopping operation" to liberate the colony. This, of course, proved exactly true.[6]

MacArthur, Eisenhower and Ord protested, had lost sight of reality and continually spoke as if his elaborate military plans were actually working. In fact, during 1936 and 1937 only a small number of Filipinos were trained. MacArthur spent most of his time socializing in Manila, arranging for President Quezon to name him field marshall of the largely paper Philippine Army. A disillusioned Ike characterized both the title and his boss's performance as "rather fantastic."

By 1937, MacArthur had become something of an embarrassment to other Americans in Manila and to civilian and military officials in Washington. In August Army Chief of Staff Malin Craig informed MacArthur that his appointment as head of the military mission would be terminated at year's end and he would be reassigned to a command in the United States. An embittered MacArthur compared this to making "President Roosevelt go back to his former functions as Assistant Secretary of the Navy." Pleading ill health, he announced he would retire from the U.S. Army effective December 31, 1937. Since MacArthur had no desire to return to America, he arranged with President Quezon to be appointed as a civilian military advisor to the commonwealth government, allowing him to continue working with the American army advisory mission.[7]

Ultimately, MacArthur's defense program depended on strong support from Washington, close cooperation with his staff, Quezon's continued faith in him, and deferral of the Japanese threat for several years. The diminished support from the Roosevelt administration was apparent by the end of 1937. Each of the remaining pillars eroded in turn, leaving MacArthur's program a hollow shell. Despite MacArthur's pleas for more money, during 1939 and 1940 President Quezon encouraged the Philippine legislature to cut defense funds. Little money was available to buy equipment or even to conscript trainees. By 1940, the Philippine army consisted of only 468 officers and 3,700 enlisted men. In meetings with visiting Americans during 1940 and early 1941, President Quezon described his field marshall's program as "idiotic." He was "sick of doling out funds to MacArthur."[8]

The defense advisor felt increasingly isolated and frustrated in his position. During 1939 he appealed to Roosevelt, through presidential aide Steve Early, to offer him a civilian job as high commissioner in Manila. Roosevelt ignored the plea and named Francis Sayre to the post.[9]

MacArthur and Sayre could not stand each other. Admiral Thomas C. Hart, commander in chief of the Manila-based Asiatic Fleet, commented upon

MacArthur's growing alienation from nearly all American and Filipino officials. In late 1940 he observed that "Douglas seems to have sunk to an unenviable official position and relationship" in which the "dignified thing to do would be to resign." If it were not for his exorbitant salary, Hart surmised, MacArthur would "duck out."[10]

In December 1940, Theodore White, a young journalist beginning his career with *Time* magazine, visited Manila to prepare a profile on MacArthur. Regular army officers ridiculed the retired general and Filipino field marshall as the "Napoleon of Luzon." Nevertheless, when White interviewed MacArthur, he declared that he would lead American forces in Asia when war broke out. Dismissing the Japanese army as "not even second class," he predicted an easy victory.[11]

Despite this bravado, MacArthur had actually made plans to leave Manila and return to the United States unless he received a civilian appointment. When it appeared that High Commissioner Sayre might depart in March 1941, MacArthur again appealed to Steve Early to lobby FDR to appoint him to the post. Besides enjoying the "complete confidence of the Filipinos," MacArthur boasted, "from Vladivostok to Singapore I am thoroughly familiar with the most intimate details, political, military and commercial. I have a personal acquaintance with everyone of importance in the Orient and I believe no American holds the friendship and respect of this part of the world more than myself." He was especially eager to serve Roosevelt—"not only our greatest statesman but what to me is even more thrilling, our greatest military strategist."

The White House replied politely but offered nothing. By the spring of 1941 a despondent MacArthur informed Steve Early and now Army Chief of Staff George C. Marshall he intended to close down the office of the military advisor and return to America. But suddenly Japan's thrust into Southeast Asia rescued MacArthur from the shadows.[12]

MacArthur's defense plan faced an overwhelming obstacle that not even his optimism could dispel. Japan resumed its military expansion in 1937, invading China and making plans to incorporate all of East and Southeast Asia into its "Greater East Asia Co-Prosperity Sphere." Ironically, the general's success during the final months of 1941 in convincing Washington to make the Philippines a bastion of American power made the islands a major military target.

Between 1938 and early 1941, Franklin Roosevelt relied on a dual strategy to resist Japanese aggression. Economic aid to China, combined with selective trade embargoes on Tokyo, would, he hoped, sustain Chinese resistance. FDR also expected Britain, France, and the Netherlands, all major Asian colonial powers, as well as the Soviet Union, to resist Japanese expansion. But the Soviet

Union signed nonaggression pacts with Germany in 1939 and Japan in 1941 that minimized its deterrent value. Germany's conquest of Western Europe by June 1940 left besieged Great Britain the only European power able to assist American efforts in the Pacific.

Following Germany's blitzkrieg in 1940, Japan occupied northern French Indochina, demanded increased access to petroleum from the Dutch East Indies, and joined the Axis alliance. While still vexed by Chinese resistance, the remaining impediments to Japanese domination of East and Southeast Asia came from the U.S. Pacific Fleet and American forces in the Philippines and British forces in Malaya and Singapore.

Initially, American strategists did not place much value on defending, much less enhancing, the Philippine garrison. Late in 1940, the War Department tentatively suggested withdrawing most American forces and equipment from the islands. By this time British and American military planners agreed that when and if the United States went to war with the Axis, the main theater should be Europe. As late as April 1941, the updated War Plan ORANGE called for nothing more than a defense of Manila Bay.

Not surprisingly, Douglas MacArthur disparaged this estimate. In interviews with journalists he opined that if Japan attacked the Western powers, "the Americans, the British, and the Dutch could handle her with about half the forces they now have deployed in the Far East." MacArthur doubted Japan would even dare attack, as it was constrained by its senior ally, Germany.[13] In retrospect, it is hard to imagine a more erroneous set of predictions.

Strategic events quickly outdated MacArthur's predictions. On June 22, 1941, the Nazis invaded the Soviet Union, eliminating a Soviet deterrent against Tokyo. The "Japs," FDR told Interior Secretary Harold Ickes, were having "a real dragdown and knockout fight among themselves" over whether "they are going to jump-attack Russia, attack the South Seas (thus throwing in their lot definitely with Germany), or whether they will sit on the fence and be more friendly to us." The president sought a way to restrain Japan without driving it to invade Russia or the oil-rich East Indies. For the present, however, he insisted on keeping control of the Atlantic by preserving "peace in the Pacific."[14]

A day after Roosevelt spoke to Ickes, Japanese Emperor Hirohito presided over an Imperial conference that ratified plans for an "Advance into the Southern Regions." Because strategic raw materials, especially petroleum, were more accessible in Southeast Asia, the Japanese deferred action against Siberia. Tokyo hoped that a dual strategy of intimidation and negotiation would secure access to Southeast Asia. If not, Japan would strike militarily.[15]

During July Tokyo demanded and obtained from Vichy French authorities air and naval bases in southern Indochina. Roosevelt hastened to retaliate and adopt measures designed to deter further expansion. On July 17, George C. Marshall, army chief of staff, recommended that the president call the Philippine army into U.S. service and appoint retired General Douglas MacArthur as overall commander of "Army Forces in the Far East." Knowing how few resources Washington could actually spare, Marshall and Secretary of War Henry Stimson believed that naming MacArthur would be a symbolic act that might bluff the Japanese into reconsidering an attack upon Western forces in the region.

Between July 24 and July 26, Roosevelt responded forcefully to Japan's move into southern Indochina. The administration froze Japanese assets in the United States, effectively stopping oil sales. MacArthur was recalled to active duty, promoted to the temporary rank of lieutenant general, and placed in charged of U. S. Army Forces in the Far East (U.S.A.F.E.). Marshall and Stimson also decided to send a large contingent of the most powerful bombers in the American arsenal, the B-17, to the Philippines, along with advanced type P-40 fighter planes.[16]

Just a few months before, MacArthur had been a virtual outcast in Manila, shunned by many Americans and Filipinos. Now leaders in Washington and Manila rallied to him. President Quezon, who had earlier called the general's defense plans "idiotic," now told MacArthur he was sure the American would "attain in this difficult assignment the same success that has crowned your every endeavor in the past."[17]

The general threw himself into the task of preparing the Philippines for the expected Japanese onslaught. He assembled a headquarters staff that included Colonel Richard Sutherland and Lieutenant Colonel Richard Marshall as chief of staff and deputy chief of staff, respectively. He named Lieutenant Sidney Huff, Colonel Charles Willoughby, Colonel William Marquart, and Lieutenant Colonel LeGrande Diller to other top positions. They formed the nucleus of what later became known as the "Bataan Gang," the loyalists who served MacArthur during the Pacific war and beyond. The general later placed Brigadier General Jonathan Wainwright in command of his ground forces, while Major General Lewis H. Brereton, who arrived in November, took command of the growing air force. Significantly, neither of these two key officers were personally close to MacArthur, and they quickly incurred the wrath of the inner circle. MacArthur took personal control of the Philippine Army in addition to his job as U.S.A.F.E commander.

Nominally, MacArthur commanded an impressive military force. This included a combined American-Filipino ground army of 100,000 men, an air force that was slated to include over 70 B-17 bombers by early December as well as over 100 advanced fighters, and the support of the Asiatic Fleet with its large submarine contingent.

Actual strength was less imposing. Philippine Army reserves, a paper force, comprised three fourths of MacArthur's ground troops. The bulk of the B-17s were yet to arrive and the airfields and anti-aircraft protection they required had not been made ready. Moreover, the general all but ignored the Asiatic Fleet, which would have to play a crucial role in interdicting a Japanese invasion.

Still, on August 30 MacArthur notified Washington that defense preparations had progressed by "leaps and bounds," and the mood among Filipinos had changed from a "feeling of defeatism to the highest state of morale I have ever seen." As air and ground reinforcements arrived, he could insure the "development of a completely adequate defense force" before a Japanese attack, which he anticipated coming not before April 1942.

MacArthur's self-assurance seemed almost manic. He told Admiral Hart they had "plenty of time" remaining before war erupted. He declared that he was "not going to follow" or be bound in any way by "whatever war plans have been evolved, agreed and approved in Washington." Strutting about and pounding his hands together, he told Hart he would soon command an army of 200,000 men in a "glorious land war." If Japanese troops came ashore, he would promptly crush them. MacArthur brushed off Hart's plea that the two commanders coordinate their efforts, declaring that the "Navy had its plan, the Army had its plans . . . and we each had our own fields." His "primary interest was in the land battle he was going to wage." Although infuriated by MacArthur's brush-off, even Hart admitted that the general radiated a contagious confidence.[18]

But the Philippine Army, in which MacArthur placed so much faith, remained largely fictive. Mobilized during the autumn of 1941, its untrained, ethnically and linguistically diverse conscripts lacked any sense of common purpose. The American instructors had so little equipment that most of the Filipinos had never fired a weapon before they saw combat. To alleviate the problem, MacArthur ordered vast quantities of supplies from the United States, but relatively little arrived before war began.

Although MacArthur could not be faulted for many of these problems, he either ignored or misunderstood the facts. As late as October he wrote to a friend how morale among his forces had risen to "a point almost of exuberance." His appointment as Philippine commander had brought "jubilation," MacArthur claimed, "throughout the Netherlands, East Indies, Malaya and China." It left Japan "dumbfounded and depressed." He would soon be able to repulse "any effort that may be made against us."[19]

Ignoring standing policy to concentrate on the defense of Manila Bay, MacArthur planned to hold the entire archipelago. Repelling an invasion would strain even a vast, fully equipped, and superbly trained army. With its several thousand major and minor islands, the Philippines had a coastline longer than that of the United States. Given the forces under his control and the resources of Japan, it hardly mattered whether MacArthur commanded 100,000 men or twice that number. Nevertheless, as D. Clayton James observed in his exhaustive study of the problem, the general's "overconfidence and unjustified optimism as to the abilities of himself, his staff and the untried Filipino soldiers . . . became a contagion which ultimately affected even the War Department and the Joint Army Navy Board." By November, the Joint Army-Navy Board agreed MacArthur should be permitted to defend the entire archipelago, not just the bays around Manila.[20]

MacArthur proved an exceptionally persuasive lobbyist, influencing the outlook of Henry Stimson, George Marshall, and Franklin Roosevelt. He all but guaranteed to deter or defeat a Japanese thrust into Southeast Asia if only given the men and supplies he requested. Moreover, his grandiose claims seemed buoyed by the appearance of a new weapon—long range airpower in the form of the B-17 bomber.

By August American factories were producing substantial numbers of the so-called Flying Fortress. The B-17C, 35 of which arrived in the Philippines before war began, had an operational radius of about 1,000 miles, allowing it to reach Formosa, Okinawa, or Shanghai from Philippine bases. The modified B-17E, some 60 of which were slated for delivery by the end of 1941, with 80 more due early in 1942, could reach southern Japan. Because of production delays and the need to fly planes along a circuitous Pacific route, only about 74 heavy and medium bombers, including 35 B-17s, reached the Philippines by early December. Air Commander Brereton also possessed about 175 pursuit planes and 55 miscellaneous aircraft. Together, this comprised the strongest American air force outside the continental United States.

As noted, the newer B-17s could deliver a payload as far as southern Japan or attack Japanese ships far at sea. Some air force planners suggested that the planes could bomb central Japan if a shuttle run were established between the Philippines and Soviet bases in Siberia. Unfortunately, the B-17 had not been tested under realistic conditions. For most of the first year of the war a host of technical defects rendered it almost useless against ships. Nevertheless, President Roosevelt and Secretary of War Stimson believed the deterrent effect of the bomber might restrain Japan from attacking either Southeast Asia or Siberia. FDR spoke of the plane's "great effect . . . upon the Japs." The Army War Plans Division asserted that the air and ground units being dispatched to the Philippines would change "the entire picture of the Asiatic area." Air power, Secretary of War Stimson predicted, would "Keep the fear of God in Japan."[21]

However, when the first Flying Fortresses reached the Philippines, no one knew how to deploy them. Since only Clark Field on Luzon could accommodate the B-17, all were concentrated in one location, making them especially vulnerable to attack. Even after Del Monte Field on the southern island of Mindinao became partly operative, most of the bombers were kept at Clark.

Unaccountably, neither MacArthur, who seemed ambivalent about the role of air power, nor the air power enthusiasts in Washington paid much attention to these operational problems. The general focused his attention on ground defenses, largely ignoring his air commander, Brereton. Rather than developing a joint plan with Asiatic Fleet commander Admiral Hart, MacArthur ridiculed him. At one point he blurted out, "Get yourself a real fleet, Tommy, then you will belong." The admiral complained to his superiors in Washington that MacArthur's behavior had grown ever more "erratic" during the autumn. He offered a more dismal assessment to his wife. "The truth of the matter is," Hart wrote, "that Douglas is, I think, no longer altogether sane. He may not have been for a long time."[22]

It remains a testament to MacArthur's persuasive powers that, despite Hart's fury, even he half believed the general might succeed in repulsing a Japanese attack. The Navy Department, however, was less sure. Fearing entrapment of the fleet in Manila, it ordered Hart to shift the bulk of his surface fleet south, to join Anglo-Dutch units and fight Japanese ships at sea in case of war.

During October and November 1941, desultory negotiations aimed at averting war continued in Washington between Secretary of State Cordell Hull and Japanese delegate Admiral Nomura. As is well-known, each side presented what amounted to mutually exclusive terms for a settlement. The Japanese offered minimal guarantees to respect the status quo and partially withdraw from southern Indochina if the United States ceased aid to China, pressed China to accept Japanese peace terms, and lifted the trade embargo. Roosevelt and his aides demanded that Japanese forces evacuate Indochina, make peace with China, pledge not to attack Southeast Asia, and drop out of the Axis alliance before the United States would resume sales of oil and other strategic items. MAGIC radio intercepts convinced American negotiators that Japanese hard-liners were not interested in a real settlement.

Still, during November, army and navy chiefs in Washington urged FDR to avoid any dramatic moves until at least mid-December. After that, they felt confident, America's growing "air and submarine strength in the Philippines" would pose a "positive threat to Japanese operations south of Formosa." By February or March, Admiral Harold Stark and General Marshall predicted, the anticipated 200-strong B-17 force in the Philippines might become a "deciding factor in deterring Japanese operations." Of course, from Japan's perspective, the buildup in the Philippines represented a growing threat that had to be dealt with before Tokyo's petroleum reserves were depleted.[23]

The collapse of negotiations in Washington on November 26, 1941, along with intelligence information revealing that a large number of Japanese troops were being transported toward Southeast Asia, convinced Roosevelt and his aides that Japan would soon attack in that region. On November 27, both MacArthur and the commanders in Hawaii received a "final alert" from the War Department and a "war warning" from the navy. The messages did not alarm MacArthur. In a meeting that day with Admiral Hart and High Commissioner Sayre, the general paced the floor confidently, puffed his cigar, and told his colleagues that the "existing alignment and movement of Japanese troops" convinced him that there would be no attack before the spring.[24]

At about the same time that MacArthur minimized the likelihood of imminent war, *Life* magazine received the draft of an article on the Philippine commander written by the publisher's wife, Clare Boothe Luce. During October she interviewed MacArthur in Manila and prepared a flattering portrait of him for the magazine. However, in a note to the editor, she apologized for what she described as the exaggerated "buildup." There were "quite a few unpleasant things to be said about the man," she admitted, but for now they must remain unspoken in public. Since American prestige "in the whole Far East" had become "indissolubly linked with the military (and personal) prestige of the General," anything lowering "his prestige in the eyes of his troops, the Filipinos, or for that matter the British at Singapore, the Dutch and the Japanese, will inevitably weaken our military effort."[25] Deterring Japan, she suggested, depended as much on pumping up MacArthur's image as on the capabilities of the B-17 and the nation's war fleets.

Shortly after noon on December 8 (Manila time), the first of three successive waves of Japanese planes attacked Clark Field on central Luzon. Seventeen B-17s, as well as most of the P-40 pursuit planes at the field, were destroyed on the ground. At about the same time, Japanese aircraft attacked nearby Iba Field, destroying another P-40 squadron. In less than one hour, about half the modern combat aircraft in the Philippines and several dozen older planes had been reduced to scrap. Seventeen B-17s based on Mindinao escaped damage. Even though only about eighty U.S. personnel died, the much touted Far Eastern Air Force had been eliminated as a combat threat.[26]

Despite the devastation wrought and the many unanswered questions about how the successful surprise had come about, not even one official inquiry took place during or after the war, either by the executive branch or Congress. The contrast with the several investigations of the attack on Hawaii is notable. Even among MacArthur's command, no shakeup or internal investigation occurred. Most of the American fliers blamed MacArthur for the debacle, while MacArthur and his chief of staff, Richard Sutherland, blamed Far Eastern Air Force (FEAF) Commander General Brereton. Since few official records survived the war, the case has been argued largely on the basis of the recollections of the principals.

The first word of the attack upon Hawaii reached Asiatic Fleet headquarters in Manila at 2:30 A.M., when radio operators picked up a broadcast. Admiral Hart and his staff began combat preparations at once and tried to contact MacArthur's headquarters. An hour later, General Sutherland learned of the attack in a commercial news broadcast and notified MacArthur. The War Department did not officially inform the Philippine commander until 5:30 that morning, about three hours after the war began. FEAF commander Brereton learned of the attack at about 4:00 A.M. and by 4:30 arrived at MacArthur's headquarters to discuss launching a B-17 strike against Japanese-held Formosa.

This sequence of events is generally accepted by all those involved. None of the three men agree upon what followed. According to Brereton, Sutherland refused to let him speak to MacArthur, saying the general was too busy. Brereton requested permission from headquarters to launch a B-17 strike against Japanese targets on Formosa. Sutherland said he should instead prepare a photo-reconnaissance mission but await permission to launch any planes. At about 7:00 A.M., Brereton tried again to see MacArthur and was again refused admission by Sutherland. He was told to await orders before sending any aircraft toward Formosa.

In midmorning radar detected flights of Japanese planes approaching the Philippines. The B-17s at Clark Field were sent aloft to avoid being caught on the ground. After a few hours passed without incident, the planes returned to the base. Radio reports confirmed that the Japanese had bombed other targets on Luzon. At 9:30 A.M. Sutherland gave Brereton permission to send a reconnaissance flight to Formosa, and shortly after that MacArthur and Brereton finally spoke. Brereton insists that he told MacArthur of his plans for a reconnaissance flight followed by a late-afternoon bombing raid. He also reports he told MacArthur he would bring up to Clark Field the 17 B-17s based on Mindinao so they could join the impending raid on Japanese targets. MacArthur later denied that Brereton had discussed with him attacking Formosa and that he would have vetoed the idea because the island was too well defended.

By noon on December 8, most of the B-17s and P-40s that had been scrambled had returned to Clark Field and nearby Iba Field for refueling and preparation for the intended raid on Formosa. They arrived just in time to be destroyed on the ground by incoming Japanese planes, which arrived with no warning, even though air defense units in outlying areas insist they broadcast an alert to Clark.

In later remarks, MacArthur, Sutherland, and Brereton blamed each other for the fiasco. MacArthur said he had not known Brereton tried to see him early on December 8 or that he requested permission to attack Formosa. If this latter fact were so, it is unclear what MacArthur and Brereton discussed in their midmorning conference. Sutherland defended himself by insisting that a photo-reconnaissance mission was vital before attacking Formosa and that Brereton had dallied for hours in arranging the mission, resulting in the B-17s being caught on the ground. All three men insist that they had earlier recommended moving the B-17s at Clark Field south, out of Japanese range, but that the others had delayed the redeployment. (In fact, airfields in Mindinao were inadequate to base all of the large bombers.)

It is by no means clear that an early mission against Formosa would have saved the B-17 fleet. The Japanese had a strong air and ground defense network on Formosa. If the B-17s had flown against the island, they would likely have been devastated. Had Sutherland allowed Brereton to see MacArthur early on December 8, and had the air commander requested permission to attack Formosa, MacArthur might well have disapproved the raid. The result, in that case, would probably have been to send most of the B-17s at Clark to the relative safety of Mindinao. Japanese aviators, in fact, had expected this and were shocked, they later reported, to discover seventeen Flying Fortresses at Clark Field.

Sutherland's arrogance and imperious style probably accounted for the bulk of the confusion, historians such as D. Clayton James have concluded. Still, as overall commander and Sutherland's patron, Douglas MacArthur bears overall responsibility for the dismal events of December 8, 1941.[27]

Over the next several days, subsequent Japanese air attacks destroyed most of the remnants of the FEAF. On December 15, General Brereton removed the remaining B-17s from the southern Philippines to Australia and on December 24 he himself flew there. That same week, Admiral Hart and most of the remaining units of the Asiatic Fleet left the Philippines, leaving MacArthur dependent almost solely on his ground force. When the Japanese began their major amphibious landings on Luzon, on December 22, they were almost unopposed. The Philippine Army dissolved quickly, forcing MacArthur to abandon his defense plan. In the end, he fell back upon the old War Plan ORANGE, ordering his remaining forces to withdraw to Bataan and Corregidor.

The Japanese offensive that began less than two weeks after MacArthur dismissed the danger of imminent war swept aside all the Allied naval and land forces in Southeast Asia. Singapore, Malaya, the East Indies, and the Indian Ocean quickly came under Japanese control. Most of the Philippines also fell rapidly. As the Japanese tightened the noose around Bataan and Corregidor, MacArthur became convinced that enemies in Washington had made him a scapegoat for the disasters in the Pacific.

In fact, during the first three weeks of the war nearly all MacArthur's designated enemies championed his cause. Even veteran MacArthur-hater Interior Secretary Harold Ickes spoke to his colleagues about the general's "magnificent" performance in holding off the Japanese. Ickes "thanked our lucky stars" that FDR had put MacArthur in charge and predicted he would soon drive the invaders out of the "entire archipelago." Contrasting MacArthur's fighting spirit to the "defeatists" in the navy, Secretary of War Henry Stimson actually threatened to resign unless the president ordered an all out effort to assist MacArthur's beleaguered command.[28]

In spite of these sentiments, it soon became clear that the losses sustained at Pearl Harbor, Japanese domination of the western Pacific, and the Europe-first strategy made it impossible to reinforce or even rescue the defenders in the Philippines. As he realized his isolation and likely fate, MacArthur lashed out at Roosevelt and other military officials, accusing them of deceit.

As early as January 2, 1942, Stimson complained of receiving messages of a "most agonizing character" from Corregidor. Soon, army officers like Dwight D. Eisenhower joined Stimson and Ickes in questioning MacArthur's abilities and motives. Why had he not "made a better showing on the beaches" or "saved his planes"? Ike believed MacArthur refused to face facts, had "lost his nerve" and proposed strategies more suitable for "plebes at West Point" than for real war.[29]

By February, MacArthur grew so despondent over his fate and the specter of so many eminent Filipinos cooperating with the Japanese that he accepted Manuel Quezon's offer of an illegal gift of $500,000. He all but endorsed Quezon's demand to FDR that the Philippines be granted immediate independence and be allowed to make a separate peace with Japan in return for a cease-fire.[30]

Roosevelt, Stimson, and Marshall were enraged by Quezon's proposal and MacArthur's tacit endorsement of it. Nevertheless, they resolved to pull MacArthur out of Corregidor and place him in command of forces assembling in Australia. Eisenhower, by now completely disillusioned with his old boss, complained that the decision by FDR and Marshall made no military sense but marked a capitulation to "editorials and public opinion."[31]

Ike referred, of course, to the MacArthur craze that was sweeping America during January and February 1942. The drama of the siege in the Philippines, combined with MacArthur's histrionic press releases, created genuine fixation among many Americans. Meanwhile, the anti–New Deal press, led by such publishers as William Randolph Hearst, Colonel Robert McCormick, Roy Howard, and Henry Luce, glommed onto MacArthur as an ideal foil to attack FDR and his Europe-first strategy. News stories and editorials stressed that even with minimal support MacArthur had frustrated Japan's war plan. Imagine what he could do with a real army!

Cities renamed buildings, roads, and bridges in the general's honor. Patriotic societies showered awards upon him. The Polish government-in-exile granted him a medal. Meanwhile, politicians in both major parties pressed FDR to name him commander in the Pacific or, perhaps, commander of all American forces. Senator Arthur Vandenberg, Republican of Michigan, spoke for several colleagues when he suggested that Roosevelt callously abandoned this "hero" in order to save the British and Russians. If the general "gets out alive," Vandenberg pledged, "I think he will be my candidate for president in 1944."[32]

Meanwhile, under the command of General Jonathan Wainwright, the beleaguered troops on Bataan surrendered on April 9, 1942; those on Corregidor capitulated a month later. Defeat in the Philippines had an especially depressing impact on Dwight D. Eisenhower, formerly MacArthur's chief aide and now a key assistant to George Marshall. Ike had labored mightily to assist the men fighting desperately in the Philippines and reacted angrily to MacArthur's effort to shift all responsibility for defeat to others. When Corregidor fell, Eisenhower poured out his spleen in a diary entry.

> Poor Wainwright! He did the fighting in the Philippine Islands, another got such glory as the public could find in the operation . . . General MacArthur's tirades to which . . . I so often listened in Manila would now sound as silly to the public as they then did to us. But he's a hero! Yah.

Nothing revealed more clearly the gap between the public's view of MacArthur and the general as he was known by his peers.[33]

About the time MacArthur, his family, and close aides reached Melbourne, Australia, on March 21, the Joint Chiefs decided to create two Pacific war theaters, an expedient to satisfy army-navy rivalries. MacArthur received command of the Southwest Pacific Area. But even while appointing the general to this important command, high officials expressed ambivalence toward him. Army Chief of Staff Marshall thought it would be a good idea to award MacArthur a Congressional Medal of Honor. When Stimson and Eisenhower expressed surprise, Marshall described it as a ploy to "offset any propaganda by the enemy" ridiculing the debacle in the Philippines and as a "morale" builder at home. The army chief may also have seen the award as a way to short-circuit efforts in Congress to press greater honors and authority on MacArthur. FDR approved the medal on March 25, without comment.

Privately, the president belittled the honor. As noted above, he told Admiral Hart that MacArthur had falsely assured him that the Philippines could be defended successfully anytime after December 1, 1941. In April, he told Supreme Court Justice Frank Murphy (formerly high commissioner in Manila) that MacArthur had repeatedly misled Washington about the true situation in the Philippines. The Philippine army had proved worthless and MacArthur's defense of Corregidor and Bataan was "more a rout than a military achievement." Why, Murphy asked, had FDR approved the Medal of Honor and given MacArthur a new command? The president described his actions as "pure yielding to Congressional and public opinion."[34]

Within a few weeks of MacArthur's arrival in Australia, Stimson and others began to discuss the "emerging problem" of MacArthur. Stimson, Eisenhower, and Ickes complained that the general's unauthorized public statements often contradicted official policy. The general's call for an early Pacific offensive provoked Assistant Secretary of War John J. McCloy and Harold Ickes to begin leaking stories to journalists that the Medal of Honor was based on "made-up" incidents. Ickes told his colleagues that MacArthur's declarations from Australia were evidence that he had begun to campaign for the White House as "our man on horseback."[35]

Soon Marshall and Eisenhower, as well as Ickes, raised questions about the $500,000 gift MacArthur received from Quezon. They thought it might be intended as a political slush fund for a presidential race or money to be used for lobbying on the general's behalf. By the summer of 1942, FDR told the White House staff that the "trouble MacArthur was making" by his calls for a Pacific-first strategy had gotten out of control. Perhaps someone should let the general know that the kind of "criminal" behavior exhibited at Corregidor might lead to courts martial for the commanders at Pearl Harbor.[36]

The bitter memories of MacArthur's performance in 1941-42 cast a long shadow on the Roosevelt administration. Although it is uncertain what FDR might have done with the general at the end of the war, Truman and others in Washington harbored grave doubts about the wisdom of sending MacArthur to Tokyo in 1945. Texas Democratic Senator Tom Connally spoke with Truman early that August to warn him that it would be a "big mistake" to appoint "Dugout Dug as Allied commander to accept the Jap surrender." Connally predicted the general would use the post to run against Truman in 1948.

Harold Ickes told Truman that it was terribly sad, but probably inevitable, that "MacArthur should be cast for this role." Truman agreed, but said it was not fair to "blame on him the appointment of MacArthur as the Chief Commander in the Far Eastern Area." Ickes admitted that politically the president "couldn't do anything else." The blame, Ickes said, was "due to Roosevelt" who made a terrible "mistake in taking MacArthur away from the

Philippines." Instead, he should have left the general "to clean up his own mess and taken Wainwright out," allowing the Japanese to solve the MacArthur problem. The president and interior secretary touched on what they saw as an irony: Most Americans considered MacArthur "an outstanding hero," while those in the know judged his wartime service a "fiasco." Ever since MacArthur's removal from Corregidor, politics had triumphed over sound strategy. Yet even now, Ickes lamented, denying the general command in Japan would only make a "martyr out of him and a candidate for president." Harry Truman disputed only one point: "MacArthur," he predicted, would "be a candidate anyway."[37]

On that note, MacArthur's postwar career in the Pacific began.

Notes

1. Hart diary entry of March 1942, quoted in James Leutze, *A Different Kind of Victory: A Biography of Admiral Thomas C. Hart* (Annapolis, M.D.: 1981), 287.
2. William D. Hassett, *Off the Record with FDR* (New Brunswick, N.J.: 1958), 88.
3. Louis Morton, "War Plan ORANGE: Evolution of a Strategy," *World Politics* 2 (1959): 221-50; Theodore Friend, *Between Two Empires: The Ordeal of the Philippines, 1929-46* (New Haven, Conn., 1965), 161-63; David J. Steinberg, *Philippine Collaboration in World War II* (Ann Arbor: 1967), 20.
4. For a fuller discussion of the Philippine and American political aspects of MacArthur's appointment, as well as the unusual financial arrangements surrounding it, see Michael Schaller, *Douglas MacArthur: The Far Eastern General* (New York: 1989), 24-28.
5. Ibid., 29-33.
6. See memorandum by Frances Sayre of conversation with Roosevelt, Nov. 16, 1936, cited in Sidney Fine and Frank Murphy, *The New Deal Years* (Chicago: 1979), 196; See also Dorothy Borg, *The United States and the Far Eastern Crisis of 1933-1938* (Cambridge: Harvard University Press, 1964), 244-46; and Entry, November 20, 1936, Diary, Harold Ickes Mss., Library of Congress.
7. Schaller, *MacArthur,* 36-38.
8. D. Clayton James, *The Years of MacArthur,* 2 vols. (Boston: Houghton Mifflin, 1970), vol. 1, 526-31 and 537-38; Murphy, *The New Deal Years,* 197; Friend, *Between Two Empires,* 193-94; and Stephen Shadegg, *Clare Boothe Luce: A Biography* (New York: 1970), 129.
9. MacArthur to Early, July 14, 1939, OF 4771, Franklin D. Roosevelt Mss, Roosevelt Library.
10. Leutze, *Hart,* 185-88.

11. Theodore White, *In Search of History* (New York: 1978), 108.
12. MacArthur to Early, March 21, 1941, OF 400, FDR Mss; Gen. Edwin Watson to MacArthur, April 15, 1941, OF 4771, FDR Mss; Early to MacArthur, April 14, 1941, Box 10, Steve Early Mss; MacArthur to Early, May 11, 1941, ibid; James, *Years of MacArthur,* vol. 1, 585-88.
13. John Hersey, *Men on Bataan* (New York: 1943), 287-91.
14. Diary entry, July 1, 1941, Harold C. Ickes Mss, Library of Congress.
15. On the Japanese debate over where and when to strike, as well as the sporadic Japanese-American negotiations and the role played by U.S. intercepts of Japanese communications, see, Robert Dallek, *Franklin D. Roosevelt and American Foreign Policy, 1932-1945* (New York: Oxford University Press, 1985), 273-75; Ronald Spector, *Eagle Against the Sun* (New York: Free Press, 1985), 85; Ronald Lewin, *The American Magic* (New York: Farrar, Straus, Giroux, 1982), 1-75; Waldo Heinrichs, *The Threshold of War: Franklin D. Roosevelt and American Entry into World War II* (New York: Oxford University Press, 1988), 118-45.
16. Schaller, *MacArthur,* 46-48.
17. MacArthur resurgent popularity among Filipinos is discussed in Carole Petillo, *Douglas MacArthur: The Philippine Years* (Bloomington: Indiana University Press, 1981), 198.
18. James, *Years of MacArthur,* vol. 1, 592-93; and Leutze, *Hart,* 212-17.
19. MacArthur to Cal O'Laughlin, October 6, 1941, Box 54, O'Laughlin Mss, Library of Congress.
20. James, *Years of MacArthur,* vol. 1, 609.
21. Schaller, *MacArthur,* 49-50; Heinrichs, *Threshold of War,* 175-76.
22. Hart's letters and diary entries of October-November 1941 appear in Leutze, *Hart,* 218.
23. Schaller, *MacArthur,* 52; and Heinrichs, *Threshold of War,* 204.
24. Francis B. Sayre, *Glad Adventure* (New York, 1957), 221; and James, *Years of MacArthur,* 616-17.
25. Clare Boothe Luce to Noel Busch, quoted in Shadegg, *Clare Boothe Luce,* 128-30.
26. The most informative summary of the events surrounding the attack of December 8, 1941, is contained in James, *Years of MacArthur,* vol. 2, 1-16. See also Louis Morton, *The Fall of the Philippines* (Washington, D.C.: 1953).
27. Ibid.
28. Entries, December 14 and 21, 1941, Diary, Ickes Mss.; and Entries, December 14, 17, and 21, 1941, Diary, Henry Stimson Mss, Yale University.
29. Entry, January 2, 1941, Stimson Mss; and Entries, January 8, 13, 17, and 19, 1942, in Robert Ferrell, ed., *The Eisenhower Diaries,* 43-44; and Eisenhower quoted in James, *Years of MacArthur,* vol. 2, 84. For a description of the

fighting on Bataan and Corregidor during this period, see James, *Years of MacArthur,* vol. 2, 50-87; Ferrell, ed., *Eisenhower Diaries,* entries of January 29 and February 3, 8, 9, 1942, 46-47; *New York Times,* February 23, 1942.

30. Schaller, *MacArthur,* 58-61.
31. Ibid., 61; Ferrell, ed., *Eisenhower Diaries,* entry of February 23, 1942, 49; James, *Years of MacArthur,* vol. 2, 98-99.
32. Entry, February 15, 1942, Diary, Ickes Mss; Gardner Jackson to Marvin H. McIntyre, March 11, 1942, PPF, 3453, Roosevelt Mss; Ltr, Vandenberg of February 1942, in Arthur H. Vandenberg, Jr., ed., *The Private Papers of Senator Vandenberg* (Boston: 1952), 76. For a detailed discussion of the "MacArthur craze," see James, *Years of MacArthur,* vol. 2, 132-39.
33. Entry, May 6, 1942, in Ferrell, ed., *Eisenhower Diaries,* 52.
34. On the decision to establish the Southwest Pacific Area Theater, see James, *Years of MacArthur,* vol. 2, 100-32; Spector, *Eagle Against the Sun,* 143-44; Marshall to Roosevelt, PSF, Fl06, Roosevelt Mss; Hart Diary, quoted in Leutze, *Hart,* 287; Murphy quoted in Sidney Fine, *Frank Murphy: The Washington Years* (Ann Arbor, Michigan, 1984), 216; Roosevelt to Marshall, August 22, 1944, PSF Fl06, Roosevelt Mss.
35. Entry, March 19, 1942, Ferrell, ed., *Eisenhower Diaries,* 51-52; and Entries, March 22 and 30, April 30, 1942, Ickes Mss.
36. References to Ickes's and other administration officials' probes into MacArthur's activities are found in Entries April 5, May 24, and September 1942, Ickes Mss; Quezon's unsuccessful effort to "bribe" Eisenhower is discussed in a memorandum by Eisenhower of June 20, 1942, in Ferrell, ed., *Eisenhower Diaries,* 63; and Entry, May 14, 1942, Diary, Stimson Mss; Hassett, *Off the Record with FDR,* 88.
37. Ickes and Truman had grown increasingly frustrated with MacArthur's handling of the internal political situation in the Philippines during the spring and summer of 1945. See diary Entries, April 29, June 9, July 21, and August 18 and 26, 1945, Ickes Mss; and Robert Ferrell, ed., *Off the Record: The Private Papers of Harry S. Truman* (New York: 1980), 47, 61.

9.

The United States, Japan, and the Panama Canal

John Major

In 1940 Charlie Chan foiled a sabotage attempt against it by a traitorous WASP lady in tweeds. In 1942 Humphrey Bogart saved it from destruction by a kamikaze prince of imperial Japanese blood. The objective in each case was the Panama Canal, and the episodes were both fiction, but the history of the Canal's role in the Pacific war is no less dramatic than the extravaganzas of the Hollywood screenwriters. This chapter delineates that role, not only in the war itself but across the previous generation, as the long-term crisis between Washington and Tokyo came to its explosive head.

To most Americans early in this century, the Canal was the jewel in Columbia's diadem. For the doyen of American navalists, Admiral Alfred Thayer Mahan, American dominion over Panama was as sacrosanct as the Monroe Doctrine and the ban on Oriental immigration. Senator Claude Swanson affirmed in 1919 that control of the Canal was "a national policy as fixed as the eternal stars. For its maintenance there is no sacrifice we would refuse." To President Franklin Roosevelt's secretary of war, Henry Stimson—who as Taft's war secretary had supervised planning of the Canal's defenses—Panama and its environs were "the one spot external to our shores which nature has decreed to be most vital to our national safety."[1]

This was no hyperbole. The lock canal dug through the Panama isthmus was nothing short of what one serving officer called "the Navy's main life artery." It gave the fleet a crucial shortcut from its Atlantic bases to its Pacific bases, freeing it from the enormously longer voyage around Cape Horn and allowing it to transfer from one ocean to the other with relative dispatch. For that reason Stimson was certain it would have been a more productive target than Pearl Harbor for the initial Japanese strike. And testifying after the war on the prelude to its outbreak, the wartime army chief of staff, General George Marshall, recalled that "the probabilities pointed to the Panama Canal and to the Philippines before Hawaii." Yet though the Canal was not hit on December 7, it lay wide open to attack. Flying down to Rio for the Pan-American Conference of January 1942, Under Secretary of State Sumner Welles was all too aware that the fate of the Canal "had suddenly become a matter of life and death" since it "might be bombed from the air or from the land and be blocked for many months." At a time when the United States was reeling from the shock of the Japanese assault such a closure could have proved an even worse bodyblow than the catastrophe visited on Oahu.[2] The perception of a Japanese menace to Panama had been current well before the Canal opened to shipping in August 1914. In 1911 the chairman of the Canal Commission, General George Washington Goethals, had all the biggest guns in the Army's coast artillery batteries placed at the Pacific terminal to counteract a Japanese naval bombardment. After a Japanese quest for concessions in Mexico's Magdalena Bay, Senator Henry Cabot Lodge put through his own corollary to the Monroe Doctrine, warning Latin American governments against giving any franchise to a foreign corporation that might endanger Washington's links with its overseas outposts. During the now-forgotten Japanese war scare of 1913, 2,500 rifles were sent down to Panama to arm the white American component of the Canal workforce, and submarines were transhipped across the isthmus by rail to guard the Pacific entrance.[3]

Come the First World War, American mistrust of Japanese intentions surfaced time and again, in spite of the fact that an amphibious expedition against the Canal was deemed well beyond Japanese capabilities. The 1914 draft of the U.S. plan for war with Japan—War Plan ORANGE—concluded that the 8,000 miles of Pacific Ocean between Japan and the waterway was an insurmountable barrier, but the war made anything seem possible. Thus in May 1915 the coincidence of Japan's attempted subjugation of China via the

Twenty-One Demands and the German sinking of the liner *Lusitania* with many American passengers on board raised the bogey of a Berlin-Tokyo alliance and a two-front war, in the Atlantic and the Pacific.[4]

The army consequently began to press for the fortification of Taboga and Taboguilla islands just south of the Pacific prism and to urge the navy to develop a submarine base at the Pacific as well as at the Atlantic terminal. Captain William Veazie Pratt, of the U.S. Navy, for his part, was positive that Japanese pearl fishermen were more knowledgeable about the Pacific coast of Panama than the Navy Department itself, while Commanding General Clarence Edwards was equally sure that "Japanese hostile schemes . . . have been and are about us here all the time." "Nothing more confounds me, when I think of the Pacific end," wrote Edwards in February 1917, "than the helplessness I would feel did I awake and fear that an enemy . . . had possession of the Saboga Anchorage [in the Pearl Islands some fifty miles southeast of the Pacific entrance]."[5]

In the event no attack materialized, but the aftermath of the war made it unmistakably clear that Japan was still seen as a serious danger to American interests across the Pacific. When the Senate debate on the League of Nations Covenant opened in the summer of 1919, former Secretary of State Philander Chase Knox insisted on inserting a declaration echoing the Lodge Corollary, namely: "We do not intend that Japan shall obtain a military base in Mexico or anywhere near the Panama Canal." In December the garrison commander in the Canal Zone urged a U.S. veto on Japanese bids to acquire land in Panama, and the Panamanian government obediently turned down the applications when they came in.[6]

The most pointed indication of American feelings, however, was a major redisposition of the navy. In July 1919 six of the navy's most modern battleships steamed through the Canal to take up station at San Diego; three years later the realignment was complete, with the fleet now based mainly on the West Coast. One of its primary functions was to deter any Japanese sortie into the Eastern Pacific, leading to a descent on the Canal "at the outbreak of hostilities, or as a preliminary strike to a declaration of war" —like the surprise attack on tsarist Russia's Far Eastern naval headquarters at Port Arthur in 1904. Under Plan ORANGE the fleet was to block the path of a Japanese task force estimated at 75,000 men and involving an aircraft carrier raid on Canal installations.[7]

To the naval commandant in the Canal Zone, it was inconceivable that Japan would go through with the operation unless it had first secured control of the Pacific in general and knocked out Pearl Harbor, but to make the assurance double sure the Zone was exempted from the freeze of fortifications in the Pacific agreed by the Washington disarmament treaty of 1922. Five years later, when the Japanese were reportedly about to propose the Zone's defortification at the Geneva naval conference, the American defense establishment dismissed the idea out of hand. Discussion of the Canal was inadmissible because it was virtually part of America's own coastline, and for Japan to broach the subject signaled "a distinctly hostile attitude." With this clear warning shot across its bows, Tokyo said no more.[8]

Meanwhile, maneuvers off the Canal tested the navy's defenses against a Japanese foray, first with Fleet Problem I in 1923, which concluded that the principal threat to the waterway now came from air power, not sea power, and that it was pointless to extend the gun emplacements installed a decade earlier to neutralize a seaborne thrust. Six years later, in Fleet Problem IX, the *Saratoga* launched her planes in what the umpires pronounced an overwhelming onslaught. The only possible answer, in the judgement of the Fleet's C-in-C, Admiral Henry Wiley, was "to put enemy carrier decks out of commission before their squadrons take the air." Otherwise, as the *New York Times* put it, "no naval base in the world is safe from a devastating blow by swift carriers properly supported by a fleet." The lesson was unquestionably not lost on the Imperial Japanese Navy.[9]

Yet no air defense screen was set up to cover the Canal against a Japanese incursion. A new army air base was built near the Pacific entrance, to improve the reaction time to marauders closing in across Panama Bay, but its runways were not concreted and it was unusable by loaded bombers during the six-month rainy season. Nor was anything done to protect the Canal against the contingency of sabotage by the Japanese colony in Panama, which the editor of the local English-language daily was convinced was a nest of subversion. Military Intelligence in Washington agreed. Wrote one apprehensive G-2 officer: "The spectacle of 8,000 men gazing out to sea for an enemy who is operating behind their backs, destroying the very thing they are sent to protect, would not be too pleasant."[10]

Fears climbed to a new pitch early in 1934, as the fleet made ready to transit. In February an ex–navy signalman told Naval Intelligence he had been approached to take part in a plot to disable the Canal after the last warship cleared the Atlantic Terminal. His story was taken seriously, and an investigation ordered by the White House revealed a scandalous state of unpreparedness. The locks had not been guarded since 1918, except by "a couple of indifferent, sleepy watchmen," while in the view of the U.S. envoy to Panama, Antonio Gonzalez, "our secret service for Panama Canal protection is perhaps less than that, say, for a tobacco warehouse in North Carolina." And this against an enemy who, in Gonzalez's words, "strikes out of a clear sky and declares war afterwards."[11]

When Japan went on to denounce the disarmament treaties at the end of 1934, military planners considered the security of the "strategic triangle" of Hawaii, Alaska, and Panama now at risk, and countermeasures began to take shape. U.S. diplomatic missions started keeping tabs on Japanese activities in Central America. They were also instructed to report any suspicious details about Japanese merchant ships that might hint at preparation for blowing up a vessel in one of the locks or in the central cut of the Canal—as the writer Hector C. Bywater had suggested back in 1925 in his disquieting piece of futurology *The Great Pacific War*. "For any nation of a certain type of psychology," wrote Governor Clarence Ridley, "such a fearful martyrdom was entirely possible in view of the priceless results it might obtain."[12]

At the same time, Panama's decision in 1935 to give the green light to unrestricted Japanese immigration raised an uncomfortable parallel with Hawaii, "where a large Japanese population has been allowed to grow up in close proximity to one of our vital elements of defense." Army and navy subsequently urged a Panamanian embargo after Japanese aircraft sank the American gunboat *Panay* off Nanking in December 1937, while President Roosevelt himself prompted a bill to control Japanese trailers off Hawaii, the West Coast, and the Canal, whose purpose was transparently to "follow the Fleet and not the fish."[13]

Meanwhile, Ridley elaborated a comprehensive package of antisabotage precautions, providing for ship inspection and transit guards, plus a ban on cargoes with more than a prescribed amount of high explosives, and allowing foreign bottoms to use one side only of the twin-chambered locks. Looking farther ahead, the governor sponsored legislation for a third set of locks at a safe distance from the existing flights and reserved for the navy. It was authorized in 1939, and the countersabotage program went into effect soon afterwards, just before the outbreak of a second world war in Europe.[14]

This still left the problem of Japanese air attack, and here the response was more sluggish by far. Since 1919, as we have seen, the first line of defense had been the navy's capital ships in the Pacific, but in 1938 and 1939 Roosevelt and his advisers were focusing increasingly on securing the Southern Hemisphere against penetration by Nazi Germany. In April 1939 a joint army-navy strategy review called for priority to go to the Atlantic and the Caribbean, even at the expense of the Pacific. In June the Army Air Corps insisted that "the approach by air from South America represents the most serious threat to the Panama Canal," via a *Luftwaffe* bomber force based in northeast Brazil. To make up for any shift of resources to the Atlantic, Commanding General David Stone therefore began to press for a distant early warning line in the Pacific, with air bases on Cocos Island and the Galápagos from which U.S. air power could reach out "to destroy the wasps in their nests before they ever begin to fly." Progress toward leasing land for the bases was astonishingly slow, however, and Ecuador did not grant permission to develop the Galápagos until October 1941.[15]

By this time the chance of Japanese sabotage had been reduced to a minimum by denying Japanese shipping access to the Canal, even though Japan had a right to transit under the Anglo-American Treaty of 1901 guaranteeing free passage to ships of all nations. The move had been discussed as early as February 1941, in spite of qualms that it might provoke Tokyo to go to war. In the event, Japanese merchantmen at the terminals in July were simply told that they would face inordinate delays owing to "repairs" to canal facilities, and they soon disappeared over the horizon. In October, after the ousting of the pro-Axis Panamanian president Arnulfo Arias, his successor was perfectly ready to intern all Japanese citizens whenever Washington gave the word. The Canal thus seemed beyond the machinations of an Asiatic enemy within.[16]

In respect to air attack the Canal was still in high jeopardy. Early in 1941 Admiral Ernest J. King's Atlantic Fleet laid claim to the Catalina flying boats of the navy's Third Patrol Wing in the Canal Zone, hitherto pledged to watch over the Pacific outskirts of the isthmus. In September Commanding General Frank Andrews complained that the navy's air arm in the Zone was so reduced that surveillance of the Pacific approaches was practically nonexistent. Eight days before Pearl Harbor, Andrews reported that his 37-mm anti-aircraft guns—the innermost defense ring against low-flying assailants—had ammunition for only one minute of fire. And when the Zone's navy commandant renewed an earlier plea for 360 scouting planes, the request was denied by Chief of Naval Operations Admiral Harold Stark on the traditional grounds that the Canal was immunized by its distance from Japan and by the presence of the U.S. Pacific Fleet at Pearl Harbor.[17]

By the forenoon of December 7, when six of the fleet's nine battleships lay sunk or disabled along Battleship Row, Stark's confident assumption had been blown sky-high. "Panama is in great danger now of an air raid," Stimson confided to his diary. "It will probably be one of the next objectives of the Japanese." The first response was to take deep aerial reconnaissance of Pacific waters out of the navy's hands and assign it to the army. At sunrise and sunset all combat aircraft in the Zone and Panama were on red alert, with pilots sitting in their cockpits, but by late February the air defenses were still rudimentary. No night fighters were on station, while the blimps of the balloon barrage were liable to burst in the tropical sun. Bomb nets made to be stretched over vital parts of the Canal mechanism had failed to withstand tests at the Aberdeen Proving Ground.[18]

Above all, there was the Achilles' heel of the Gatún Dam, containing the artificial lake that provided the locks with most of their water supply. "The loss of the water in Gatún Lake—and this is what I fear," Andrews told Washington, "would be a strategic calamity," which Stimson knew could close the Canal for over two years. After being flown by Andrews over the lake during an inspection tour in March, Stimson landed deeply shaken by his realization that the dam was "vulnerable to heavy sustained bombing . . . more possible than I had believed."[19]

In his following report to Roosevelt, Stimson stressed the need for a 1,000-mile defense cordon, since the radius of the existing aircraft warning system was too short to detect a carrier before she released her planes for a dawn attack. The army's patrol squadrons were to be fitted immediately with airborne radar, while new land-based radar equipment would be rushed into place on Panamanian territory west of the zone to give all possible notice of an incoming threat. As things were, radar installations were disturbingly inadequate, and in a February exercise a simulated raid had not been spotted until it was less than 15 miles from Gatún.[20]

Over the next three months the defensive structure was assembled at breakneck speed, though on June 6, 1942, an Army Intelligence evaluation claimed that at any time between six in the evening and three in the morning, a carrier and her escorts could cross the patrolled area and get within striking distance of the Canal. Just as well, then, perhaps, that 48 hours earlier Japan had lost four of its fleet carriers at the Battle of Midway. Although eight months later Military Intelligence thought it possible that Tokyo might sacrifice two carriers on a one-way mission against Panama, the conclusion was that Japan's manifold commitments elsewhere, its severe losses in aircraft and pilots, and the perfection of the long-range interdiction force made it an unlikely prospect.[21]

A progressive rundown of the garrison thus began early in 1943, so much so that in December *Newsweek* could compare the atmosphere in the Canal Zone with the mood in Honolulu on the eve of Pearl Harbor, marked by "a spirit of carefreeness and gayety that one doesn't associate with an all-out war effort." A year later Stimson noted of the Zone's military overlord, General George Brett: "He's got a rather discouraging command, because the menace of a Japanese surprise attack which livened up the situation two and a half years ago now is dim in the distance as the Japanese fleet has been pounded to pieces across the Pacific." On May 12, 1945, shortly after the unconditional surrender of Japan's Axis partner, the Third Reich, Brett's fiefdom was designated an inactive theater.[22]

Yet for the Canal the war was not quite over. "There is little doubt," Colonel Carl Strong had asserted in 1943, "that the Japanese are fanatical, desperate, and in their insane desire to conquer, will no doubt follow what appears to us to be the most illogical and unexpected line of action." Stimson himself had written of Panama that "although it might lie dormant for a long while, if attacked it was capable of being an almost fatal disaster." He felt this way partly because of his doubts about General Brett. "I had hardly ever seen an ineffective man appointed to a position in the hope that it would not require supreme abilities," he told Marshall, "without lightning almost immediately striking that spot with disastrous results."[23]

Stimson's foreboding was justified, in the sense that Japan *was* planning an attack on the Canal in the wake of Germany's capitulation, to delay the transfer to the Pacific of American forces from Europe. The discovery of the wrecks of two midget submarines in the Gulf of Panama in 1973 suggests an aborted suicide venture against Miraflores lock, next to the Pacific terminal. And there was certainly a scheme to mount an air strike by floatplane bombers carried aboard two giant 5,000-ton submarines completed in January 1945. The target, however, was switched to Ulithi Atoll in the Caroline Islands, stagingpost for the U.S. invasion force gathering for its landing on the Japanese home islands. As the project's leader, Captain Ariiyumi, was graphically to put it: "A man does not worry about the fire he sees on the horizon when he sees other flames licking at his kimono sleeve." So when Japan too surrendered on August 14, 1945, the Canal had come through unscathed.[24]

Its contribution to the war effort was immense. If the alternative subcontinental route around South America had to be used in the event of a closure, American policymakers might well have been forced to choose between reducing the protection given to Atlantic convoys and limiting Pacific shipments to what could have been sent to the West Coast by road and rail. The Canal removed the necessity for that choice, and combat vessels and supply ships could be shuttled readily from one ocean to the other. Between July 1941 and June 1945 more than 23,000 transits were recorded, an average of nearly 16 per day. It was a remarkable performance, and in bringing it off, the Canal more than justified itself as one of the country's prime strategic assets.[25]

Yet the war also tolled its passing bell. When it elevated the United States to global power, the worldwide responsibilities taken on demanded far more than the effort to reconcile the competing claims of Atlantic and Pacific through the medium of Panama. Meeting those responsibilities required a vast new range of armaments, and these too drastically impaired the Canal's significance. The construction of a two-ocean navy inevitably marginalized a waterway designed to make the most of a one-ocean fleet. Locks built to handle dreadnoughts were dwarfed by the huge Midway-class carriers laid down as flagships of the navy's ultimate offensive against Japan.

Above all, what Japan failed to achieve before it succumbed came about paradoxically through the very weapon that clinched its defeat. The new "high explosives" currently being brought to fruition, Stimson rightly predicted in June 1945, were likely to make any lock canal such as Panama "dangerous and easily destroyed." Stimson was talking about the atomic bomb, and his comment was an epitaph on the work he had helped consummate not long before the First World War. Then, belief in the pivotal importance of the Canal was unquestioned, but World War II shattered many of the axioms of Stimson's generation, not least the belief that the Canal was the hinge of U.S. national security. Though still the symbol of American might for years to come, Washington's victory in the death struggle with Japan made certain it would never again be its vital center.[26]

Notes

1. Maflan letter in *New York Times,* April 2, 1912, 1/4; Swanson speech in *The Congressional Record,* Senate, July 14, 1919, 2537; and Henry L. Stimson and McGeorge Bundy, *On Active Service in Peace and War* (New York: 1948), 186.
2. United States National Archives, Record Group 80, Secretary of the Navy, Secretary and Confidential Correspondence 1919-26, PD 198-2, Commander, Destroyer Squadrons, Atlantic Fleet to Daniels, February 26, 1920; hereafter cited as NA. Stimson and McBundy, *On Active Service,* 183; U. S. Cong., Senate and House of Representatives, *Hearings before the Joint Committee on the Investigation of the Pearl Harbor Attack,* Part 32 (Washington, D.C.: 1946), 562, quoted in Gordon Prange, *Pearl Harbor: The Verdict of History* (London: Harmondsworth, 1991), 257. Sumner Welles, *Seven Major Decisions* (London: 1951), 102-3.
3. U.S. Congress, Senate, Committee on Interoceanic Canals, Hearings H.R. 21969 (Washington, D.C., 1912), 71. Thomas Bailey, "The Lodge Corollary to the Monroe Doctrine," *Political Science Quarterly,* 48 (1933): 223-24. NA, RG 94, Adjutant General of the Army 1784-1917, 2283996, Adjutant General to Commanding General, Eastern Department, July 27, 1915.
4. Edward Miller, *War Plan ORANGE; the U.S. Strategy to Defeat Japan, 1897-1945* (Annapolis: Naval Institute Press, 1991), 41. As a fine example of wartime Nipponophobia see Cleveland Moffett's novel *The Conquest.*
5. NA, RG 94, AG 2298940, Cronkhite to Scott, June 19, 1915. Ibid., AG 2314751A, War College Division to Scott, January 3, 1916. Operational Archives, Naval Historical Center, Washington Navy Yard, Washington, DC, Papers of the General Board, 426-1, S.618, Pratt to Operations, June 26, 1916; ibid., Edwards to Wood, August 1, 1916; hereafter cited as OA, GB. NA, RG

165, Records of the General and Special Staffs, War College Division 1903-1917, 6178-139.

6. CR, Senate, August 7, 1919, 3687. NA, RD 38, Office of Naval Intelligence, C-1O-J, 12469, Kennedy to Price, December 10, 1919 and Price to Lansing, December 17, 1919.
7. *New York Times,* July 28, 1919, 6/3. William Braisted, *The United States Navy in the Pacific 1909-1922* (Austin: University of Texas Press, 1971), 458-60. NA, RG 225, Joint Board of the Army and Navy, 325, S.84, Mission, US Forces in Canal Zone, October 10, 1919; ibid., S.117, Day to Craven, September 20, 1920; hereafter cited as JB. NA, RG 407, Adjutant General of the Army 1917-1925, AD 660.2 Panama Canal Department (October 7, 1920), Revised Project for Defense of Panama Canal, October 10, 1920.
8. NA, RD 80, Secretary of the Navy Secret and Confidential Correspondence 1919-1926, PD 197-15, Taylor to Sturgis, undated (probably February 1922). Ibid., PD 226-103, October 19, 1921 NA, RG 165, War Plans Division, 2938, Davis to Kellogg, April 28, 1927; hereafter cited as WPD. NA, RG 225, JB 338, Joint Board to Davis, May 10, 1927.
9. NA, RG 165, WPD 639-6, Weeks directive of July 16, 1923. NA, RG 80, Confidential Correspondence 1927-1939, Whiting comment of January 30, 1929; CINCUS Report, 16. *New York Times,* February 11, 1929, 14/1.
10. *New York Times,* January 6, 1929, III, 6/6. NA, RG 165, WPD 3531, Sampson to Simonds, May 16, 1931. U.S. Army, Caribbean Defense Command, Historical Section, History of the Panama Canal Department, I (Quarry Heights, CZ, 1947), 69-701; hereafter cited as HCPD. NA, RG 165, Military Intelligence Division, 1766-R-22(1), Military Attaché, Costa Rica memorandum of April 25, 1933; ibid., (6), memorandum of August 30, 1933; hereafter cited as MID.
11. NA, RG 165, MID 1766-R-22(17), Smith memorandum, of February 14, 1934. NA, RG59, Department of State, 811F.312 Protection/9, Dern to Flint, March 10, 1904; ibid.,/5, memorandum, of March 27, 1934. NA, RG 165, MID 1766-R-22(21), Military Attaché, Costa Rica, memorandum of February 23, 1934.
12. NA, RG 165, WPD 3804, Dern to Roosevelt, December 27, 1934. RG 59, 894.20219, Welles circular of June 4, 1936; 811F.812 Protection/55, Hull circular of May 8, 1939. Hector C. Bywater, *The Great Pacific War: A History of the American-Japanese Campaign of 1931-33* (London: 1925), 21-25. See also William Honan, *Visions of Infamy: The Untold Story of How Journalist Hector C. Bywater Devised Plans That Led to Pearl Harbor* (New York: 1991). NA, RG 165, MD 3730-12, Ridley memorandum of April 18, 1938.

13. NA, RG 59, 819.628/23, Dern and Swanson to Hull, April 13, 1935. NA, RG 165, WPD 3730-12, Leahy and Woodring to Hull, August 18, 1937. NA, RG 59, 819.628/42, Corrigan to Hull, January 25, 1938. NA, RG 107, Secretary of War Classified File, Dern to Flint, May 14, 1935; hereafter cited as SWCF.
14. NA, RG 165, WPD 3730-12, Hidley memorandum of April 18, 1938. NA, RD 197,SWCF, Ridley to Woodring, December 23, 1938. NA, RG 59, 811F,812/1062, Dern to Hull, February 6, 1936. NA, RG 80, General Correspondence 1927-1939, QH(15)Panama/A1-1, Chief, Bureau of Yards and Docks, memorandum of October 2, 1939. Stetson Conn and Byron Fairchild, *Guarding the United States and Its Outposts* (Washington, D.C.: 1964), 310.
15. NA, RG 225, JB 634, Report of April 21, 1939, by Colonel Frank Clark and Captain Russell Crenshaw, IV, 1-2; V,1; VI,1. NA, RG 165, WPD3748-17, Air Board Report of June 26, 1939, TAB X2 (Caribbean). WPD 3782-3, Stone—to Adjutant General, January 5, 1939. NA, RG 18, Army Air Forces, Central Decimal Files 1939-1942, Series 2, AAG 400 Panama-Caribbean, Dargue memorandum of September 19, 1939. NA, RG 165, WPD 3782-11, memorandum of October 16, 1941.
16. NA, RG 59, G11F.812 Protection/257, memorandum of February 20, 1941; 258, undated; 259 of April 24, 1941. RG 165, MD 3730-22, War Plans Division to Adjutant General, July 9, 1941. MD 4319-5, Marshall to Welles, October 27, 1941.
17. The navy's commitment to maintain the Pacific patrol was made on December 9, 1939: see NA, RG 165, MD 3689-14, memorandum of March 3, 1940. VPD 4452-3, Lynd report of May 1, 1941. WPD 3730-42, Andrews to Adjutant General, September 17, 1941. MD 4544-13, Andrews to Adjutant General, November 29, 1941. The call for 360 patrol planes was first made in August 1940: see CNO/SECNAV Files 1940-1947, (SC) HG/A-16-1, Sadler to Stark, August 29, 1940 and Stark to Sadler, October 21, 1940. The second refusal is in OA, Strategic Plans Division Files 1919-1947, Stark to Sadler, October 9, 1941. See also NA, RG 165, WPD 3730-42, Marshall to Stark, October 14, 1941, and Stark to Marshall, October 25, 1941.
18. Sterling Memorial Library, Yale University, Diary of Henry L.Stimson, entry for December 12, 1941; hereafter cited as Stimson Diary. NA, RG 165, MD 2917-34 of December 12, 1941 and 2917-35 of December 16, 1941. OA, SPD Files, memorandum of January 1, 1942. NA, RG 165, WPD 4452-16, Andrews to Marshall, December 16, 1941. MD 1992-121, minutes of conference of February 23, 1942.

19. NA, RG 165, WPD 4452-19, Andrews to McNair, January 15, 1942. Stimson Diary, entry for March 11, 1942.
20. NA, RD 107, Secretary of the Army Subject File 1940-1942, Stimson to Roosevelt, March 14, 1942. Welles, *Seven Major Decisions,* 103. NA , RD 165, WPD 1992-121, minutes of conference of February 23, 1942.
21. Conn and Fairchild, *Guarding the United States,* 424-29. NA, RG 165, Operations Division 1942-1946, 452.1 Caribbean Defense Command, Case 9, memorandum of June 6, 1942; hereafter cited as OPD. NA, RG 18, Air Adjutant General, Bulky Files 1942-1944, Military Intelligence Service memorandum of February 8, 1943.
22. HCPD, IV, l. NA, RG 165, OPD 000.7/109, Hull to Brett, December 7, 1943. Stimson Diary, entry for December 14, 1944. HCPD, IV, 8.
23. NA, Washington National Records Center, Suitland, Maryland, Military Intelligence Division, Regional File, 9185, Strong memorandum of June 11, 1943. Stimson Diary, entry for October 17, 1942.
24. Letter to the author from Colonel Robert Sprague, February 12, 1982. A. J. Watts and B. G. Gordon, *The Imperial Japanese Navy* (London: 1971), 365-70, 351-53. Zenji Orita and Joseph Harington, *I-Boat Captain* (Canoga Park, CA: 1976), 318-19. E. John Long, "Japan's 'Underseas Carriers'," *U.S. Naval Institute Proceedings* 76 (1950): 609.
25. NA, Washington National Records Center, RG 185, The Panama Canal, 9-A-14, ICS memorandum of May 28, 1948, "Military Value of the Panama Canal, 1942-1946," 18 & 20, *New York Times,* November 10, 1945, VI,6.
26. Stimson Diary, entry for June 7, 1945.

10.

Saturday, December 6, 1941

Jon Bridgeman

John Toland argued that most of the mysteries of Pearl Harbor could be quite easily solved if we only knew what Roosevelt really did during the critical 24 hours prior to the attack.[1] Toland may or may not be right. This chapter attempts to trace in as great detail as possible the president's activities from noon on Saturday December 6, when Secretary of the Navy Frank Knox called to inform Roosevelt that two large Japanese convoys had been sighted entering the Gulf of Siam, until 1:35 P.M. on Sunday, when Knox again called him to report that the Japanese were bombing Pearl Harbor. The president spent most of his waking hours during that last day of peace in a final effort to head off war by means of personal diplomacy.

Whether the president was using his diplomatic efforts as a smokescreen to cover up some deep-laid plot, as the conspiracy buffs insist, or was making a sincere effort to preserve the peace, as the court historians claim, can probably never be established with absolute certainty. It can be asserted with considerable confidence, however, that Roosevelt had two very good reasons for not wanting a war with Japan. First and most important, the president knew that in December 1941 the American armed forces in the Pacific were not ready for a war with Japan. The chief of naval operations, Admiral Harold Stark, and the army chief of staff, General George C. Marshall, had made no secret of the fact that they needed several more weeks at least before they could undertake a war with any degree of confidence. Second, since Roosevelt and his War Council—an informal group consisting of Secretary of State Cordell Hull, Secretary of War Henry Stimson, and Knox, as well as Marshall and Stark—were committed to the proposition that Nazi Germany was the principal danger to the security of the United States, while Japan was at most a second-line threat, it followed that anything that detracted from defeating Germany was a danger to the overall security of the nation.

"Germany first" was a recurrent theme in all American grand strategic planning, from Stark's Plan Dog of November 1940 and the ABC-1 agreement with the British in March 1941 to the American war plan Rainbow Five and the Victory Plan.[2] This is not to suggest that Roosevelt was willing to pay any price to appease the Japanese, but he was willing to consider the possibility of some modest concessions to preserve peace in the Pacific, concessions he surely would not have been willing to extend to Hitler's Germany.

Roosevelt's actions during this final phase of the crisis, when viewed in a larger perspective, are what common sense tells us a leader would do in such circumstances. Each successive move he made during those 24 hours seems to be consistent with the "official" version of the Pearl Harbor disaster, which finds the president "not guilty" of any wrongdoing in respect to the attack. But if we examine the president's day in greater detail, some of the clarity dissolves. There are hints of incoherence, irrationality, and obscurity. Does this murkiness suggest that there is some deeper truth we are missing in accepting the commonsensical interpretation of the president's actions and motives? Or does it only reveal the commonplace—that if any highly contentious historical event is examined in great enough detail, it is likely to dissolve into a muddle?

We may well start our consideration of the last 24 hours of peace by examining the account of the president's day as given out by his Press Office:

> The President stayed over at the White House yesterday, vetoed any ideas his secretaries had about official appointments and went to work in the comparative privacy and quiet of the upstairs study. After a slight huddle with his staff of aides, the President shooed them, rang for private secretary and right-hand lady, Grace Tully. In front of him was a formidable stack of papers representing a little work to be cleaned up.
>
> After time out for lunch, the President did some phoning, kept an eye and ear bent toward the Pacific, did some checking on lend-lease and then went back to the barely dented mountain of paper work. The

> executive office staff, convinced that the lid was on for keeps, began filtering outward, Christmas-shopping bound. The President and Grace Tully continued to dig away at the week-long accumulation of correspondence, memos to be answered, reports crying for opinions. Midafternoon someone suggested a little air and a ride in the country but the boss had made up his mind, shook his head and continued to pull off layers of the paper tower.
>
> Knocking off before dinner, the President went to his room, climbed into a dinner jacket for the first company dinner the Roosevelts have had in a long time. A handful of friends, whose viewpoints as well as company Host Roosevelt has missed, dined quietly in the small dining room, saw a movie in the upstairs sitting room afterward.
>
> Today (that is Sunday, December 7) the President has promised, somewhat vaguely, to take it easy; get in an afternoon snooze and a drive in the Virginia countryside. Personal friends are due for a small, informal supper this evening. [3]

Thus the White House press office described the president's activities on Saturday and his plans for Sunday. It is a curious document in that most of the information in it, while not actually wrong, although some of it is, is tilted in such a way that a cynic might think it was deliberately designed to deceive. That being the case, one might legitimately ask whether the president's press secretary, Steve Early, or the president himself had something he wanted to hide and, if so, what? Just what did the president do and say from Saturday to Sunday up to the time of the attack? Considering that we are dealing with the last 24 hours before the United States was plunged into war, the documentary record is rather thinner than one would have expected. The White House telephone logs for the day are missing;[4] the appointment book is incomplete;[5] there is often no evidence at what time the President saw various documents;[6] few of those who saw the President that day left a written record; and Roosevelt himself, as was his custom, kept no notes of any kind on the conversations he had. There are lacunae; there is contradictory evidence; there are frustrating instances when the witness stops recording just as the story is getting interesting; there are the occasional statements that hang in the air because we do not know the context in which they were made, but for all that the president's actions can be followed reasonably closely. For the routine aspects of the day we have assumed that, if there is no compelling reason to doubt that the normal routine was not maintained, it probably was.

In January 1941, *Life* commissioned a well-known New York writer, Geoffrey Heilman, to prepare a piece on a typical presidential day.[7] Heilman began his article by pointing out that the president was a man of well-established habits and that his daily routine was distinguished by "a continuing consistency that is rivaled by few men." That judgment is amply borne out by the memoirs and comments of many White House insiders. Based on Heilman's account, we have assumed that the president arose that Saturday morning at about 9:00 A.M. as was his custom, that he was served breakfast in bed—soft boiled eggs, ham or bacon, coffee, toast and fruit juice, and three cigarettes—and that while eating FDR glanced at a selection of the morning press including, of course, the *New York Times*. The *Times* of December 6 took a guardedly hopeful view of the crisis in the Pacific: "an impression prevailed in diplomatic circles that something approaching a status quo may have been reached temporarily that might permit the exploratory conversations to continue with less disturbance," according to Bertram Hulen, a *Times* Washington correspondent, on December 6.[8]

As soon as it was known that the president was awake, his personal staff began to gather in his bedroom on the second floor of the White House. Early was there, as was the appointment secretary, General Edwin "Pa" Watson, and the president's physician, Admiral Ross McIntire. Watson customarily began the proceedings by telling the president a joke or two, setting the tone for the conference. Amid much chaff and lighthearted banter two bits of business were always transacted: the doctor inevitably asked his patient how he felt—and almost always got the same answer, "Just fine," although on this day Roosevelt's sinuses were bothering him—and Watson briefed the "Boss" on any appointments, meetings, et cetera, that were on the docket; this is the "slight huddle with his staff of aides" referred to in the press release quoted above. As soon as the last of the staff left, the president's valet, Chief Petty Officer Arthur Prettyman, arrived and assisted his charge in dressing; after which Prettyman wheeled the president to his office and settled him at his desk. On this Saturday, Roosevelt chose to work in the relative privacy of his study located next door to his bedroom. The time was about 10:00 A.M.

Early, in the meantime, had gone to the press room to give the president's schedule out to the reporters gathered there. On December 6, Early told the assembled press that since the president had no appointments scheduled and planned to do nothing more exciting than trying to catch up on some routine paperwork, they might as well spend their time Christmas shopping. At just about the time Early was giving out this information, the first of the president's appointments, Justice William O. Douglas, was being shown into FDR's study.

The appointment book indicates that Douglas was with the president for an hour, which would suggest that the call was something more than a formality, routine calls being generally limited to 15 minutes. There is no evidence to indicate what the two men talked about. Politics and the Court are the best guesses, and it is unlikely that the crisis in the Far East was on the agenda. At 11:15 A.M., the director of the budget, Harold Smith, arrived to keep Roosevelt's second and last scheduled appointment that day. In this case we do have some indication of what transpired during the meeting because Smith kept a daybook. [9] In it he noted two specific matters upon which the president asked him to take action. First, the president told Smith that he wanted the number of Marine Corps trainees inducted during the next fiscal year to be cut from 40,000 to 20,000 because, as he explained, plans were being formulated to replace Marine guards at naval yards and stations with special security guards, thus releasing a substantial number of Marines for more serious purposes. All very reasonable, but to cut back the Marine Corps for any purpose whatsoever just 24 hours before the bombs rained down on Pearl Harbor does seem a bit strange.

Next, the president discussed with Smith a plan he was working on that would require each young man serving in the National Youth Administration upon finishing his stint to spend a year doing either conservation work or serving in the military. In reference to this proposal, Roosevelt asked Smith to talk with Lyndon Johnson—then, of course, a congressman from Texas—about a plan he had to combine the NYA with some other youth agencies. "Report back to me on Monday about what you and Lyndon Johnson agree to," the president said.

At this point in the conference, the president took a call from Frank Knox. When FDR hung up, he turned to Smith and, according to Smith's account, told him first that large Japanese convoys were moving into the southern Pacific; second, that the Japanese explanation of those convoys had just come in and was unsatisfactory, barely an acknowledgment of the president's inquiry; and finally, that he was going to send a message to Emperor Hirohito but was not optimistic about the chances of preserving peace in the Pacific. "We might soon be at war with Japan," said the president. Either Smith misheard or misremembered what Roosevelt said or the president made some very strange remarks indeed.

First the convoys. In this instance, the president's remarks as recorded by Smith are generally in accord with the historical record. Early on Wednesday morning, December 4, late Tuesday afternoon Washington time, four regiments of Japanese assault troops on Hainan Island boarded 19 transports and set sail for the south escorted by the light cruiser *Sendai* and 12 destroyers. Twenty hours after this convoy had left Hainan, a second convoy consisting of seven transports covered by a light cruiser and four destroyers left Saigon.

This second formation took a position some 50 miles in advance of the Hainan convoy. As each convoy in turn reached a point about 80 miles to the south of Cape Cambodia, the southernmost point of Indochina, it turned to the west and headed into the Gulf of Siam on a course of 2700. Their first objective was a rendezvous point in the geographic center of the gulf, which they were to reach on Sunday morning (Saturday evening in Washington). At the rendezvous point, the 26 transports and their escorts (joined by two additional transports coming from Phu Quoc Island and carrying air personnel) were to split up into six different task groups and proceed to assigned landing beaches on the coast of Thailand and Malaya. At about noon Saturday (Singapore time; midnight in Washington), the lead convoy had already doubled the cape and was heading directly for the rendezvous point on a course of 310; the second larger convoy was still 50 miles from the turning point.

At 12:12 P.M. (Singapore time), a Hudson reconnaissance aircraft flying out of an airfield at Kota Bharu, piloted by a Lieutenant J. C. Ramshaw of the Royal Australian Air Force, sighted the first of these convoys. He radioed to his base that he had in sight a small convoy consisting of three transports, covered by three small naval vessels that he identified as minelayers and minesweepers. He estimated that the ships were 185 miles from Kota Bharu bearing 020, on a course of 340, and proceeding at slow speed. Insofar as the course, speed, and location of the force, Ramshaw's report was reasonably accurate, but he was a bit off as to the makeup of the convoy. He made it out to be three transports rather than six; three small escorts rather than a cruiser and four destroyers. About a quarter of an hour later, Ramshaw reported a second, much larger convoy made up of 22 transports covered by a battleship, five cruisers, and seven destroyers. He estimated the course of this convoy as 2700, speed slow, and he located it at a point about 80 miles south of Cape Cambodia.

Ramshaw was a good observer. Again he got the position, course, and speed about right, and though he overestimated the type of ships in the escort force, he had the numbers right and his estimate of 22 transports was off by only three—a good piece of work considering the fact that he was sighted by the Japanese, who launched a seaplane to drive him off, obliging him to scurry for cover into a nearby cloud bank. A few minutes after Ramshaw sighted the second convoy, a Hudson searching the next sector to the right, commanded by a Lieutenant J. G. Emerton, reported seeing a "comparably large" convoy to the east of the one Ramshaw had sighted.

After making their sightings, Ramshaw and Emerton headed back to Kota Bharu, where they landed sometime between 2:30 and 3:00 P.M. (about three o'clock in the morning in Washington) and were debriefed. The intelligence officers at Kota Bharu believed, rightly as it turned out, that Ramshaw and Emerton had in fact sighted the same convoy. Upon the completion of the debriefing, Kota Bharu sent on to Singapore the report of the sightings and their analysis of it. The Singapore intelligence officers, for no apparent reason, decided that there were indeed two very large convoys entering the Gulf of Siam in addition to one small one.

It was this evaluation that the commander of the British forces in the Far East, Air Marshal Sir Robert Brooke-Popham, sent on to the chiefs of staff in London, as well as to Admiral Tom Philips in the Philippines. Earlier in the week, Philips had arrived in Singapore with Force X, consisting of the HMS *Prince of Wales,* HMS *Repulse,* and four destroyers. On Friday, Philips had flown off to Manila to confer with his American counterpart, Admiral Thomas Hart. The two men were in a meeting when Philips received the news of the convoys. The conference was brought to an abrupt end and Philips left almost at once by flying boat for Singapore. Hart, in turn, radioed the news of the sightings to the Chief of Naval Operations, Admiral Stark, with Admiral Husband E. Kimmel as an information addressee. The message read:

> Report by CinC China "25 ship convoy with escort of 6 cruisers and 10 DD's Lat 08-00 N, 106-00 East at 0316 GMT today. Convoy of 10 ships with two cruisers and 10 destroyers 07-40 North, 106-20 East two hours later. All on course west. Three additional ships 07-51 north 105 East at 0442. Course 310. This indicates all forces will make for Kontron." Sighted by my scouting force anchored Camranh Bay 30 ships and one large cruiser. [10]

While it is true that the times of sighting and makeup of the convoys given in this message seem to be the product of some imaginative reworking of the raw data received, nevertheless the message correctly conveyed the larger truth: large Japanese forces were moving into the Gulf of Siam, objective unknown, but pretty obviously up to no good. The only odd part of the message is the totally unsupported assumption that the Japanese ships were heading for Kohtron, an anchorage in southern French Indochina. If this was indeed the destination of the convoys, their appearance in the Gulf would have been serious but not immediately threatening. The arrival of Japanese troops at Kohtron there would not lead to an immediate crisis since they would not have violated any international frontier.

Hart's message was the one that Knox passed on to FDR while he was meeting with Smith. Knox had received it shortly after he arrived at his desk that morning and it was the subject of discussion at the conference he held every morning with his top naval advisors at 11:00 A.M. [11] He asked the admirals bluntly whether this new move on the part of the Japanese suggested that they were about to take on the Americans. Admiral Richmond Kelly Turner, speaking for the assembled brass, assured the secretary that the Japanese were not yet strong enough to challenge the Americans. After the meeting broke up, Knox called Roosevelt and gave him the gist of the Hart message. Just why no one had thought to call the president before is baffling, but this certainly seems to be the case since Smith's notes clearly imply that Roosevelt knew nothing of the convoys before he received Knox's call.

According to Smith's account, the president, after telling him about the convoys, said that the Japanese explanation of the movement of these ships had just come in and it was unsatisfactory. This makes no sense at all. The Japanese never gave any explanation for these convoys and none was ever asked for. Almost surely, FDR was referring to a Japanese note given to Hull on Friday explaining why they were massing troops in southern French Indochina. This note was considered by the Americans to be "unsatisfactory," as Roosevelt said, but by no stretch of the imagination could one say it had "just come in." Roosevelt had seen it Friday morning and the text had been released to the press later that day so it could appear in the Saturday morning papers. Quite obviously, either Roosevelt was confused, which seems unlikely, or Smith misheard the president, which is less unlikely but still odd.

Roosevelt's third comment to Smith was that the appearance of the convoys might well lead to war. Interestingly enough, no one else who saw the message that day drew this conclusion. After all, it was not self-evident why the appearance of Japanese convoys in the Gulf of Siam presented any clear and present danger of war for the United States. After all, the Japanese ships were hundreds of miles away from the nearest American territory and they were moving away from it. Nothing in Hart's message suggested that he thought the Japanese were about to attack the Philippines, nor did Brooke-Popham take that view. The American admirals meeting with Knox that morning concurred. True, General Marshall, unlike the navy leaders who thought that the appearance of the convoys was not a direct threat to the United States and required no action on their part, did take some action, but what he did strongly suggested that he did not believe there was any immediate danger of war that Saturday (emphasis should be placed on "immediate" meaning in the next two or three weeks—in the longer view, of course, the convoys were surely a threat to peace in the Far East).

Marshall discussed Hart's report with Stimson and the two men concluded that the proper response was to continue and, if possible, accelerate the flow of reinforcements to the Philippines.[12] They rejected any idea of recalling the ships then on the high seas carrying men and materials to MacArthur. Since these ships were all ten days or more from their destination, Marshall and Stimson, by implication at least, apparently were operating on the assumption that war was unlikely to break out before Christmas. Later that day, Marshall phoned General H. H. Arnold, who happened to be on the West Coast, and ordered him to get a flight of B-17s at Hamilton Field near San Francisco into the air as soon as possible. [13] These planes were the next installment in a buildup of a heavy bomber force in the Philippines. To get to their final destination, the Flying Fortresses had to fly ten days or more hopping from island to island—Oahu, Midway, Wake, New Guinea, northern Australia, and finally Manila—across the Pacific. Again this order implies that Marshall did not believe war would break out before the planes arrived.

Nothing in the recorded statements or the actions of the highest military leadership of the United States indicate that Stimson, Marshall, Knox, or Stark thought that the appearance of the two convoys in the Gulf of Siam meant war was likely in the near term, say two to three weeks. For what it is worth, no one thought it necessary or appropriate to inform the president about what was being done in the Munitions Building and the Navy Department, nor did the White House make any inquiries.

Is there any reason that the President would have taken a more alarmist view of the convoys than his top military advisors? The answer is quite simply yes. Roosevelt knew something that Marshall, Stark, Stimson, and Knox did not. On Thursday night, he had met secretly with the British ambassador, Lord Halifax, and assured him that should the British find themselves at war with Japan they could count on American military support. And the president went even further, promising that if the British launched a "forestalling" attack into neutral Thailand to block a Japanese landing at the Isthmus of Kra, he would stand foursquare behind them.

It is worth reflecting for a moment just what the implications of the president's commitment were. He had committed the United States to going to war against Japan if the British invaded neutral Thailand—the Thais incidentally had threatened to fight back if their frontier was violated—in order to defend their colonial empire in the Far East. Such a commitment may have been strategically sound, but it was also politically reckless and constitutionally suspect. If Roosevelt's commitment to the British ever got into the hands of Charles Lindbergh, Burton Wheeler, Hiram Johnson, and the rest of the big guns of the America First Committee, they would have had a field day accusing him of going to war to save the British Empire by "pulling England's chestnuts out of the fire," in the phrase of the day. So when FDR said to Smith that "we might soon be at war," he was not speaking just for effect. He knew that the appearance of the convoys meant just that: The United States could easily be at war in a matter of hours if the convoys held their course. Once the Japanese landed at the Isthmus of Kra, Roosevelt would either have to support the British with armed measures or go back on a solemn pledge he had made to Churchill not once but three times in the preceding week. [14] It was because the members of the War Council had not an inkling of this commitment that they interpreted the sighting of the convoys in a less alarmist way than did their commander in chief.

Finally, Roosevelt told Smith that he proposed to send a message to the emperor in a last-ditch effort to avoid a conflict in the Pacific. The idea of communicating directly with the emperor had been in Roosevelt's mind for several weeks, but every time he brought it up, his War Council raised so many objections that he had invariably dropped the idea. Their objections were three: first, if the message was nothing more than a pious appeal to the Emperor, as a peace-loving man, to stop his nation's headlong plunge toward war, it would be a waste of time. Second, they argued that if the message was to have chance of success it would have to contain a substantive proposal, but what would it be? After six months of hard bargaining, there simply were no more proposals left to be made. All had been tried and all found wanting. "We keep going around and around in the same circle," as Hull said. Third, they rejected any idea that the message contain a warning because, in the view of the State Department experts, it was deemed diplomatically inappropriate to "warn" an emperor. No one but FDR thought much of the idea of a direct appeal to the Mikado,and even he had not thought enough of it to push the proposal very hard. Nevertheless, on this Saturday Roosevelt's first inclination on hearing of the convoys was to revert back to the idea of a direct appeal to the emperor.

The President had lunch at 1:00 P.M. and started drafting his message to the emperor at about 2:00 P.M. [15] For the next five hours he worked on the message. First, he requested and received a draft from the State Department but rejected it and wrote out his own version. He dictated it to Grace Tully and sent it to Hull for corrections; saw the Australian Minister R. G. Casey and the British ambassador, Lord Halifax. At about 7:00 P.M., FDR had finished his work and dressed for dinner. While he was composing his draft he received several messages, that shaped his thinking. Early in the afternoon, he received a message from the American ambassador in London, John Winant. It read:

> TRIPLE PRIORITY AND MOST URGENT 5918. December 6, 4 P.M. (Received 10:40 A.M.) PERSONAL AND SECRET TO THE SECRETARY AND THE PRESIDENT
>
> British Admiralty reports that at 3 A.M. London time this morning two parties seen off Cambodia point, sailing slowly westward toward Kra 14 hours distant in time. First party 25 transports, 6 cruisers, 10 destroyers. Second party 10 transports 2 cruisers, 10 destroyers. [16]

The Pearl Harbor Investigation Minority Report notes: "State Department file copy of this message bears stamp 'Sent to President' but does not indicate hour." Winant's assertion that the two big convoys were heading for Kra, while literally true—the large convoys when sighted were on a course of 2700 and had they continued on that course they would have been off the isthmus in a few hours—was at sharp variance with the assumption that Singapore intelligence had made as to their probable destination, that is, "this indicates all forces will make for Kohtron." The chiefs of staff in London, after discussing Brooke-Popham's message at length, concluded that the convoys might be headed for Kohtron or Kra or might be "cruising round as a bluff." [17] Just where Winant might have gotten the impression that the British chiefs thought the Japanese were on the way to Kra is not known, but if Winant's assumption had in fact been right and Kra was the destination, then Roosevelt's blank check to the British given Thursday night might well have been presented for cash much sooner than even the President had expected.

In midafternoon a second message was received from Winant:

> TRIPLE PRIORITY AND MOST URGENT 5923, December 6, 7:00 P.M. (received at 3:05 P.M.) PERSONAL AND SECRET FOR THE SECRETARY
>
> Again from Cadogan. Admiralty conference on information just forwarded, Cadogan attending. They are uncertain as to whether destination of parties is Kra or Bangkok. Latter would not be reached before Monday.
>
> Note a discrepancy in time reported by me and time reported in our naval despatch, latter stating 3 A.M. Greenwich time, my dispatch as given me 3 A.M. London time. Believe former correct.
>
> British feel pressed for time in relation to guaranteeing support Thailand fearing Japan might force them to invite invasion on pretext invasion before British have opportunity to guarantee support but wanting to carry out President's wishes in message transmitted by Welles to Halifax.
>
> Leaving to spend evening with Eden in order to go over with him your number 5682, December 5 although I have previously pressed on him each of the points you outlined prior to reception your message with the exception of paragraph seven which I agree is not clear and which I will clear up with him this evening. I want you to know that I had nothing to do with the insertion of the reference to the I. L. O. I am having lunch

> with the Prime Minister tomorrow at his usual place in the country and will be constantly in contact with the Embassy over private wires in case you wish to communicate with me.[18]

Although this message was not addressed to the president, it would seem quite likely that Hull informed FDR of its contents in the course of the afternoon. Several comments are in order. By adding Bangkok as a possible destination Winant somewhat defused the very alarming impact of his 10:40 A.M. message. Whereas a landing at Kra could trigger a British forestalling attack, and this in turn would obligate Roosevelt to give military support to the British, a landing at Bangkok was quite another matter. Whether the British would consider a Japanese landing there a casus belli or not is debatable, but the American military hierarchy had agreed some weeks before that any Japanese incursion into Thailand that did not go west of 100 degrees East and/or south of 10 degrees North—a somewhat complex formula which meant, in essence, if they did not land at the Isthmus of Kra—would not threaten any vital American interests. As for Winant's comment on the time discrepancy, he apparently did not realize that Greenwich mean time and London time are in fact the same. The most interesting part of the message is his cryptic comment about the "President's wishes in message transmitted by Welles to Halifax."[19] Under oath before the Pearl Harbor Investigating Committee, Sumner Welles professed to have no memory at all as to what this comment might refer. A search in the State Department files failed to turn up any such message. The investigators, particularly those unfavorably disposed to FDR, were suspicious that there was some sculduggery here but they could not divine what it was. With the publication of the Australian documents covering this period, some light has been shed on the mystery. We now know that Roosevelt told Welles on Tuesday to inform Halifax that when he had promised the British support in the event they became involved in a war with Japanese, he had meant military support. This apparently is the message referred to, although it is still not known what the president's "wishes" were.

Besides the two Winant messages, Roosevelt also received sometime that same afternoon a message that Churchill had given to W. Averell Harriman to be relayed to Harry Hopkins for transmittal to the president. (Why this complex form of delivery was used is not explained. Churchill routinely sent messages directly to the president.)

> The President should be informed of Churchill's belief that in the event of aggression by the Japanese it would be the policy of the British to postpone taking any action—even though this delay might involve some military sacrifice—until the President has taken such action as, under the

> circumstances, he considers best. Then Churchill will act "not within the hour, but within the minute." I am seeing him again tomorrow. Let me know if there is anything special you want me to ask. [20]

In effect, Churchill was saying: We (the British) will not launch our planned "forestalling" attack into Thailand, codenamed Operation Matador, unless or until the president acts, that is to say, he sends a warning to the Japanese that if they land at the isthmus the United States will respond militarily. Why would Churchill have sent this message? Not to put too fine a point on it, the fact is he did not completely trust the president, knowing from experience that FDR sometimes promised more than he could deliver. Thus Churchill, despite the extremely explicit nature of Roosevelt's promises given on Tuesday to Halifax, confirmed by Welles that same day and repeated on Thursday, was concerned that Roosevelt might not be as good as his word. We know now, but Roosevelt did not know then, that Churchill's implied threat to postpone Matador until the Americans acted was empty. On Friday, Churchill had authorized Brooke-Popham to execute Matador if and when he deemed appropriate without further reference to London, explaining that London now had absolute assurances of American military support. [21] Having given this authorization to Brooke-Popham, Churchill in effect washed his hands of Matador and for all he knew when he was talking to Harriman, Brooke-Popham might have already given the order for his troops to move across the Thai frontier.

These three messages Roosevelt almost surely had in hand that afternoon, or at least he knew of their contents. It is probably also the case that at about 4:00 P.M. his naval aide, Captain John R. Beardall, told him that the Japanese reply to the American Ten Point Proposal of November 26 was then being deciphered and would be delivered to him sometime that evening.[22] Whether Beardall also told him of the arrival of the so-called Pilot Message cannot be established. [23] That message, which was received by the army codebreakers at 12:05, alerted Nomura and Kurusu that an extremely important message would be sent to them shortly, that it was in 14 parts, that it was to be handled with the greatest of care, and that it was to be delivered only upon receipt of explicit orders from Tokyo to do so. The Pearl Harbor Committee was never able to ascertain whether or not the Pilot Message was delivered to Roosevelt, or anyone else for that matter, on Saturday afternoon. One might think that such a question could be easily answered by simply consulting the relevant logs, but surprisingly enough, there was no log showing at what time Japanese intercepts were deciphered, translated, or delivered.

Thus as Roosevelt was drafting his message to the emperor, he had in hand or received the following information: 1) Two large convoys had entered the Gulf of Siam in the early hours of Saturday morning (Washington time) and were heading for either Kohtron, Kra, or Bangkok. If they were headed for Kra or Kohtron, they could be at their destination as early as midafternoon, that is, at the same time the President was drafting his message to the emperor. If, on the other hand, their destination was Bangkok, they would arrive there at the earliest Sunday night (Washington time). 2) Churchill threatened to do nothing even if the Japanese landed at the isthmus unless or until the president sent a warning to the Japanese. 3) The Japanese answer to the American Ten-Point Proposal was coming that afternoon.

As a first step in preparing the message to the emperor, Roosevelt asked Hull to send him a draft embodying a proposal for a modus vivendi, or a "standstill agreement."[24] This is a strange request because on November 26 the president, with the concurrence of his War Council, had abandoned completely any idea of offering the Japanese a "standstill" proposal and instead had decided to give Nomura and Kurusu the Ten Point Proposal. Hull, who must have been amazed to find that the president was intending to resurrect the idea of a modus vivendi, nevertheless sent the requested draft to the White House without comment. The critical paragraph of the State Department draft read:

> I propose now the conclusion of a temporary arrangement which would envisage cessation of hostilities for a period of ninety days between Japan and China and an undertaking by each of the Governments most concerned in the Pacific area to refrain from any movement or use of armed force against any of the other parties during the period of the temporary arrangement. If the Japanese Government is favorably disposed toward conclusion of such an arrangement I would be glad promptly to approach the other Governments concerned with a view to obtain their assent and commitment.[25]

The draft went on to propose that the Japanese reduce their troop strength in Indochina to the levels that prevailed on July 26. In return, the Americans would undertake to "suggest" that Japan and China "enter into negotiations."

Sometime after Roosevelt received the State Department draft, he thought better of the idea of the modus vivendi and decided instead to make the thrust of his message a veiled warning. The president's decision was somehow known outside the White House almost at once by the most interested parties, the British and Australians. At 3:37 P.M., the Australian minister, Mr. R. G. Casey, sent a message to his home government reporting that he had just learned that Roosevelt was "working on his proposed message to the Japanese emperor. As I understand it this message will have some sting in it, but will not in itself constitute the 'warning.'"[26] Why did FDR change his mind? Perhaps the absurdity of calling for a standstill when the Japanese were already on the move influenced him. Or, more likely, he received the Harriman message with its implied threat that the British would sit on their hands unless he issued a warning. In any event, Roosevelt completely scrapped the State Department draft and worked up one of his own. He started by taking the opening and concluding portions of a draft dated November 29 and sandwiching between them some original thoughts of his own. As Casey said, this message had some sting to it. The key passage read:

> I am sure that Your Majesty will understand that the fear of all these peoples (in East Asia) is a legitimate fear in as much as it involves their peace and their national existence. I am sure that Your Majesty will understand why the people of the United States in such large numbers look askance at the establishment of military, naval and air bases manned and equipped so greatly as to constitute armed forces capable of measures of offense.
>
> It is clear that the continuation of such a situation is unthinkable. None of the peoples whom I have spoken of above can sit either indefinitely or permanently on a keg of dynamite. [27]

Just as Grace Tully was leaving for a cocktail party, she was summoned to the president's study, where he dictated his message to her for transcription. [28] When a smooth copy was ready Roosevelt sent it over to Hull in the State Department Building with a note reading: "Dear Cordell: Shoot this to Grew—think can go in gray code—saves time—I don't mind if it gets picked up." Before sending out the president's draft, Hull had it vetted by the chief of the Division of Far Eastern Affairs, who edited out a few words and phrases which, in his view, might tend to upset the Chinese. As most of the corrections were on the third page of the draft, this page was retyped. Before sending the corrected version to FDR, Hull called and told him of the changes. The revised version was then sent over to the White House with a note from Hull:

> There is attached your message to the Emperor of Japan with page three of the message amended to take care of the point with regard to which I spoke to you on the telephone. If you approve the draft as it now stands, we will see that it gets off to Grew at once.

Roosevelt sent the revised version back with a note reading: "C. H. OK—send the amended p. 3 to the British Ambassador & send a copy to me. FDR." [29]

At 8:00 P.M., the State Department sent a telegram to Grew alerting him that an important telegram "is now being encoded." An hour later the text itself was sent out with covering instructions that ordered Grew to communicate the contents to the emperor in such a way as seemed most appropriate to him and to do it at the earliest possible moment. Furthermore, Grew was told that the press was being informed that the president was dispatching a message to the emperor.

At the same time that the appeal to the emperor went out, Hull also sent a message to the ambassador in China that Roosevelt had drafted:

> In communicating copy of this message to Chiang Kai Shek, please state orally as from the President that the quoted message has already been sent by the President to the Emperor; that this message, as the situation now stands, would seem to represent very nearly the last diplomatic move that this Government can make toward causing Japan to desist from its present course; that if the slender chance of acceptance by Japan should materialize, a very effective measure would have been taken toward safeguarding the Burma Road; and that it is very much hoped that Chiang Kai Shek will not make or allow to be spread in Chinese Government circles adverse comment. [30]

This message, as it stands, is baffling. It is quite obviously an attempt to prevent Chiang from scuttling the standstill proposal, but that proposal had been scrapped several hours before. The message actually sent to the emperor was a warning, and there would be no reason to imagine that Chiang would have any objection to it. The only reasonable explanation is that Roosevelt had drafted this message while he was still toying with the modus vivendi idea and he forgot to tell Hull not to send it.

To summarize: The President learned of the appearance of the convoys and feared war was in the offing. The only possible course he could think of to avoid the war or, at least, put it off was to make a direct appeal to the emperor. His first inclination was to revive the modus vivendi or standstill idea, but for whatever reason he abandoned that and instead made the thrust of the message a warning.

As for the question of whom the president saw that afternoon while drafting his message, there are some problems. All members of his War Council testified under oath that they did not see the president on the afternoon of December 6, and only Hull said he talked to him on the telephone. The record confirms their testimony. So FDR operated without the advice of his War Council in deciding to make a direct appeal to the emperor. (Hull is not really an exception. Roosevelt consulted him only on matters of form, not content.) Of Roosevelt's inner circle, Grace Tully can be definitely placed in the White House that afternoon, and Hopkins may have been there.[31] Beardall did not have an office in the White House, working normally out of the Navy Department Building on Constitution Avenue, and probably was not there, but the evidence here is not conclusive. This much, however, can be established: besides Tully, and perhaps Hopkins, the president saw only two people that afternoon, Casey and Halifax—neither of them Americans—and it was to them that he revealed his innermost thoughts about the crisis and how he proposed to handle it. Casey saw the president sometime after he, Roosevelt, had completed his original draft of the message to the emperor (5:00 P.M. would be a good guess).[32] Sometime after Casey left, Halifax appeared. Since he telegraphed to London his report of his meeting with the president at 7:00 P.M., he must have arrived at the White House sometime between 6:00 and 6:30 P.M. and stayed for perhaps thirty minutes.

> I communicated this (Telegram Number 6729 thanking the President for his promise of support given Thursday night) to the President when I saw him this evening. He is sending message to the Emperor as in my immediately following telegram for delivery, by Japanese time, Sunday morning.
>
> If no answer has been received by Monday evening, Washington time, he will publish here.
>
> As at present advised, if no reply is made, or if answer is unsatisfactory, he will send warning note to the Japanese Government on Tuesday afternoon or evening, and suggested that we and Dutch should act similarly on Wednesday morning.
>
> All this time table is subject to speeding up if the Japanese move faster. The President does not think they will but Hull does.
>
> He told me the best information the United States could obtain was that the Japanese had about 105,000 troops in IndoChina, 30,000 in North and 75,000 in the South. These figures did not include numbers on troop transports that the President thought might be another 20,000 or 30,000.
>
> He told me that he thought seriously of possible Japanese threat to Rangoon from land or air. [33]

The visits of Casey and Halifax were not only not revealed to the press, but the evidence is overwhelming that no member of the War Council knew about them either. It does seem very odd indeed that the president of the United

States, believing the nation was on the verge of war, chose to make all his decisions in private and then reveal them to foreign diplomats.

At 6:30 P.M. or thereabouts, the president, having done all he could to head off the crisis, gave the impression to those who saw him that he felt he had done a good piece of work. His mood was relaxed, almost jocular. Eleanor Roosevelt had been spending the day with Judge Justine Wise Polier working on civilian defense problems. Before the judge left for the day, the first lady took her coworker in to see the president, who jovially said: "Well, Justine, this son of man has just sent his final message to the Son of God."

Normally the president ended his working day at about 4:00 P.M. and was then taken to the White House pool for a swim. This was a daily routine until the beginning of 1941, when the press of business had forced him to limit himself to three sessions in the pool per week. The swim was followed by a rubdown, a physical checkup, and a nap. Given the fact that Halifax could not have left much before 6:30 P.M. and the president had a dinner scheduled for 8:00 P.M., it seems unlikely that he had time for a swim or nap on this Saturday.

Shortly before 8:00 P.M., Mrs. Roosevelt brought the dinner guests to the president's study for a cocktail. Just before dinner was served, she escorted the guests down to the dining room slowly enough so there was time for the president to be taken down privately and seated before the guests made their way into the dining room. That night there were 34 at dinner, ranging from a visiting British admiral, Sir Wilfred French, to a White House aide, Lieutenant Wilkie A. Rambo. [34] In between, there were a number of Adamses who were relatives of the president (they were Delanos on the distaff side); two generals and their ladies; and two members of Donovan's organization—the president's son James and Conyers Read. Sometime before the main course was served an aide appeared and whispered something to the president, who immediately left the dinner without explanation. His departure mystified the guests—some thought he must have been indisposed—but the dinner went on, with Mrs. Roosevelt doing the honors as hostess.

What the guests did not know was that Roosevelt had just received word that the Japanese answer to the last American Proposal was about to be delivered. At about 8:00 P.M. the deciphering of the first 13 parts of the 14-part Japanese message was finished, but the last part had not yet been received. Though the message was incomplete, the head of Op-20-GZ, Commander Alwin Kramer, decided to go ahead and deliver what he had in hand without waiting for the missing part. Step one was to send six locked cases to his counterpart on the army side, Colonel Rufus Bratton, who was responsible for seeing that General Marshall, Secretary Stimson, and Secretary Hull received their copies. Bratton took the view that an incomplete message whose contents had already been heavily discounted—the Japanese had made no secret for some days past that they intended to reject the American proposal out of hand, or more accurately that they were contemptuous of it—did not warrant disturbing anyone unnecessarily on a Saturday evening.

Precisely what Bratton did that night was the subject of considerable investigative time and energy at the Pearl Harbor hearing, although very little was ever learned, but one fact stood out. None of the three men he was responsible for delivery to (Hull, Stimson, and Marshall) received their MAGIC pouch that night. Bratton left Hull's pouch with a State Department duty officer with strict instructions to get it to the secretary as soon as possible, but for whatever reason, Hull never received it. Neither did Stimson or Marshall. Why Marshall was left out was the subject of many hours of testimony, much of it muddled, but through the fog of words one fact stood out: Bratton never got the pouch to the chief of staff.

Kramer, in sharp contrast to Bratton, believed the Fourteen-Part Message to be of the highest importance, and he made every effort to see that the recipients not only got the document, but also were alerted to its extreme importance. Before leaving his office in the Navy Department, Kramer made a series of phone calls. First, he contacted his immediate superior, Admiral Theodore Wilkinson, head of the Office of Naval Communications, to inform him that the message was ready for delivery and to get formal permission to deliver. Next he called Admirals Stark, Royal Ingersoll, and Turner. As none of them were in, he canceled their names from the list. Next he called Secretary Knox, found him in, and told him he would be delivering an important message shortly. He did not call the White House since he knew that a duty officer was there awaiting his arrival. At about 9:00 P.M. Kramer, with his wife acting as his chauffeur, left the Navy Department Building for the five-minute drive to the White House. Kramer gave the sealed pouch to a Lieutenant Lester Schulz, telling him that the contents were of great importance and should be taken to the president at once. [35]

There followed one of the most memorable set pieces of the day. Schulz, who had been an aide for less than a week, was fortunate enough to witness a bit of actual history-in-the-making. Rather by chance the Pearl Harbor Committee learned that he was the duty officer that night and had a story to tell. He was duly called to testify in March 1946. Schulz, by this time a commander and executive officer of the battleship *Indiana*, said that Captain Beardall had told him at about 4:30 P.M. that he, Schulz, was to stay at his post in the White House—he had a small cubicle off the mail room—to await an important message that would be delivered by Commander Kramer. About 9:30 P.M. Kramer arrived and handed the pouch to Schulz. He was taken at once by an usher to the president's second floor study. Schulz unlocked the pouch, handed the contents to the president, stepped back, and awaited orders. As he was not dismissed, he heard quite by chance the reaction of FDR and Hopkins to the message.

The president read the message first and then handed it to Hopkins. When Hopkins finished, the president said, "This means war." Hopkins agreed with him and suggested the possibility of getting in the first blow. To this the president countered by saying, "No, we can't do that. We are a democracy and a peaceful people." He then raised his voice and said (Schulz testified he was sure these were Roosevelt's exact words), "But we have a good record." The gist of the conversation from that point on concerned French Southeast Asia, where the two men thought the fighting would start. Roosevelt mentioned sending a message to the emperor and Schulz recalled that he emphasized that the message was to the emperor himself and not the premier. Schulz also had the definite impression that the president did not expect anything to happen as soon as the next day. At some point in the conversation Roosevelt put a call in to Admiral Stark, but on learning that he was at the theater declined to have him paged for fear of causing public alarm. Roosevelt said or implied that he intended to talk to Stark later, after he returned to his quarters. [36]

Considering the fact that Schulz knew very little of what had happened that day at the White House, his account dovetails quite well with what we know now. The President told Halifax that he did not expect the Japanese to do anything for several days, and from the tenor of his conversation Schulz inferred the same thing. When the President talked with Halifax on Thursday evening, the two men agreed that the point of greatest danger was Southeast Asia—Thailand, Malaya, Burma, and the Dutch East Indies—and neither man even so much as mentioned Pearl Harbor. Schulz testified that he was certain Pearl Harbor was never mentioned by Roosevelt or Hopkins. As for the possibility of a preemptive strike, Stimson had brought that up a week before and Roosevelt had rejected it then as he rejected Hopkins's suggestion on Saturday night. The most interesting aspect of the scene is the president's assertion that "this means war."

No one else seeing the message that night interpreted it that way, partly because it was as yet incomplete and partly because it really did not contain anything new. Wilkinson thought it was only "diplomatic" and not of direct interest to the navy; Knox withheld judgment, ordering Kramer to bring the fourteenth part to him as soon as it was received. Bratton did not think it was necessary to get it to Marshall that night. And Stark, when he learned of it, took no action. Everyone assumed the Japanese would reject the Ten Point Proposal, and now they had. Why then would the confirmation of what everyone took to be the case lead the president to say, "This means war"? Did Roosevelt again, as was the case with the convoys, know something his War Council did not, and if so, what? In the case of the convoys, we can give a plausible answer, but in this case no obvious explanation is at hand. Is it possible that the president was talking just for effect? Possible, but not probable.

Schulz estimated he was in the president's study for 30 minutes. So at about 10:00 P.M., the president returned to his office with the pouch. His account, at this point, presents us with a minor problem. Schulz said that when he returned to his office, Kramer was waiting for him. He was sure this was the case because at that time he had no secure place to store the pouch overnight. Kramer quite explicitly said that as soon as he dropped off the pouch at the White House he proceeded on his way. At any rate, Schulz then called Beardall, who was having dinner with Wilkinson, reported that the president had received the material, and was given permission to go home.

It was now close to 10:00 P.M. Roosevelt and Hopkins were in the President's study, but what they talked about after Schulz left is forever lost in the mists of history. This much can be said with some assurance: The president made only one telephone call (all members of the War Council swore under oath that they did not talk with him that evening); he saw none of his top advisers; he asked for no further information from his intelligence services; he issued no orders of any kind or any warnings.

Beyond that negative evidence there is just one brief but tantalizing flash of light. Admiral Stark had testified under oath that he had no memory whatsoever about how he spent Saturday evening. Despite repeated proddings by various members of the committee, Stark failed to recall any detail of any kind about the evening. Then, as the hearings were coming to a close in 1946, a close friend of Admiral Stark, Captain H. D. Krick, reminded the admiral that they spent the evening together. Stark recommended that his friend give his story to the committee, which he did. It turns out that Captain Krick and his wife joined the Starks for dinner that night, and, after dining, the foursome proceeded to the theater to see *The Student Prince.* Upon returning to the admiral's quarters for a post-theater drink, Stark was informed by his servant that the president wanted him to call. Stark retired to his study for about ten minutes and, on rejoining his guests, said something to the effect that the situation in the Far East was serious but did not elaborate.[37]

If the president called Stark, is it possible that he called others? Is it even possible that he called a meeting of the War Council late that evening? There is a persistent rumor to this effect. [38] There is no evidence at all to confirm the story, but then there is no evidence either that it did not take place. The probabilities are, however, strongly against it. If Roosevelt avoided his War

Council that afternoon, and he seemed to be doing just that, why would he want to see them that evening? He did not think "the balloon was going up" in the next few days, and he was scheduled to see them the next afternoon anyway, so what would be the point of a meeting Saturday night?

By midnight or so, the president retired, as was his wont. If, as his detractors insist, he knew that a Japanese task force was then some 500 miles north of Oahu, then he must have slept well knowing that his deep-laid plot had succeeded; not even his closest friends and advisors had penetrated his plan to bring the United States into the war by sacrificing the fleet at Pearl Harbor.

From the time Roosevelt finished talking to Admiral Stark (about 11:00 P.M. EST) until midmorning the next day, the president disappeared from the historical scene. This is natural enough—even great world leaders have to eat and sleep. There is no reason to think that this was not how Roosevelt spent those hours. There is no evidence that he called anybody or received any calls; or that he received or sent any messages; or that he saw anyone from the time he retired until he awoke the next morning. During these 12 hours when the president was off the stage the crisis proceeded on apace.

In Singapore, the president's night coincided with the afternoon and evening of December 7, 1941. That morning, Brooke-Popham had decided against launching Operation Matador. For one thing, it would require 36 hours of lead time and he was not sure that much time would be granted to him. More importantly, he did not want to take the responsibility for initiating a war.

As the British forces in Malaya were on full alert, Brooke-Popham spent the day waiting for some news about the convoys, which since their initial sighting 24 hours before had disappeared from view. A number of reconnaissance flights had been sent out, but as the Gulf of Siam was under a blanket of heavy clouds, none of them had been able to regain contact with the Japanese ships. Early that morning a long-range PBY had taken off from Seletar but had not been heard from for several hours. We know now, but the British did not know then, that the PBY had been shot down by the Japanese before its crew was able to use their radio to alert Singapore that it was under attack. Finally in the late afternoon, a Hudson from Kota Bharu reported spotting a Japanese transport heading south off the coast of the Isthmus of Kra, its decks crowded with troops in khaki.

Brooke-Popham received this news calmly enough and waited for the Japanese to make the first overt move. He did not inform London of the sighting, and of course, Washington remained completely in the dark. The only communication received that night from the Far East was a telegram from Hart reporting that he had learned from an American liaison officer in Singapore that Roosevelt had given the British absolute assurances of support in the event they found themselves at war with Japan.[39] As this was the first Hart had heard of such assurances, he quite reasonably asked for clarification from his superiors in Washington.

When the president retired at about midnight, it was still early evening at Pearl Harbor. Admiral Kimmel had spent an anxious day conferring with his staff about what to do with the fleet now that war appeared to be imminent in the Far East—this being his interpretation of the Hart message reporting the appearance of the Japanese ships heading into the Gulf of Siam. The issue was whether to sortie the fleet or not. Generally speaking, when hostilities are about to commence, it is better to have a fleet at sea than in a harbor, particularly one so crowded and with such a narrow entrance as Pearl Harbor.

Kimmel's first instinct on receiving the Hart message was to take the fleet to sea, but his staff argued against any precipitous action. They pointed out that to cancel shore leave and make an emergency sortie on a Saturday afternoon would surely trigger wild rumors and panic and that was just what Washington wanted to avoid. Furthermore, fuel was always a problem and a sortie before hostilities commenced would drawn down vital fuel supplies, which would be needed when the shooting actually started. Finally, there was the fact that with all the carriers at sea, if the battleships went out they would be without air cover in waters known to be infested with Japanese submarines. These were weighty arguments and they convinced Kimmel to sit tight and wait events out.

Uncharacteristically, Kimmel had agreed to attend a dinner party that night of all nights. He retired early because he had a golfing date the next morning with his army counterpart, General Walter C. Short. Kimmel's decision to leave the fleet in harbor was made without knowing that the first 13 parts of the Japanese answer to the last American proposal was then known in Washington, although there is no reason to think he would have acted any differently if he had known of the message. His decision to leave the fleet at Pearl Harbor was not communicated to his superiors in Washington, nor did they make any inquiries concerning the whereabouts of the fleet. Both parties agreed that it was his responsibility and his alone.

In the Old Munitions Building and the Navy Department all was quiet on the night of December 6-7, 1941. The fourteenth and final part of the Japanese final message arrived at 4:18 A.M. EST and was decrypted and ready for distribution by 7:30 A.M. (as it was in English it required no translation). The duty officer saw no reason that this message should not be handled in a routine fashion and it was. A little later, another message came in from Bainbridge. It, too, was broken out by 7:30 A.M., but since it was in Japanese, it was sent to the Army translators who did not work on it until after the start of the daytime shift at 8:00 A.M. Roosevelt knew nothing of either of these messages until midmorning nor did any member of the War Council.

The president arose at about 9:00 A.M., had his usual breakfast, and looked at a sampling of the morning press. There is reason to believe that no members of his inner circle were present until somewhat later in the morning. He was apparently still lounging in bed at 10:00 A.M. when Captain Beardall was shown into the presidential bedroom to deliver this latest MAGIC, which included the fourteenth part of the Japanese message. [40] The president read the final part with its ominous last sentence: "The Japanese Government regrets to have to notify hereby the American Government that in view of the attitude of the American Government it cannot but consider that it is impossible to reach an agreement through further negotiations." [41] After Roosevelt read the document, he commented that he assumed this meant that the Japanese were breaking diplomatic relations. One cannot help but be struck by the fact that on seeing the first 13 parts Roosevelt said, "This means war," while on seeing the last and much more inflammatory part he thought it meant only a break in diplomatic relations.

When Kramer returned to the Navy Department at 10:20 A.M. from delivering the fourteenth part, he found waiting for him the just-completed army translation of the One O'Clock Message. It was only 31 words long and on the surface at least seemed a routine message. It read: "Will the Ambassador please submit to the United States Government (if possible the Secretary of State) our reply to the United States at 1:00 P.M. on the 7th, your time." [42] To Kramer, however, the One O'Clock Message was anything but routine. The delivery of an important diplomatic message on a Sunday was unusual enough and to give a precise time for delivery even more so. Kramer automatically calculated that 1:00 P.M. EST would be shortly after dawn in Hawaii and two or three hours before first light in Manila. He drew no particular conclusion from this calculation, but he did assume that the Japanese planned to take some military action at or about 1:00 P.M. EST. In great haste, Kramer made up the delivery pouches and half ran and half walked first to Stark's office and then to the White House and the State Department. Every time he handed over a pouch, he pointed out the possible significance of the 1:00 P.M. delivery time. Marshall, who had been out riding and therefore could not be immediately contacted when the One O'Clock Message first came in, arrived at his office at 11:25 A.M., read quickly through the accumulated MAGIC and decided at once to send a warning to all army commanders in the Pacific to be on the qui vive. After some hesitation, Stark agreed to join Marshall in sending this warning.

All witnesses agree that there was a palpable sense of anxiety in both the Old Munitions Building and the Navy Department. At the White House, however, there was no evidence of any similar tension. Dr. McIntire and Captain Beardall, who were with the president that morning, did not later recall any particular sense of urgency in the two hours between the time the president received the fourteenth part and noon or so when they left. [43] The fact that the president made no calls to any member of the War Council confirms the impression that FDR, as opposed to his military commanders, did not seem to anticipate any immediate Japanese military action. At about 11:00 P.M., the Japanese embassy asked Hull for a meeting at 1:00 P.M.[44] Hull reported this to the president, who did no more than ask to be kept informed.

At 12:30 P.M. FDR saw the Chinese ambassador, Dr. Hu Shih, who had just arrived from New York at the request of the president.[45] "With an air of leisure and gusto," Roosevelt read the entire text of his message to the Japanese Emperor, pausing here and there to explain a word or phrase. At about 1:00 P.M. Mrs. Roosevelt put her head in the door of the president's study to remind him that a family luncheon would be served shortly. Hu Shih took this as a hint that he should leave, but FDR motioned him to resume his seat and continued to read the document. "This is my last effort for peace," the president said, "I am afraid that it may fail."

Roosevelt added that if he received no reply by Monday, he planned to publish the text. He also told Hu Shih that "those fellows" (Kurusu and Nomura) had asked for an urgent appointment with Hull, presumably to give him Tokyo's answer to the last American note. In conclusion, the president said that he expected "foul play" within 48 hours and added that he thought something "nasty" might happen in Thailand, Malaya, the Dutch Indies, and "possibly" the Philippines.

At 1:10 P.M., Hu Shih left. The president sent word to Mrs. Roosevelt that he would not be able to be present at the planned luncheon. He then ordered a tray to be delivered to his study and he was joined by Harry Hopkins. At 1:35 P.M., Roosevelt was still waiting for Hull's call when Knox called to report that the Japanese were bombing Pearl Harbor.

To summarize, in the last 24-plus hours before the attack, Roosevelt saw several members of his inner circle: McIntire, Early, Hopkins, Grace Tully, Captain Beardall, and General Watson; three ambassadors—Hu Shih, Halifax, and Casey; his wife; Judge Polier; Lieutenant Schulz; and Chief Petty Officer Prettyman, in addition to the 34 guests at the dinner on Saturday evening. But he did not see any member of his War Council. Without the telephone logs it is impossible to say exactly whom the president talked to, and we know for sure only that he talked with Hull several times on Saturday afternoon and once on Sunday. He also talked with Stark on Saturday night and, perhaps, once early on Sunday morning. He had no communication of any kind with Stimson and Marshall, and as for Knox, his two calls neatly frame the last 24 hours: He called at noon on Saturday to inform FDR of the sighting of the convoys and again on Sunday afternoon to inform the commander-in-chief of the attack on Pearl Harbor.

One cannot help but be struck by the fact that Roosevelt handled the crisis by himself, without seeking the advice of his War Council or even informing them of what he was up to. His very private way of managing the crisis was certainly not because he underrated its seriousness: on five separate occasions the president said that he expected the country to be at war very soon. But despite his obvious concern, he displayed a remarkable lack of curiosity. On learning of the convoys, Roosevelt (in sharp contrast to Churchill, who badgered his chiefs of staff repeatedly for more information about the convoys) never asked if there were any further sightings; he never asked his own naval experts for their evaluation of the evidence; nor did he seem to be much aware of the fact that the report he received was already 12 hours old and the Japanese ships could that Saturday afternoon be at their destination. On Sunday morning, Roosevelt did not inquire whether the fourteenth part had arrived and he took the One O'Clock Message in stride. Here the contrast to Marshall and Stark is very striking.

The president devoted about six hours to "handling" the crisis—most of it on Saturday afternoon. Half of the time he worked on the message and the other half he was consulting with Casey, Halifax, and Hopkins. The balance of the time he spent eating, drinking, sleeping, socializing, and chatting with his intimates. This is not to suggest that the president was in some way derelict in his duty, but it does highlight the fact that he did not feel any overriding sense of urgency such as characterized the actions of the men in the Munitions Building and the Navy Department.

Finally, one cannot help but be struck by the numerous oddities that characterized the president's actions and statements. These include the confusion he evinced in telling Smith about the sighting of the convoys; his request for the draft of an appeal to the emperor including the modus vivendi; his secrecy in seeing Halifax and Casey; his overreaction to the 13-part message; his odd protest to Hopkins, "But we have a good record"; his failure to call anyone but Stark on Saturday night; and his strange calm on Sunday morning.

Notes

1. John Toland, *Infamy* (Garden City, New York: Doubleday, 1982).
2. In November 1940, Admiral Stark wrote: "The vital theater *is* the eastern Atlantic and the western Pacific is a secondary one." American planners had interpreted ABC-I to mean that the American Pacific Fleet should be used "to influence Japan against further aggression." Rainbow 5 specifically stated that

after M-Day no reinforcements would be sent to the Far East. Finally, the Victory Plan did not even factor Japan into the strategic equation.

3. *Washington Post,* December 7, 1941, 8.
4. The White House logs, which recorded calls placed through the White House switchboard, do exist, but the logs that show what calls the president received and made do not.
5. The appointment book for December 6, 1941, does not show that Halifax saw the president late that afternoon, and there is no entry in the log of December 7 that the president had scheduled a family luncheon at 1:00. These are just examples of the incompleteness of the book.
6. None of the messages received by the president on Saturday have any sort of time stamp on them.
7. Geoffrey Heilman, "Roosevelt: From Breakfast in Bed to Wisecracks at Movies, President Retains His Bounce After Eight Years." *Life,* 10, January 20, 1941.
8. *New York Times,* December 6, 1941. 1.
9. Quoted in Leonard Baker, *Roosevelt and Pearl Harbor* (New York: Macmillan, 1970) 298.
10. Pearl Harbor Attack, Hearings, Part 15, Exhibit #66, p. 1680. Hereafter cited as PHA.
11. Frank E. Beatty, "The Background of the Secret Report," *National Review,* 3, no. 50 (December 13, 1966). Beatty is not the most reliable witness and this piece was written a quarter century after the attack. Nevertheless, the meeting that described almost surely did take place, and given the fact that Stark took no action at all after he heard about the convoys, there is nothing inherently improbable in his account. As Beatty remembered it, Knox asked: "Gentlemen, are they going to hit us?" and Turner, speaking for the assembled admirals, replied: "No, Mr. Secretary. They are going to attack the British. They are not ready for us yet."
12. On November 21-22 three troop transports escorted by the *Pensacola* left San Francisco for the Philippines. They were scheduled to arrive on January 4, 1942. On December 5-6, four more transports sailed from San Francisco.
13. H. H. Arnold, *Global Mission* (New York: Harper Brothers, 1949), 268-69.
14. See Sir Llewellyn Woodward, *British Foreign Policy in the Second World War,* vol. 2 (London: *Her Majesty's Stationary Office,* 1971), 170-75 for a summary of the three meetings. In the first meeting Roosevelt said that if the Japanese attacked Malaya "we'd all be in the same boat." He then assured the British that by this statement he meant the United States would give military support to the British in the event they became involved in a war with the Japanese. While it is true that in a sense FDR was only reiterating a policy decision made

by the Joint Board in November, there is a significant difference. The American military planners assumed that the decision to go to war would remain in Washington, while Roosevelt had, in effect, let London make the decision.

15. The appointment book shows that the president had lunch at 1:00 P.M. No guests are noted, but as the president very rarely ate alone, perhaps he was joined by Harry Hopkins and/or Grace Tully. Both were known to be in the White House that afternoon.
16. PHA, Hearings, Part 14, Exhibit #21, p. 1246.
17. Arthur Bryant, *The Turn of the Tide: A History of the War Years Based on the Diaries of Field-Marshal Lord Alanbrooke, Chief of the Imperial General Staff* (Garden City, NY: Doubleday, 1957), 225. The entry for December 6 reads: "We examined situation carefully, but from the position of the transports it was not possible to tell whether they were going to Bangkok, to the Kra Peninsula, or whether they were just cruising round as a bluff."
18. PHA, Part 14, Hearings, Exhibit #21, 1247-48.
19. Raymond Esthus, "President Roosevelt's Commitment to Britain to Intervene in a Pacific War," *Mississippi Valley Historical Review,* 50, no. l (June 1963).
20. Robert Sherwood, *Roosevelt and Hopkins: An Intimate History* (New York: Harper & Brothers, 1948), 424.
21. Martin Gilbert, *Finest Hour: Winston S. Churchill, 1939-1941* (London: Hamish Hamilton, 1983), 1264.
22. PHA, Hearings, Part XI, 5270-72.
23. PHA, Hearings, Part XI, 5269ff.
24. We do not have FDR's request for a draft containing the modus vivendi (perhaps it was made by telephone), but we do have Hull's covering letter which refers directly to the president's request. PHA, Hearings, Part XIV, Exhibit #20, 1231.
25. PHA, Hearings, Part XIV, Exhibit #20, 1232ff.
26. W. J. Hudson & H. J. W. Stokes, eds., *Documents on Australian Foreign Policy, 1937-1944,* 7 vols. (Canberra: Australian Printing Office, 1982), vol. 5, 283.
27. *Foreign Relations of the United States,* 1941, vol. 4, pp.723-25. Hereafter *FRUS.*
28. Grace Tully, *FDR: My Boss* (New York: Charles Scribner's Sons, 1949), 253.
29. *FRUS,* 1941, vol. 4, 723-25. The footnotes contain the covering notes and marginalia.
30. Ibid., 727.
31. Was Hopkins with the president on Saturday afternoon? The fact that Harriman sent a telegram to him for transmission to the president suggests that he was if for no other reason than there is no suggestion anywhere that the telegram was not delivered. However, that evening when the president

talked to Hopkins about the 13-part message, he explained that he had sent an appeal to the Mikado that afternoon—a statement which would seem to imply that Hopkins did not know the president had spent the afternoon drafting such a message.

32. William Langer and S. E. Gleason, *The Undeclared War, 1940-1941* (New York: Harper, 1953). They note that Casey "saw President Roosevelt late on Saturday afternoon," and add that "the fact that the State Department has no record of this conversation is not unusual, since many of Roosevelt's negotiations were not recorded." See also Roberta Wohlstetter, *Pearl Harbor: Warning and Decision* (Stanford: Stanford University Press, 1962). She too speaks of the Casey-Roosevelt meeting as an established fact. Nevertheless, Casey's telegram relating to Roosevelt's message to the emperor is ambiguous and could be read as an account of Halifax's meeting with Roosevelt.
33. Hudson and Stokes, *Australian Foreign Policy,* vol. 5, 277-79.
34. PHA, Hearings, Part 12, Exhibit #58, pp. 1633-34.
35. PHA, Hearings, Part 7, pp. 3893ff. Kramer was repeatedly questioned as to the exact times he made deliveries on Sunday morning. His testimony is for the most part not terribly clear, but he was quite certain about the times he was at the White House.
36. PHA, Hearings, Part 10, pp. 4659-72.
37. PHA, Hearings, Part 9, p. 5555ff.
38. Edwin T. Layton, *And I Was There: Pearl Harbor and Midway: Breaking the Secrets* (New York: William Morrow, 1985), 295.
39. PHA, Hearings, Part 10, pp. 5080-89.
40. PHA, Hearings, Part 11, pp. 5271 and 5275.
41. PHA, Hearings, Part 12, Exhibit #1, p. 245.
42. Ibid., 248.
43. Ross T. McIntire, *White House Physician* (New York: G.P. Putnam's Sons, 1946), 137. "I sat with him on that Sunday morning from ten to twelve o'clock, while Mr. Hull was waiting in the State Department for the Japanese envoys to bring their Government's reply to the American note, and the President made it clear he only counted on the usual evasions."
44. Cordell, Hull, *The Memoirs of Cordell Hull,* 2 vols (New York: Macmillan, 1948), vol. 2, 1095-97.
45. Herbert Feis, *The Road to Pearl Harbor* (Princeton: Princeton University Press, 1950), 340.

11.

FDR as Commander in Chief

Robert W. Love, Jr.

Many historians have assessed President Franklin Roosevelt's performance as commander in chief of the army and the navy, most of them dwelling on wartime grand strategy, his relations with his great chiefs of staff—General of the Army George C. Marshall, Admiral Harold R. Stark, and Fleet Admiral Ernest J. King—and his epic dealings with Churchill, Chiang Kai-shek, Charles de Gaulle, and Joseph Stalin. Overall assessments of FDR's conduct of military and naval policy over his entire presidency are surprisingly rare; indeed, only longtime Hyde Park Library Director William Emerson, in a brief essay in Ernest May's 1960 collection on the president as commander in chief, *The Ultimate Decision,* and journalist Eric Larabee in his 1987 book *Commander in Chief,* have attempted to assess the entire 12 years.[1] Nonetheless, both Larabee and Emerson focused on the war years and agreed that Roosevelt had earned high marks. This chapter revisits the issue, identifies some anomalies, and suggests the need for a revision of the traditional view.

Until the 1947 National Security Act unified the military and naval establishment and created a single secretary of defense, the president as commander in chief was the lone manager of the War and Navy departments.

Representing the president's elected political authority, under an 1816 arrangement crafted by President James Madison, the secretary of war and an assistant headed the War Department—which managed the army—and the secretary of the navy and, occasionally, an assistant secretary, headed the Navy Department. Owing to reforms enacted by the Progressives, law dictated that their immediate subordinates would be the uniformed service chiefs: the chief of staff of the army, a post created in 1904, and the chief of naval operations (CNO), a billet established in 1915. These jobs were quite different. The army's general staff, under the chief of staff, was responsible for every activity within the army. Whereas the chief of staff planned operations, he did not conduct them. The CNO, on the other hand, shared responsibility for naval activity and policy with the powerful shore-based General Board of the Navy, first chaired by the legendary Admiral George Dewey, and the influential Washington-based technical, staff, and materiel bureau chiefs. Unlike the chief of staff, the CNO exercised unquestioned, ongoing everyday operational authority for the composition, training, movements, deployments, and operations of the entire seagoing fleet. As a result, OpNav, the CNO's general staff, naturally functioned quite differently from its army counterpart.

As a result, the chain of command from the White House to the armies in the field or the fleets at sea was short and understandable. Roosevelt inherited this system and did nothing to damage it, except to agree to revise the membership of the Joint Army-Navy Board at the onset of American belligerency, to change its name to the Joint Chiefs of Staff, and to allow the Joint Chiefs as a body to exercise "ad hoc" command authority. The practical importance of these steps for the conduct of the war has been greatly overrated, however.

Roosevelt's entire national security apparatus was intended to preserve his authority. He acted as "his own Secretary of State," often defining and redefining American foreign policy without reference to the Department of State, and tightly controlled the conduct of higher-level American diplomacy. Owing to a lack of staff support, however, the results of FDR's system, or lack thereof, were often counterproductive. "Roosevelt was at his worst when he had to coordinate conflicting views of foreign policy," concluded historian Jonathan Utley.[2] Moreover, a case might be made that Roosevelt more or less constantly mismanaged national security policy—for example, military and naval affairs, both before the war and thereafter. Some historians and political scientists have argued that Roosevelt governed by means of "creative tension," pitting subordinates against one another, protecting his ultimate authority as chief executive, and postponing decisions until he divined the most sensible bureaucratic and political outcome. One means of doing this was to keep his subordinates in the dark about his views on key questions, to postpone decisions until the last moment, or to suspend the last moment, and to obfuscate in the meantime.

This method may have worked well in the arena of partisan politics, with Chicago ward heelers and the protected groups that formed the New Deal coalition, but it failed when it came to military and naval policy. "Duty, honor, and country," surely defined the ideals of navy and army men, but understood routine, orderliness, precision, and obedience were the standards by which they conducted daily business. As president, Roosevelt might reasonably expect his political subordinates to disobey him or distort his policies, but he could also expect a very high level of obedience to his instructions and conformance with his policy preferences from his military subordinates. "My problems with dealing with him [Roosevelt] . . . arose from his habit of rapidly changing his mind and from his carelessness in not always making his word his bond," recalled Admiral J. O. Richardson, who served as the navy's budget officer and chief of the Bureau of Navigation in the 1930s.[3] According to Admiral King, Roosevelt was a "tricky" man who "liked to pull things."[4]

What hampered Roosevelt most as commander in chief, and as manager of the War and Navy departments, was his inattention to truth-telling. He could not bring himself to be candid about his interpretation of events, his desired policies, or the outcomes he sought. This often led unnecessarily to unwanted, unforeseen results. Many of Roosevelt's defenders have hailed his manipulation of men toward the elusive end of what Eleanor Roosevelt called his "secret purposes," but the president's concealment of his purposes, if he indeed really had any, often meant that he forfeited the chance to shape the outcomes. And his unsettling practice of delaying decisions to protect presidential power and to keep his options open frequently meant that new events foreclosed older, more desirable options and unleashed unfriendly, unforeseen forces.

These habits, in practice, had devastating results. Roosevelt hesitated to appoint truly strong men to official posts, especially to service secretaryships. Upon joining the cabinet, Attorney General Anthony J. Biddle wrote in his diary that it was not an outstanding group of men. Roosevelt's service secretaries were a mixed lot. Only one, James Forrestal, deserves the accolade of true greatness; but Forrestal succeeded to the secretaryship of the navy by accident, upon Secretary Frank Knox's death in early 1944, and he was bitterly frustrated by his inability to accomplish anything during the last year of the Roosevelt presidency. Forrestal's predecessors were a mixed lot. Claude Swanson was an aging, seedy Virginia machine politician when he entered the department in 1933. Owing to two decades of service on the House and Senate naval affairs committees, he understood the legislative aspect of naval policy and had the makings of an outstanding official. In 1934, however, Swanson fell, fractured his ribs, and contracted pleurisy two weeks later. "From this point," concluded his biographer, "he was an invalid." [5] According to Lieutenant Commander William Smedberg, who worked in the Navy Department, "Nobody even thought of him because they knew he was almost 'non compos mentis.'"[6] Roosevelt nonetheless kept Swanson in office until he finally succumbed in 1939. "Give my regards . . . to the Secretary," wrote the CNO, Admiral William Standley, from the London Naval Conference on March 3, 1936, "if he is still with us."[7]

With Swanson disabled and Standley often out of town, Henry Latrobe Roosevelt, the assistant secretary, became acting secretary, but Standley and Henry Latrobe hated one another, and their turbulent relationship disrupted the work of the Navy Department and the arrangement of naval policy. The result was that for long stretches the navy had no effective political spokesman to deal with Congress or to represent the department to the White House. Roosevelt allowed Charles A. Edison to succeed Swanson in 1939, but he rather callously told him at the same time that he was neither his first nor even his second choice for the job, and that he might be displaced at any moment. For his part, Edison liked the navy, but he was little interested in naval policy and devoted his time to advancing new technology and promoting various research and development projects. Frank Knox, who relieved Edison in June 1940, was an intelligent, dynamic figure, but he knew nothing about the navy, had little influence on Roosevelt where naval policy was concerned, and admitted at the time the Japanese attacked Pearl Harbor that he was still learning about the department. Knox did a fine job during the war, but by 1942 the most important decisions were strategic, organizational, and operational, and they fell to the new CNO, Fleet Admiral King. Knox's successor, Forrestal, inherited the billet when Knox died. He was a great public servant, but when Roosevelt appointed him to the secretaryship the president surely knew that Forrestal and Admiral King simply hated one another for no clearly tangible reason.[8] Unwilling to challenge King, whose ability and prestige were immense, Forrestal was virtually paralyzed until the end of the war. Indeed, a good argument can be made that Forrestal's most important work was done outside of the Navy Department. In short, it should not surprise us that the most important civilian associated with naval policy during the Roosevelt administration was Carl Vinson, the able chairman of the powerful House Naval Affairs Committee.[9]

Walter Dern, a former governor of Utah, joined Roosevelt's cabinet as his first secretary of war in 1933. Hoover's last budget virtually emasculated the army, and Dern and General Douglas MacArthur, the chief of staff, soon learned that the first New Deal budget aimed for even more drastic cuts. In the context of explaining how Roosevelt went about "the taming of Douglas MacArthur," Larabee recounted a dramatic 1933 scene in the White House when Dern and MacArthur confronted Roosevelt over the issue. "Dern argued that with Germany rearming and Japan becoming aggressive," Larabee wrote, "it would be a 'fatal error' to economize on defense, and MacArthur said the country's safety was at stake, but Roosevelt heaped scorn on them."[10] While Larabee trumpets Roosevelt's oratorical defeat of MacArthur, the outcome of the meeting was that most of the cuts remained intact and the army was weakened. But Dern was demoralized and soon took ill; his influence on the New Deal, never great, thereafter eroded.[11] Why Roosevelt selected Harry H. Woodring as Dern's successor, and his archrival, Louis Johnson, as assistant secretary of war, has to be one of the great mysteries of this presidency. The Woodring-Johnson feud, a stainless example of management by creative tension, made the War Department the butt of Washington humor, unnecessarily embarrassed two great chiefs of staff—Generals Malin Craig and George Marshall—left the army without an effective spokesman in the Cabinet or on Capitol Hill, and enfeebled the attempts of Craig and Marshall to rearm. Marshall depicted the Woodring-Johnson feud as "the most miserable experience of my life. They not only didn't make any secret of how they hated and despised each other, they ran to the president behind each other's back."[12]

Woodring's relief, Secretary Henry L. Stimson, a longtime Republican placeholder, presents something of an enigma to serious military historians. He was lionized by his legion of former assistants, led by protégé McGeorge Bundy, and early postwar liberal historians for his commitment to public service—some might say the truest symbol of the "revolving door" syndrome. Only the distinguished historian Richard Current took a critical view.[13] Stimson's most important service to the army was to advance the Selective Service Acts of 1940 and 1941, but in most other respects he was a rather poor manager who had little idea of the major issues at stake in his own department. He was devoted to General Marshall and usually left important army decisions to the chief of staff, with the result that no counterweight to Marshall existed within the War Department after 1940. He loyally supported Marshall's 1942 reorganization of the army, which created the ground, air, and service forces, and, according to General Eisenhower in 1945, unwittingly divorced the general staff from logistics and administrative questions—a criticism also voiced by Richard Leighton and Robert Coakley. A stronger secretary of war might have challenged the army's decision to establish uniformly light, highly mobile divisions to fight German panzers in World War II or questioned the wisdom of establishing the virtually independent overseas heavy bomber commands in ETO and POA.[14] On at least one occasion when Stimson took a hand in military policy, in this case antisubmarine operations in 1942-43, the outcome was to delay the effective use of land-based bombers against the U-boats and prolong the agony of the Battle of the Atlantic.[15] More comfortable dealing with the larger issues of grand strategy and international relations, Stimson felt left out of wartime planning and resurfaced as a major player on this field only after Roosevelt's death.

Rebuilding the army before Pearl Harbor clearly took a second seat at Roosevelt's table to the navy, the department of government Roosevelt clearly knew best. Indeed, Marshall once complained that it was unfair of the president to refer to the navy as "us" and the army as "them."[16] Having served as assistant secretary from 1913 to 1920, Roosevelt believed that he understood the navy and how the Navy Department functioned. Working familiarity often expressed itself in arrogance, however. "I do not have to have military and naval operations explained to me at length," Roosevelt boasted to a confidante.[17] He repeatedly said that he loved the navy, but his jocular air, his hollow pretensions, and the patronizing, chummy use of Naval Academy nicknames for the admirals did not always sit well. Roosevelt might have studied what his onetime mentor, Admiral Bradley Fiske, labeled the "genius of the Navy," but the evidence suggests that it was a lesson FDR did not learn.

Until March 1942, the navy's principal management problem was as obvious as it had been in World War I. Only the civilian secretary was empowered to coordinate the overlapping work of OpNav, the General Board, and the materiel bureaus. Without going into too much eye-glazing detail, the problem was to enhance the authority of the CNO over naval policy without making him more powerful on industrial and manpower issues than the political secretary. Roosevelt had seen firsthand that a weak or incompetent secretary compounded the basic problem. Perhaps—understanding his management style—this explains why he waited so long to do something about it. Roosevelt served under Navy Secretary Josephus Daniels, perhaps the worst executive in modern American military history, excepting Robert Strange McNamara, who belongs in a special category. Daniels provided Roosevelt with a model. He was suspicious, arrogant, willful, and more or less consistently wrong on policy issues. Moreover, he disrupted the navy's established chain of command. He was also likeable, pleasant, friendly, outwardly well-meaning, and usually cheery. Anyone searching for the source of Roosevelt's proclivity for repeatedly postponing important decisions need look no further than Josephus Daniels' habits in office.

As for Roosevelt's role in selecting the major military figures of his time, we can dismiss Larabee's claim—that the president plucked them from obscurity—on this score out of hand, as have most reviewers. MacArthur, who served as chief of staff until 1935, was a holdover from the Hoover administration. By all accounts, he was unwelcome by the New Dealers. There were two candidates for his relief, Major General Simonds, the assistant chief of staff, and Major General Malin Craig, the head of the Army War College. MacArthur backed Simonds, and this was perhaps held unfairly held against the assistant chief by the White House. In any case, General Pershing backed Craig, and no interwar president dared to oppose Pershing's choice for his old billet. What is illustrative is that Roosevelt did not consult Secretary Dern and even waited until Dern was entrained to the Pacific coast, en route to the Philippines, to announce Craig's appointment. It was a testament to Dern's maturity that he did not hold this against Craig and supported the new chief of staff loyally, but Roosevelt had publicly affronted his secretary of war in a way that ill served the army. Craig was an officer of stainless honor, extraordinary ability, and high intentions. Army historian Russell Weigley considered Craig's "hardheaded realism and determination reminiscent of Pershing himself." Although Craig is little remembered today, Weigley concluded that no "soldier did more than he to make possible American military accomplishments in World War II."[18] Yet Craig's finest achievement was to lay the groundwork for an expanded Army, for the president refused to support the chief of staff in enlarging the peacetime army. Roosevelt paid little attention to War Department issues, seldom conferred with MacArthur, Craig, or even George Marshall until 1940, and provided the War Department with little assistance on Capitol Hill. When Congress, in 1936, enacted a measure empowering the chief of staff with explicit command authority over expeditionary forces, Roosevelt was apparently oblivious to the issue.

A dissonance survives between Roosevelt's thundering against the Axis powers and his unwillingness to rearm. "Our national defense is inadequate for purposes of national security and requires increase," he declared in January 1938, but he went on to ask Congress for only $17 million for that purpose, largely for an increase in aircraft and anti-aircraft guns.[19] When Craig left office in September 1939, Roosevelt had rejected his four requests to bring the army up to the strength envisioned in the 1920 National Defense Act, there was not one combat-ready division, and the weapons budget was so low that the infantryman carried a modified 1903 Springfield rifle and fired the World War I 3-inch Stokes mortar. Only one major step had been taken to reverse this unhappy trend: on Capitol Hill in mid-1939, overriding the president's demand that the army be limited to 165,000 men, Congress lifted the permanent ceiling altogether. Randy Kolton, Craig's biographer, sadly concluded that the "deficiencies at the end of Craig's tenure fundamentally reflected flaws in the Roosevelt administration's defense policy."[20] Indeed, Roosevelt's one abortive attempt to enlarge the army, by purchasing 10,000 planes for the air corps in

1938-39, was an unmitigated fiasco, demonstrating less the president's commitment to airpower than his failure to understand that air forces needed base defense troops, communications networks, spares, air and ground crews, training programs, navigational aids, and a huge quantity of munitions before they could operate against an enemy. The administrative chaos ensuing from the War Department's effort to put into effect the president's 10,000-plane plan lay at the root of the scandalous shortages affecting the army air corps in December 1941.

One of Craig's more important legacies was his relief, George C. Marshall—surely one of the two best chiefs of staff in American history. Larabee credited Roosevelt with his selection and put this forth as evidence of Roosevelt's greatness as commander in chief, but the situation was far more ambiguous. As Forrest Pogue pointed out many years ago, Marshall really had only one or two competitors, the most important being General Hugh Drum. Craig paved the road for Marshall's ascendancy. He saw to it that Colonel Marshall received his first star, brought him to Washington as head of the War Plans Division, promoted him to deputy chief of staff, and arranged that he serve as acting chief when Craig's last illness kept him out of action in mid-1939. By this time, Drum's entanglement in partisan politics wrote the end to his candidacy. Marshall was the army's institutional choice, and Roosevelt accepted it.

Roosevelt had virtually ignored the Army until late 1938, when, alarmed by the apparent influence of the German Air Force on diplomacy at Munich, he asked Congress to increase the size of the army air corps. On the eve of the European war, however, the army was greatly understrength. There were 190,000 men in the regular army, roughly 20,000 under its authorized strength, another 200,000 partially trained, poorly equipped National Guardsmen, and an inactive Reserve Corps of roughly 110,000. This body was organized into four skeleton field armies, without staffs or corps headquarters organizations. General Marshall did yeoman work persuading the president and Congress to begin to rearm after war erupted in Europe in September 1939, but the evidence suggests that the foreign crisis, especially the fall of France in June 1940, did more to accelerate rearmament generally than did Roosevelt's new support for greatly increased War Department appropriations. We should not be blinded to Marshall's extreme skepticism about the president at the time, however. As late as June 1941, Marshall expressed shock and anger to Brigadier General Leonard Gerow about the president's indifference to exposing the army's recently conscripted, poorly trained, ill-equipped recruits to possible combat.[21] Indeed, Marshall threatened to resign that summer if Roosevelt carried out his plan to order the Atlantic Fleet to land the army's 1st Division and the 1st Marine Division in the Azores, a successful tactic the chief of staff used with increasing frequency against a president who could ill afford such a stunning repudiation. If Larabee's thesis, that Roosevelt was in charge, is true, then the army's inability to take to the field in early 1942, the deficiencies in the army air corps so evident to Admiral Nagumo's pilots when they descended on Pearl Harbor, and the shortages that plagued army operations until 1943 and later surely must be laid at the president's doorstep.

Roosevelt clearly felt more kinship with navy men, who looked to him to reverse the navy's decline during the Hoover presidency. "The Navy's destinies go with the man Roosevelt," explained the CNO, Admiral Standley.[22] Standley seems to have been a unanimous choice to succeed Admiral Pratt as chief of naval operations in 1933, but he was Roosevelt's personal appointment. What is surprising is that while Standley felt uncomfortable at the White House and distrusted Roosevelt's circle, he became a New Deal placeholder, later chairing the prewar Maritime Commission and serving as Roosevelt's first wartime ambassador to Russia. His successor, Admiral William D. Leahy, clearly owed his ascendancy to his position as a presidential confidante; when Roosevelt was elected, the Assistant CNO, Rear Admiral Joseph Taussig, told Standley that "Leahy and the Gun Club" would now be in charge.[23] He was an able CNO, and from mid-1942 until 1949 served as the first chairman of the Joint Chiefs. Any fair assessment of this service, however, must admit that he grew overly entangled in presidential matters, became too involved in foreign policy, and failed repeatedly to exploit the latent potential of his billet to resolve interservice problems. By 1944, he had supplanted Hopkins as the president's most important national security advisor, a role for which he was ill suited and ineffective. Leahy's successor as CNO, Admiral Harold R. Stark, owed his selection in 1939 not only to his relationship with Roosevelt but also to his outstanding ability as a naval leader. Stark's peacetime record of accomplishment is without parallel; the 1940 Two Ocean Navy Act, Plan Dog, the Rainbow Plans, and the 1941 establishment of the Atlantic Fleet alone make him one of our foremost navy leaders. Stark initiated each of these projects, however, and in no case did Roosevelt provide him with significant support. Indeed, one of Stark's more important accomplishments was to use gross flattery and cheery goodwill to win the president to his side, or at least to thwart some of Roosevelt's more ill-considered schemes. Yet in the end, in March 1942, he asked to be relieved as CNO because the president had put him in an untenable position. Since mid-December 1941, he had coexisted as CNO alongside CominCh (Commander in Chief, U.S. Fleet), the more dynamic Admiral King, in a situation in which neither officer had any clearly defined authority.[24] Stark's resignation was a thorough, resounding rebuff to Roosevelt's single, foolish attempt to reorganize the Navy Department's chain of command.

Unlike Leahy and Stark, Admiral King had little association with Roosevelt until 1933, when this stern and driven figure became chief of the navy's Bureau of Aeronautics.[25] Roosevelt passed over King in 1939 for CNO, but Stark on his own restored him to sea duty in the fall of 1940 when he gave him command of the small Neutrality Patrol. This led to his King's selection as commander in chief of the Atlantic Fleet in February 1941, with the result that he was the only American service chief during the war to have commanded a major formation in combat. His appointment as CominCh in December 1941 was clearly Secretary Knox's idea, and his assumption of a second hat as CNO in March of the following year came about as a result of Stark's decision to resign.

New Deal naval policy bore the burden of the disarmament system erected at the end of World War I. Inspired by Wilson and adopted by Harding, Coolidge, and Hoover, naval disarmament was embodied in the 1922 Five-Power Treaty of Washington and the 1930 First London Naval Treaty. In effect, these agreements limited the U.S. Fleet to 15 battleships, all designed and built before or shortly after the Great War, and five heavy carriers, or an equivalent tonnage mix of fewer heavy and more light carriers. There were severe limits on new heavy cruiser construction and restrictions on destroyers and submarines. When Roosevelt entered the White House, bloc obsolescence had begun to reduce the strength of the fleet and the preliminary fencing with London and Tokyo over extending the disarmament regime was already under way.

Roosevelt adopted naval disarmament as the keystone of his foreign policy. Whereas Harding and Coolidge saw the regime as a vehicle for fiscal economy in unthreatening times, and Hoover viewed it as an ethical measure on the grounds that force was an immoral means of advancing foreign policy interests, Roosevelt truly believed in Wilson's diagnosis that arms caused wars and in the idea that disarmament would make waging war impossible. On June 26, 1941, only days after the German Army invaded Russia, Roosevelt told Adolf Berle, his assistant secretary of state, "Don't forget that the elimination of armaments is still the keystone—for the security of all little nations and for economic security."[26] This was a thorough reversal of cousin Theodore's analysis of the likely outcome of the 1908 Hague Conference. Roosevelt did everything he could to keep the disarmament regime alive; to bring Germany into some arms limitation system; to keep Japan under the umbrella of the Five-Power Treaty from 1933 to 1938; to keep Britain, France, and the United States under the regime even after Japan denounced it in 1934; and to keep from abandoning the policy until December 1939, two and a half years after Japan had invaded China and three months after Germany had conquered Poland. The one disarmament agreement he negotiated, the 1936 Second

London Naval Treaty, did not include Japan as a signatory, but it provided a model for continuing the policy, heartened liberal and isolationist opponents of naval expansion, and constricted the design of replacement battleships, carriers, and cruisers until 1940. Explained historian Stephen Pelz, "From May 1933 to September 1939, the United States . . . built five carriers to an equal number for Japan, seventeen cruisers to Japan's twelve, sixty-five destroyers to Japan's fifty-seven, and forty-one submarines to Japan's thirty-nine. The United States had a 10:8 ratio [in combatant tonnage] with Japan in 1936, which . . . steadily worsened in subsequent years."[27] The result of Roosevelt's dedication to disarmament and the disarmament regime was that the U. S. Fleet was deficient in modern warships when the Japanese attacked the old battleships at Pearl Harbor. The carriers that fought the battles of the Coral Sea were "treaty class" vessels, and treaty limitations dictated many of the early design specifications of the 24 *Essex*-class fast attack carriers. Roosevelt had been president for nearly nine years when Japan attacked Pearl Harbor, yet not one modern fast battleship—capable of operating with the *Saratoga*-class carriers—was ready for service. According to Pelz, the admirals did not complain more about the uneven, slow pace of Roosevelt's naval rearmament program because "the leadership of the navy . . . did not twist the President's arm; after the famine of the Hoover years, they remained satisfied with the 'hors d'oeuvres' that Roosevelt provided."[28]

Roosevelt "vacillated between pacifism and militance," according to John Walter, the foremost student of the naval legislation of the decade.[29] He first pointed out that the $238 million 1933 National Industrial Recovery Act (NIRA) appropriation was spread over eight years, thus making it a fairly modest increase, and that it and the 1934 First Vinson Acts were the product of Vinson's legislative skills, not Roosevelt's navalism. The 1934 act articulated the goal of building up to a "treaty fleet" within eight years, the same year in which Japan denounced the treaty regime altogether. Roosevelt resisted a battleship replacement policy in 1935 and 1936, accepting a limited measure in 1937 with great reluctance. Only Admiral Leahy, Admiral Stark, and Congressman Vinson, working together, persuaded Roosevelt to abandon his dangerous order that the new fast battleships carry 14-inch guns. As for oceangoing escorts and auxiliaries, Roosevelt refused to approve several plans for austere, mobilization-type escorts beginning in 1938; as late as 1941, even after he ordered the Atlantic Fleet to begin escorting British convoys from Newfoundland to Iceland, he rejected plans for a large ocean escort program. Not until late 1942 did this program reach the top of the president's priority list for materials and manpower. He rejected all large scale plans for ship-to-shore landing craft construction until late 1941 and did the same with several plans to build troop transports. At the time Japan attacked Pearl Harbor, the army and navy operated fewer than ten large transports, and many of these were overage.

The "court historians," exemplified by Larabee, portrayed a dynamic chief executive who moved secretively but vigorously to rearm the nation and take a stand against the Axis, in James MacGregor Burns's memorable phrase, as a "soldier of democracy." Roosevelt not only struggled to undermine isolationism, they suggest, but also to rearm. Congress moved slowly, they insist, refusing to abandon isolationism and expressing this policy by voting against rearmament. This argument does not bear the burden of the evidence. The War Department's proposals for expansion until 1940 were modest. Roosevelt, often acting through his budget director, cut every one of them. The major manpower legislation of the summer of 1939 came at the insistence of Congress, not the White House. As for the navy, Roosevelt's addiction to disarmament retarded reconstruction of the World War I fleet until the 1940 Two Ocean Navy Act, a measure in which the president took no role. Roosevelt's major contribution to naval policy prior to Pearl Harbor was to continue a failed treaty regime and to trim Navy Department shipbuilding and manning plans. He often complained that he had no forces with which to menace his overseas opponents, but he did almost nothing to rectify the problem.

How wisely did Roosevelt allocate American military resources among U.S. allies and between the army and navy? About the only measures he took in the 1930s were to provide $25 million in credit to the Nationalist Chinese and provide the French with a handful of army air corps aircraft. The latter policy, however, illustrated Roosevelt's general approach to overseas military assistance. He demanded no comprehensive analysis of the state of French forces nor any independent assessment of what they needed the most. He simply decided that they needed planes, with little thought as to the air logistics or training features of such a program. The famous Destroyer Deal of September 1940 continued this approach. Churchill first asked for destroyers days before he became prime minister in May 1940, owing to British losses off Norway. Not once between this initial contact and the consummation of the bargain did Roosevelt insist that Churchill explain how he intended to deploy them or why he was holding so many escorts in the Home Fleet and the Mediterranean. This was the first of many opportunities to get the British to explain their grand strategy and their maritime strategy, but Roosevelt passed it up—and in doing so gave away the U.S. Navy's ready reserve of mobilization escorts. The army and navy attempted to rationalize the escalating assistance policy, but the sorry record of the Coordination Committee and its successors, which Roosevelt largely ignored, suggests the dimensions of the problems they faced. The result was that at the time the Japanese attacked Pearl Harbor, roughly 75 percent of

U.S. military aircraft production had been earmarked for the British and Russians. The March 1941 Lend-Lease Act was the foundation of Roosevelt's wartime military assistance program, the vehicle by which U.S. production was transferred to Britain, Russia, China, and other allied powers. Roosevelt's confidante, Harry Hopkins, administered Lend-Lease, and his pro-Soviet views are a matter of record. As Professor Kimball and Professor George Herring have demonstrated, Roosevelt and Hopkins enforced a policy of no quid pro quo. The president refused to use Lend-Lease as a lever against the Soviets or as a means of inducing the British to agree to American strategic concepts. While the post-Vietnam New Left applauded this line, from the vantage point of military history it defies comprehension. In fine, Roosevelt's military assistance policy was generous, but it also effectively neutralized the thorough exploitation—to American ends—of the strongest arrow in Washington's quiver.

Roosevelt made little effort prior to 1940 to allocate resources between the U.S. Army and Navy, nor was there much need to do so. The issue became critical that summer, however, but it was not until late 1941 that the services crafted the Army-Navy Victory Program, and that document was not fully digested until early 1942. By that time, a parade of powerless, leaderless "alphabet soup" economic agencies had been established, leading ultimately to the appointment of Donald Nelson as head of the War Production Board. Owing to his tremendous sense of insecurity, however, Roosevelt refused to endow Nelson or any of the heads of these agencies with much authority or to clarify their authority and responsibilities. Creative tension ruled the day, the result being stupendous inefficiencies, mismatches between strategy and production, and widespread dissipation of industrial effort. Long ago, Harvard political scientist Samuel Huntington asserted that Roosevelt let the military run the war, but the existing relationship between the White House and the service departments meant that only Roosevelt had the power of ultimate decision.[30] His failures to act are legion. He failed to insist that the army allow the navy and marines to conduct all amphibious training, and he refused to order the army air force to turn over enough B-24 Liberators to the navy—or to operate them themselves—to provide effective air cover to coastal shipping in early 1942 or to cover the Atlantic Air Gap in spring 1943. He allowed Marshall to ignore a long-standing prewar agreement to transfer all army troop transports to the navy, a system that worked well in World War I, with the result that from 1942 to 1945 the War Department operated a huge seagoing Transportation Force—as did the navy for its own movements and for the marines—and the navy provided the escorting defenses. The result in the months after Pearl Harbor, for instance, was chaos and a particularly inefficient use of scarce escorts.

Few questions of modern history have received more attention than Roosevelt's handling of grand strategy in World War II. He clearly had no settled views. In the 1930s, he wanted to stiffen British and French resistance to Germany and uphold the Open Door in China against Japan. Condominiums and informal fronts attracted him, as did various forms of undeclared economic and maritime warfare: embargoes, moral and otherwise, quarantines, and distant naval blockades. He had little use for carefully negotiated alliances or precisely defined treaty obligations. None of his various prewar schemes bore fruit. Indeed one, a December 1937 plan to impose a distant Anglo-American blockade of Japan following the *Panay* incident, was described by its author, Captain Royal Ingersoll, as completely "impractical."[31] Roosevelt's grand strategy, his measures short of war in 1939-41, surely constitute the most important of the century. He accepted Admiral Stark's Plan Dog, which articulated a "Germany-first" strategy, committed the United States to defense of the Stalinist regime in the Soviet Union in mid-1941, used the oil embargo to give spine to the Open Door against Japan at the same time, and employed the Atlantic Fleet to provoke Germany that fall. Atlantic Fleet task forces conducted battleship-cruiser sweeps against German raiders, contributed to the British blockade of the German surface fleet, instituted a Denmark Straits Patrol, and in September commenced escort-of-convoy operations in defense of British merchant shipping between Newfoundland and Iceland. Other than Plan Dog, and its embodiment in Rainbow 5, however, Roosevelt's strategic moves in 1941 betray no hint of strategic synthesis. He allowed himself to remain in the dark about Soviet strategy and failed to insist that the British agree to a concerted Anglo-American strategic plan at the abortive August Argentia conference. Churchill found an untended strategic field when he appeared at the White House at Christmas 1941.

Roosevelt insisted shortly after Pearl Harbor that he would follow a "Germany-first" strategy, but in practice in 1942 he allowed Fleet Admiral King, General MacArthur, and the British to dilute its meaning beyond recognition—and there is substantial evidence that the president did not truly understand what was afoot.[32] He allowed Marshall to desiccate the Atlantic Amphibious Force and permitted the rather mysterious transfer of the 1st Marine Division to the Pacific coast. The unintended result was that the Joint Chiefs could not identify any trained American landing force when they agreed upon a cross-Channel movement, Operation Sledgehammer-Roundup, in April. By that time, Roosevelt was in Churchill's maw. The prime minister agreed to Sledgehammer in April and shortly thereafter undermined it. Roosevelt had lost control of events. On June 10, he agreed to Admiral King's plan to launch an expensive campaign in the Lower Solomons, but five days later he rejected Marshall's proposal that the Americans present London with a "Pacific alternative" to lever them into honoring their April pledge. Roosevelt's acceptance of Churchill's peripheral strategy, which dispersed scarce Allied resources, resulted in the North African and Mediterranean campaigns, which the foremost historian of the Royal Navy has recently admitted to be wasteful.[33] Roosevelt's inability to make any overall sense of the Mediterranean and South Pacific campaigns, or to insist on some collaborative grand strategy with the Soviets, left the Allies completely adrift in 1943. At Casablanca in January 1943, Marshall and King were in a sense defeated in detail. Everyone walked away with something. The army air force got daylight bombing of Germany. The navies got a statement that the Battle of the Atlantic was serious, but neither Roosevelt nor Churchill made the slightest move to act on this. Roosevelt allowed the British to pull the Americans deeper into the Mediterranean, while the U.S. Navy was permitted to continue its costly war of attrition in the South Pacific. Vacillation reminiscent of Roosevelt's handling of rearmament characterized the president's policy in 1943, until Stalin, of all people, forced the issue at the November summit at Tehran.

Roosevelt's treatment of the war against Japan surely deserves more study than it has received. After agreeing to the Guadalcanal operation, the president allowed the Pacific Fleet's position there to deteriorate considerably before insisting that the army and Army Air Force provide promised support. There is evidence that the White House inspired the utterly wasteful Aleutians landings in 1943. Roosevelt may have appeared at Hawaii in July 1944 to discuss strategy with Nimitz and MacArthur, but the evidence suggests that he misunderstood the issues at stake and probably played no hand in the final decision—one of the times Admiral King clearly needed White House support. Roosevelt took little interest in post-Luzon strategy, although some presidential attention might have prevented the dreadful situation Truman found that April: Nimitz was moving forward to Guam to prepare to invade Kyushu, whereas MacArthur was clearing out every Philippine island and intending to turn south and assault the Dutch East Indies. As for Roosevelt's China policy, the president supported General Stilwell's plan to get Chiang Kai-shek, then still holding out in Chungking, to send his best divisions into Burma to reimpose British colonial rule. Both Stilwell and Roosevelt expressed surprise when Chiang resisted their strategy. More broadly, Roosevelt never quite grasped Admiral King's basic concept of forcing Japan to fight on two widely separated fronts by amphibious operations in Southeast Asia. King's white-hot anger when Roosevelt abandoned the best of these operations at the second conference at Cairo was grounded in a ruthless, sharp-eyed appreciation of Japan's extraordinary predicament. Roosevelt's failure to insist that Japan be pressed in both the Indian

Ocean and Pacific theaters led directly to the need to bring Russia into the war as articulated in the Yalta accords.

Regardless of how these arrangements affected the postwar politics of Europe and the Far East, Roosevelt's openhanded Lend-Lease policy, his suspension of Sledgehammer-Roundup until 1944, and his strategy against Japan had created a situation in which the United States had no choice but to appeal to one of the most sinister figures of our century to deal the final blow in the Pacific war.

Yalta may provide the final clue to the commander in chief's strategy.[34] A recurrent theme of what little is known of Roosevelt's strategic preferences in the 1930s involved some collaboration with the Soviets. This is consistent with his unabashed pro-Soviet foreign policy. It was illustrated during the war by his adoption of the term "second front"—a scurrilous phrase of Communist origins that suggested unfairly that the Allies were not fighting the Axis powers. The constant wartime bench test for American strategy was how it would assist the Soviets. Not once, until Yalta, did Roosevelt insist that Soviet operations support American strategy. Indeed, he refused to demand that Stalin explain how he was using Lend-Lease materiel and countenanced Soviet secrecy by accepting it as an acceptable feature of the Soviet regime—a regime he and other liberals accepted as legitimate.[35] Roosevelt tolerated numerous Soviet outrages against various Allied personnel who found themselves in Russia during the war, and he fired Admiral Standley, his loyal servant, when Standley merely suggested that they had shown no signs of gratitude for American assistance. Standley was replaced by Averill Harriman, who championed an even less confrontational style.

What was Roosevelt's legacy as commander in chief? He failed to rearm in the 1930s and later wrongly blamed Congress for the lack of prewar preparedness. The result was that his diplomacy had virtually no influence on Germany or Italy before 1939. This is all the more surprising considering Roosevelt's eccentric view that the European Axis represented the "Gods of Force" and understood only military threats and power. The attack on Pearl Harbor surely illustrated the utter failure of Roosevelt's policy of menacing and deterring Japan. In 1942-43, Roosevelt allowed the Battle of the Atlantic to develop into an unnecessary crisis, caved in to Churchill's scheme to postpone the cross-Channel movement, and prodded Chiang Kai-shek to fight to save British colonialism in Southeast Asia. Meanwhile, thanks to the lack of quid pro quos attached to Lend-Lease, the Soviets not only survived, but also took the offensive. Owing to Roosevelt's pro-Soviet policy, the United States did not have the slightest notion of Stalin's military or political objectives. In 1944, the "brute force" of Western capitalism was at last brought to bear on Germany.

The German Army collapsed after only 11 months of fighting on two fronts. In the Pacific, the Tojo cabinet, which had approved Operation Hawaii in 1941, fell after only eight months of fighting in the Gilberts, Marshalls, and Marianas.

The Axis surrender in 1945 was an occasion of great joy, but within a year or so the West would be faced with Roosevelt's true legacy: a thorough imbalance of power in Europe and a vacuum of power in the Far East such that the Soviet Union, on the verge of collapse at the time of Pearl Harbor, emerged only four years later to once again menace the West. In sum, the 50-year-long Cold War struggle can surely be labeled the most lasting legacy of Roosevelt's tenure as commander in chief.

Notes

1. William Emerson, "Franklin Roosevelt," in Ernest May, ed., *The Ultimate Decision* (New York: George Brazillier, 1958), 135-77; and Eric Larabee, *Commander in Chief: Franklin Delano Roosevelt, His Lietenants, and Their Way* (New York: Harper & Row, 1987).
2. Jonathan Utley, *Going to War with Japan* (Knoxville: University of Tennessee Press, 1985), 115.
3. George Dyer, ed., *On the Treadmill to Pearl Harbor* (Washington, D.C.: U.S. Government Printing Office, 1973), 125.
4. King, "Roosevelt: Misc. Notes," c. 1950, King Mss, Whitehill-Buell Collection, Library, Naval War College, Newport, R.I.
5. Henry C. Ferrell, Jr., *Claude A. Swanson of Virginia* (Lexington: University Press of Kentucky, 1985), 214.
6. Admiral William Smedberg Oral History, vol. I, 134, Special Collections, Nimitz Library, U.S. Naval Academy.
7. Standley to Taussig, March 3, 1936, Taussig File, Standley Mss, University of Southern California.
8. Townsend Hoopes and Douglas Brinkley, *Driven Patriot* (New York: Knopf, 1993), 178-80.
9. John Walter, "Congressman Carl Vinson and Franklin D. Roosevelt: Naval Preparedness and the Coming of World War II, 1932-40," *Georgia Historical Quarterly,* Vol. 64, No. 1 (1980), 294-305.
10. Larabee, *Commander in Chief,* 307.
11. Randy J. Kolton, "Malin Craig," in Robert W. Love, Jr., ed., *Chiefs of Staff of the U.S. Army,* forthcoming, 12.

12. Kolton, "Craig," 16.
13. Richard Current, *Mr. Secretary Stimson* (New Brunswick, N.J.: Rutgers University Press, 1954).
14. See Russell Weigley, *Eisenhower's Lieutenants,* (Bloomington, Ind.: Indiana University Press, 1981).
15. Jeffery G. Barlow, "The Views of Stimson and Knox on Atlantic Strategy and Planning," in Timothy J. Runyan and Jan G. Copes, eds., *To Die Gallantly: The Battle of the Atlantic* (Boulder, Colorado: Westview Press, 1994), 22-37.
16. Robert W. Love, Jr., "Fighting a Global War," in Kenneth J. Hagan, ed., *In Peace and War* (2nd ed. ppb.; Westport, Connecticut: Greenwood Press), 264.
17. FDR to Lindsay Rogers, September 11, 1939, in Elliott Roosevelt, ed., *F.D.R.: His Personal Letters 1885-1945,* (New York: Duell, Sloan and Pearce, 1947-50) vol. 2, 920.
18. Russell Weigley, *A History of the U.S. Army* (New York: Macmillan, 1967), 415.
19. Weigley, *Army,* 417.
20. Kolton, "Craig," 49.
21. Leonard Gerow, "Notes for a Diary," June 19, 1941, Exec. Office File No. 10, Item No. 1, OPD, RG 165, National Archives.
22. Standley to Admiral Frank Upham, April 15, 1936, File: Corr, William Standley Mss, Library, University of Southern California, Los Angeles.
23. Taussig to Standley, August 20, 1936, File: Corr-Taussig, Standley Mss.
24. B. Mitchell Simpson, "Stark," in Robert W. Love, Jr., ed., *The Chiefs of Naval Operations* (Annapolis, MD: Naval Institute Press, 1980), 130-31; and B. Mitchell Simpson, *Admiral Harold R. Start: Architect of Victory* (Columbia, S.C.: University of South Carolina Press, 1989), 126-35.
25. Love, ed., *The Chiefs of Naval Operations,* 137-81.
26. Roosevelt to Berle, June 6, 1941, Box 212, Adolf Berle Mss, Roosevelt Library, Hyde Park, N.Y.
27. Stephen E. Pelz, *Race to Pearl Harbor: The Failure of the Second London Naval Conference and the Onset of World War II* (Cambridge: Harvard University Press, 1974), 205.
28. Pelz, *Race,* 203.
29. John Walter, "Carl Vinson and Franklin D. Roosevelt," 303.
30. Samuel Huntington, *The Soldier and the State* (Cambridge: Harvard University Press, 1964), 319-21.
31. Robert W. Love, Jr., *The History of the U.S. Navy* (Harrisburg, Pennsylvania: Stackpole Books, 1992), vol. 1, 604.
32. Love, "Fighting a Global War," p. 287. For an analysis of the 1942-43 cross-channel plans, see Walter Scott Dunn, Jr., *Second Front Now, 1943* (University, Ala.: University Press of Alabama, 1980).

33. Corelli Barnett, *Engage the Enemy More Closely* (New York: Norton, 1991).
34. The more documentation from Soviet archives that becomes available, the more critical the assessment of Roosevelt's policy becomes. See Amos Perlmutter, *FDR and Stalin: A Not So Grand Alliance, 1943–1945* (Columbia: University of Missouri Press, 1993).
35. Russell Buhite, *Decisions at Yalta* (Wilmington, Delaware: Scholarly Resources, 1986), 85.

ABOUT THE AUTHORS

I selected our contributors in an attempt to reflect the best and most recent transatlantic scholarship in the field. **Donald Cameron Watt**, longtime Stephenson Professor of International History at the London School of Economics, recently published the best-selling *How War Came.* His student **G. A. H. Gordon** is writing an official history for the Cabinet Office in London; his first book is *British Seapower and Procurement Between the Wars.* **Frederick W. Marks**'s wide-ranging interests have resulted in important reinterpretations of the Constitutional Convention, Theodore Roosevelt's foreign policy, and John Foster Dulles and the Cold War. His *Wind Over Sand* revises completely our understanding of Franklin Roosevelt's statesmanship. **Marleen Kassel**'s studies of Japanese historical texts have been widely published. Professor **J. Thomas Sanders** of the U. S. Naval Academy has worked to open Soviet Navy archives and is completing a major study of Soviet-era history writing. **Stephen E. Ambrose**, director of the Eisenhower Center at the University of New Orleans, has published several studies of Dwight Eisenhower's career, a biography of Richard Nixon, and, most recently, the best-selling *D-Day, June 6, 1944.* **Waldo Heinrichs**, who teaches at San Diego State University, won the Nevins Prize for his *American Ambassador,* a biography of Joseph Grew; his most recent work is *Threshold of War: Franklin D. Roosevelt and American Entry into World War II.* Professor **Michael Schaller** of the University of Arizona has written extensively on American relations with China and Japan, Ronald Reagan's presidency, and Douglas MacArthur, the subject of his highly regarded *MacArthur: Far Eastern General.* **John Major** of the University of Hull coauthored the best-selling *Send A Gunboat* and, most recently, *Prize Possession,* a study of the United States and the Panama Canal. The work of **Jon Bridgeman**, a senior scholar at the University of Washington, ranges widely across European and American history; currently he is writing an account of the weeks before Pearl Harbor. After editing two collections of essays on naval history, **Robert W. Love, Jr.** of the U.S. Naval Academy recently published a two-volume work, *History of the U.S. Navy.*

INDEX

ABC-1 Report, 144
Abe, Nobuyuki, 47
Afghan War (1980), 78
Aleutian Islands, 187
Alexander of Tunis, Field Marshall Harold, Lord, 10
America First Committee, 151
Analects of Confucius, 68, 71
Andrews, General Frank (USAAF), 135, 136, 137
Anglo-American [Canal] Treaty, 136
Anglo-German Naval Treaty (1935), 23
Anglo-Japanese Alliance (1902), 1, 16
Argentia Conference, 9, 49
Arita, Hachiro, 47
Ark Royal (RN carrier), 28-29, 32
Aruba, 46
Asiatic Fleet (USN), 114, 115, 117, 118, 123, 164
Atlantic Amphibious Force, 180, 186
Atlantic, (Battle), 98, 106, 178, 188
Atlantic Conference. *See* Argentia Conference
Atlantic Fleet (USN), 136, 180-81, 183, 186
Australia, 4, 44, 111, 151, 154
Automedon (UK merchantman), 26, 27
Azores, 104, 180
Barbarosa, Operation, 97, 100, 108
Barham (RN battleship), 28
Baruch, Bernard, 40, 42
Bataan Peninsula, 111
Beardall, Captain John R. (USN), 155, 166
Beatty, Admiral of the Fleet David, Lord (RN), 15
Bell, Daniel, 41
Beria, Laverenti, 75
Berle, Adolf, 182
Biddle, Anthony J., 175
Bratton, Colonel Rufus (USA), 160, 161, 162
Brereton, General Lewis (USAAF), 117, 119, 120, 121, 122-23
Brest-Litovsk Treaty, 107
Brett, General George (USAAF), 137, 138
Brezhnev, Leonid, 75, 78, 81, 82, 93
Brooke-Popham, Air Marshall Sir Robert (RAF), 149, 153, 164
B-17 Flying Fortress, 117, 119-120, 121, 122, 123
Bullitt, William, 39
Burdzhalov Affair, 77
Burma, 8
Burnett, Malcolm, 30, 31
Bywater, Hector, 135

Canada, 4, 47
Casablanca Conference, 187
Casey, R. G., 152, 156, 167, 168
Central Pacific (Campaign), 189
Chamberlain, Neville, 3, 18-19, 22, 45
Chatfield, Admiral of the Fleet Ernle, Lord (RN), 15, 17, 18, 20, 22, 23, 24
Chiang Kai-shek, 7, 40, 49, 106, 158, 173, 187-88
Chiang Tso-lin, 46
Chikao, Fujisawa, 65, 66
China Affair. *See* Sino-Japanese War
Churchill, Winston S., 9, 10, 11, 28, 29, 30, 31, 32, 47, 49, 94, 154, 168, 173, 187
Clark Field (Philippine Islands), 97, 119, 120, 121, 122, 123
Committee on Imperial Defence (CID), 9
Corregidor Island, 111, 124, 127
Courageous (RN carrier), 28
Craig, General Malin (USA), 114, 177, 179, 180
Craigie, Sir Robert, 8
Czechoslavakia, 23

Daniels, Josephus, 178
Davis, Norman, 42, 46
Del Monte Field (Mindinao), 120
Dern, Walter, 176-77
Destroyer Deal, 7, 96
Dewey, Admiral George (USN), 174
Dodd, William, 41, 50
Dreyer, Admiral Sir Frederick (RN), 18
Dutch East Indies, 99, 115-16, 123, 162

Eagle (RN carrier), 28
Early, Steve, 47, 115, 145
Edison, Charles A., 176
Edwards, General Clarence (USA), 133
Eighth Army (British), 11
Eisenhower, Major Dwight D. (USA), 113, 124-25, 177
Emperor System Ideology, 61
Essex (USN carrier class), 183
Ethiopia (Abyssinia), 20

Falklands, (Battle), 29
Far Eastern Communications Bureau (FECB), 31
1st Infantry Division (USA), 180
1st Marine Division (USMC), 180
Fiske, Admiral Bradley (USN), 178
Fleet Air Arm (RN), 10
Force Z, 29, 30, 31, 32
Forrestal, James, 175
Formidable (RN carrier), 28
Formosa, 122
French, Admiral Sir William (RN), 160
Furious (RN carrier), 28

Gangut (Russia), 85
General Board of the Navy (USN), 174
Geneva Naval Conference (1927), 2, 134
Glorious (RN carrier), 28
Goethals, General George Washington (USN), 132
Gonzalez, Antonio, 134
Gorbachev, Mikhail, 75, 82
Greater East Asia Co-Prosperity Sphere, 61, 66, 115
Greenland, 46
Grew, Joseph, 7, 42, 47, 157, 158
Groton School, 44

Hainan Island, 46, 147
Halifax, 3rd Viscount, Lord, 42, 151-52, 159, 167
Hamilton, Matthew, 49

Harriman, W. Averell, 154, 188
Hart, Admiral Thomas (USN), 30, 114, 118, 120, 122, 123, 150, 165
Hearst, William Randolph, 41, 124
Heilman, Geoffrey, 145-46
Hepburn Board (USN), 41
Hermes (RN carrier), 28
Hirohito, Emperor, 116
Hiroshima, 80, 87
Hitler, Adolf, 3, 24, 79, 81, 93, 102, 104, 107
Home Fleet (RN), 184
Hopkins, Harry, 154, 159, 162, 167, 168, 181, 185
Hornbeck, Stanley, 42, 49
Howard, Roy, 41, 47, 124
Hull, Cordell, 3, 6, 37, 42, 120, 144, 152, 154, 157, 158-59, 160-61

Iceland, 46, 183
Ickes, Harold, 116, 126
Illustrious (RN carrier), 28
Imperial Japanese Navy, 37, 38, 42, 43
Imperial Rescript, 62, 63, 64
Imperial Rule Association (Japan), 65
Indochina (French), 26, 101, 116, 147-48, 149, 150
Indomitable (RN carrier), 28-29
Ingersoll, Captain Royal (USN), 186
Inner Mongolia, 46
Iran, 9
Iraq, 9, 43

Japan's Ethical Code, 62
Jimmu, Emperor, 64
JN-25 (IJN Cipher), 30
Johnson, Lyndon Baines, 147

kami-kaze, 69
Khrushchev, Nikita, 75, 77, 78, 93
Kimmel, Rear Admiral Husband (USN), 111, 149, 165
King, Fleet Admiral Ernest J. (USN), 135, 173, 175-76, 181-82, 186
King George V (RN BBS), 28
Knox, Frank, 42, 143, 144, 147, 149, 150, 175, 182
Knox, Philander, 133
Kohtron, 149, 153, 156
Kongo (IJN battleship-class), 15
Konoye, Prince Fumimaro, 47, 65
Kota Bharu, 145, 148, 164
Kramer, Commander Alwin (USN), 160
Kra Peninsula, 153, 154, 156
Krick, Captain Harold D. (USN), 163
Kurita, Admiral Takeo (IJN), 31
Kurusu, Sabaru, 155
Kyushu, Japan, 187

Lansing-Ishii Agreement (1917), 50
Layton, Admiral Sir Charles (RN), 31
Leahy, Fleet Admiral William D. (USN), 40, 181, 183
Lend Lease Act, 96, 97, 185, 188
Life Magazine, 145
Lodge, Henry Cabot, 132
London Naval Conference (1930), 17, 62, 182
London Naval Conference (1935-36), 19, 1976, 182-83
Luce, Henry, 124
Lusitania, 133

MacArthur, General Douglas (USA), 10, 111-12, 113, 114, 115, 116, 117, 118, 119, 120, 121-27, 176-78, 187

MacMurray, John van Antwerp, 42, 49
McIntire, Rear Admiral Ross (USN), 146, 166
Madison, James, 174
Magic. *See* Ultra
Mahan, Rear Admiral Alfred Thayer (USN), 131
Malaya (RN battleship), 28
Malaya (Singapore), 10, 17, 25, 27, 28, 29, 30, 99, 100, 105, 123, 148, 149, 164
Manchuria (Manchukwo), 2, 5, 18, 38, 44, 45, 46, 47, 62, 80, 96
Mandate of Heaven, 67, 71
Manila Bay, 112, 116, 118
Marshall, General of the Army George C. (USA), 42, 115, 117, 119, 120, 144, 173, 186-87
Maryknoll Missionaries, 37
Matador, Operation (British), 155
Meiji Restoration, 61, 62, 65, 70
Mertsalov, A. N., 83
Midway, (Battle), 10, 86, 137
modus vivendi (proposal), 49
Molotov, V., 84
Monroe Doctrine, 131
Morgenthau, Henry Jr., 42, 99
Morskoi sbornik, 85
Munich Conference (1938), 79, 180
Mussolini, Benito, 5

Nagano, Admiral Osumi (IJN), 42
Nagasaki, 80, 87
Nagumo, Vice Admiral Chuichi (IJN), 181
Nara Period, 69
National Foreign Trade Council, 45
National Industrial Recovery Act (NIRA), 183
National Security Act (1947), 173
Naval Historical Journal (Russia), 85
Nazi-Soviet Nonaggression Pact (1939), 5, 99
Nekrich, Alexsandr, 78
Nelson, Donald, 185
Neutrality Patrol (USN), 182
New Zealand, 4, 44
Nichiren, 69
Nimitz, Fleet Admiral Chester (USN), 187
Nomohan (Campaign), 5
Nomura, Admiral Kichisabaru (IJN), 37, 38, 49, 120, 155, 156

Office of Strategic Services (OSS), 105
Oil Embargo (1941), 9, 37, 38, 42, 43, 48, 95, 97, 186
Open Door Policy, 99, 186
Orange War Plan (US), 112, 116, 123, 132-33
Oshima, General Hiroshi, 5

Pacific Alternative (1942), 187
Pacific Fleet (USN), 116, 187
Panama Canal, 131, 132, 133, 134, 135, 136, 137, 138, 139
Panay (USN gunboat), 135, 186
Pearl Harbor, 30, 32, 64, 79, 86, 94, 103, 106, 111, 112, 123, 124, 126, 136, 143, 144, 162, 181-84, 186, 189
Perkins, Francis, 103
Philippine Army, 112, 113, 114, 115
Philippine Islands, 98, 99, 111, 112-13, 114, 150, 151
Phillips, Vice Admiral Sir Tom (RN), 22, 29
Plan Dog Memorandum, 144, 181, 186
Port Arthur, (Battle), 133

Pratt, Admiral William Veazie (USN), 133, 181
Prince of Wales (RN battleship), 10, 28, 29, 30, 31
Poland, 24

Quarantine Speech, 6
Queen Elizabeth (RN battleship), 28, 32
Quezon, Manuel, 113-14, 117

Rambo, Lieutenant Wilkie A. (USN), 160
Ramilles (RN battleship), 28
Ramshaw, Lieutenant J. C. (RAAF), 148
Red Army, 11, 94, 102
Renown (RN battlecruiser), 28
Repulse (RN battlecruiser), 10, 28, 29, 30, 31
Resolution (RN battleship), 28
Revenge (RN battlecruiser), 28
Ribbentrop, Joachim von, 5
Richardson, Admiral James O. (USN), 175
Rodney (RN battleship), 28
Roosevelt, Eleanor, 160, 167, 175
Roosevelt, Franklin D., 7, 8, 9, 37, 38, 39, 40, 41, 42, 43, 44, 46, 47-49, 50-51, 94, 95-96, 97, 98, 99, 100, 101, 102, 103, 104, 105, 106, 111, 112, 113-14, 143, 144, 173, 174, 175, 176, 177, 178, 180, 181, 182, 183, 184, 185, 186, 187, 188, 189
Roosevelt, Henry Latrobe, 176
Root-Takahira Agreement (1907), 50
Royal Sovereign (RN battleship), 28
Russell and Company, 44
Rzheshevskii, O. A., 83, 84

Saito, Admiral Viscount (IJN), 47
Samsonov, Aleksandr Mikhailovich, 82, 83
Saratoga (USN carrier-class), 183
Sayre, Francis B., 39, 48-49, 115
Schulz, Lieutenant Lester (USN), 161, 162, 163
Semiriaga, M. I., 83
Short, Major General Walter (USA), 111, 165
Showa Restoration, 64, 65, 70
Siam, Gulf of, 143, 148, 149, 150, 151, 164, 165
Sino-Japanese War (1937-45), 5, 62, 106
Sledgehammer-Roundup (Operations), 186-87
Smedberg, Lieutenant Commander William (USN), 176
Smith, Harold, 147
Smuts, Field Marshall Jan Christian (S. Africa), 3
Solomons (Campaign), 186
Stalin, Joseph, 77, 83, 98, 107, 108, 173, 187
Stalingrad, (Battle), 81, 86
Standley, Admiral William (USN), 4, 176, 181, 188
Stark, Admiral Harold R. (USN), 97, 120, 136, 144, 173, 181, 183, 186
Stilwell, General Joseph (USA), 187
Stimson, Henry L., 42, 49, 117, 123, 132, 136, 137, 138, 139, 177
Stone, General David, 135
Suez Canal, 9
Sutherland, Colonel Richard (USA), 117, 121
Swanson, Claude, 131, 175-76
Syria, 9

Taussig, Rear Admiral Joseph (USN), 181
Ten Point Proposal (1941), 154, 155, 156, 162
Thailand (Siam), 26, 155, 162
Tirpitz (German battleship), 28
Tirpitz, Grand Admiral Alfred von, 13
Tojo, General Hideki, 42
Tokagawa Period (Japan), 61
Tokyo Earthquake (1923), 63
Tripartite Pact (1940), 8-9, 63, 101
Truman, Harry S, 124, 187
Tsushima (Battle), 14
Tugwell, Rexford, 42
Turner, Admiral Richmond Kelly (USN), 149
Twentieth Party Congress (SU), 77
Twenty-first Party Congress (SU), 77
Twenty-One Demands (1915), 14, 133
Two-Ocean Navy Act (1940), 42, 181, 184

Ultra, 120, 155, 161, 166
U.S. Army, 96, 107, 112, 113, 114, 176-78
U.S. Army Air Corps, 39, 112, 135, 179-80, 184
U.S. Army Air Force, 185, 187
U.S. Army Transportation Command, 185
U.S. Fleet, 132
U.S. Marine Corps, 147, 185
U.S. Navy, 133, 178, 183, 184, 185, 187

Valiant (RN battleship), 28, 32
Vansittart, Sir Robert (UK), 3
Versailles Treaty, 62
Victorious (RN carrier), 28
Victory Plan (1941), 141, 185
Vinson Act (1934), 39, 183
Vinson, Carl, 176, 183
Voenno istoricheskii zhurnal, 82, 83
Voprosy istorii, 83

Wainwright, General Jonathan, 117
Wang Ching-wei, 47, 106
War Production Board, 185
Warspite (RN battleship), 28
war warning message, 121
Washington Conference and Treaties (1921-22), 1, 2, 15, 24, 50, 133, 182
Way of Subjects, 62, 63-64, 71
Welles, Sumner, 6, 11, 42, 132, 154
White, Theodore, 115
Wiley, Admiral Henry (USN), 134
Wilkinson, Admiral Theodore (USN), 161, 162, 163
Wilson, Woodrow, 182
Winant, John, 152, 153

Yalta Conference, 188

Zen Buddism, 69, 71
Zero-type (Mitsubishii fighter), 42
Zhukov, Marshal of the Red Army Georgi, 78